THE HISTORY OF THE IMPERIALL ESTATE OF THE *Grand Seigneurs*:

Their Habitations, Liues, Titles, Qualities, Exercises, Workes, Reuenewes, Habit, Discent, Ceremonies, Magnificence, Judgements, Officers, Fauourites, Religion, Power, Gouernment *and* Tyranny.

Translated out of *French* by
E. G. S. A.

LONDON,
Printed by *William Stansby*, for *Richard Meighen*,
next to the middle Temple in Fleetstreet.
1635.

THE HISTORY

OF THE SERRAIL,

AND OF THE COVRT

of the *Grand Seigneur*, Emperour of the *Turkes*.

WHEREIN IS SEENE the Image of the *Othoman* Greatnesse, A Table of humane passions, and the Examples of the inconstant prosperities of the Court.

Translated out of French *by* Edward Grimeston *Serjant at* Armes.

LONDON,
Printed by *William Stansby*.

TO THE RIGHT
WORSHIPFVLL
HIS WORTHY
Kinsman,

S. Harbottell Grimeston
Knight and Baronet.

SIR,

T is the vsuall manner of Men, whom GOD hath bleſt with the goods of Fortune, when Death ſummons them to leaue the world, with all their wealth, they are then ſollicitous and carefull how to diſpoſe of that which

The Epistle Dedicatorie.

which they cannot carrie with them. Then they call for Counsell to aduise them in the drawing of their last Wills and Testaments, bequeathing large Legacies to their Children, Kinsfolke and best respected Friends, to remayne as a future testimonie of their bounties: But it fareth not so with mee; I must say with poore *Bias*, *Omnia mea mecum porto*. I am now creeping into my Graue, and am freed from that care, how to dispose of my worldly estate. But I seare that my disabilitie will leaue some staine of Ingratitude vpon mee, when I dead; that I haue left no testimonie of my thankfulnesse to so worthy a friend as your selfe, from whom I haue receiued so many fauours. To make any reall satisfaction, I cannot, neither doe you need it. Yet to free my selfe (in some sort) of this imputation of ingratitude, I haue bequeathed you a verball Legacie, the last of my fruitlesse labours. I hope you will giue it acceptance and countenance it for your owne, where you may at your best leisure (without any labour, trauell, or expences) enter into the great *Turk's Seraglio* or Court, and there take a suruay of the life, lusts, reuenewes, power, gouernment, and tyranny of that great *Ottoman*. I bequeath it
you

The Epistle Dedicatorie.

you as a testimonie of my thankfulnes when I am gone. If you make it your recreation after more serious affaires, I hope you will receiue some content, to reade the State of the proudest and most powerfull Monarch of the World. If it please you, I shall thinke my selfe very happy, hauing performed this last dutie. And will euer rest,

Your truly affected poore

Vnckle,

Edward Grimeston,

THE GENERALL
HISTORY OF THE SERRAIL,
and of the Court of the Grand SEIGNEVR, Emperour of the TVRKES.

The first BOOKE.

He wisest among Men aduise vs to goe vnto Kings as vnto the fire, neither too neere nor too farre off: It burnes when wee approach indiscreetly, and doth not warme him that stands farre off: The glorious lustre of Royall Maiestie, consumes the rash presumption of those which approach too neere, and the beames of their bounty doe neuer warme those sauage humours which recoile in flying from them. The true examples which Histories supply, haue confirmed the excellency of this counsell: yet a desire of the publique good hath enforced me to violate this respect, and my vowes to serue it carries mee into the danger there is in gazing too neere vpon Kings. I approach vnto the proudest of all other Princes, and the most seuere of Men, yea so neere as I diue into his secrets, visit his person, discouer his most hidden affections, and relate his most particular loues. If I loose my selfe, yet

B

I shall giue proofes of this veritie, that in the age wherein wee liue, whosoeuer imployes himselfe wholy for the publique, in the end ruines himselfe: But Man is not borne only for himselfe, and the barbarous ingratitude of the times cannot serue for a pretext but vnto idlenesse: He that will labour, must passe ouer these obstacles; for he is not worthy of life, which doth not imploy it well, and to consume himselfe for the publique good, is to reuiue againe gloriously out of his ashes, like vnto a new Phœnix. I haue conceiued, that hauing giuen you the History of the Turkish Empire, from its beginning vnto our times, it would not be vnprofitable to let you see what their manners are, their kind of liuing, their conuersation, and the order of their gouernement, which so powerfull and redoubted a Conquerour doth obserue. To doe it safely wee must enter into the Serrail, where the secret of all these things is carefully shut vp. But for that in going thither we must crosse thorough the Citie of Constantinople, let vs speake something of the situation, antiquitie, and beautie, of this pompous Citie, the fatall abode of the most powerfull Emperours of the Earth.

CHAP. I.
Of the Citie of Constantinople.

THe Grecians consulting with the Oracle of *Apollo Pythean*, what place they should choose to build a City in Thrace, had for answere that they should lay the foundations right against the Territory of blind Men; so terming the *Calcidonians*, who comming first into that country, could not make choice of the fertility of a good soyle, and were seated vpon the other side of the Sea vpon the borders of Asia, in a place which was vnpleasing and vnfruitfull, in old time called the Towne of Calcedonia, but now the Borough *Scutari*. *Pausanius* Capataine of the Spartians had the charge to build it, and *Byzas* Generall of
the

the Megarian Fleet, gaue it his name, and called it Byzance: It hath carried it for many ages with the glory to be esteemed among the Grecians, the most fertile of their Townes, the Port of Europe; and the Bridge to passe thither from Asia; vntill that Great *Constantine* leauing Italy retired into the East, and carried with him the most powerfull Lords which might trouble that estate: He built after the Modell of Rome, a stately Citie vpon the Antiquities of Byzance, where he erected the Eternitie of his Name, and called it Constantinople, or new Rome. The greatnesse of the Wals, the safety of the Forts, the beautie of the Houses, the riches of Columnes, which seemed to haue drawne into that place all the Marble, Iasper, and Porphyry of the Earth, were the rare wonders of the Architecture, but aboue all these things appeared a magnificent Temple, which the pietie of this Prince had consecrated to the Diuine Wisdome, vnder the name of *Saincta Sophia*, whose building and riches seemed in some sort to enuie the glory of King *Salomon*, in the like designe; at the least according to the time, and the power of *Constantine*. Seuen rich Lampes ministred occasion to curious spirits to obserue their rare art, they all receiued at one instant the substance which did nourish their flames, and one being extinct all the rest were quencht. This was in the yeare of Grace, three hundred and thirty: Since two tumultuous factions grew in the Citie, who after they had cast the fire of an vnfortunate Sedition into the spirits of Men, brought the flames into this goodly Temple and burnt it. For this cause *Iustinian* the Emperour employed in the restoring thereof, a part of the Treasures which he had greedily gathered together: He caused it to be re-edified with more state then it had beene, and in seuenteene yeares he imployed thirty foure Millions of gold, which was the Reuenew of Egypt for that time: He laid a foundation of eight hundred thousand Duckets of yearely rent, and caused this holy and reuerend place to be serued by nine hundred Priests, Men who had the merit of their beginning from Learning and Pietie. The Citie being the Queene of the World, within few yeares after, saw her restorer triumphing ouer the

King of *Persia*, and had the grace to keepe in her bosome, the precious treasure of Christianity, a part of the Crosse of the Redeemer of the World, found by the carefull pietie of the Emperours Mother: her joy, pompe, and lustre, were growne to that height, as it seemed there could be nothing to be added: it is by succession of time the seate of the greatest Monarches of the Earth: *Seuerus* and *Anthonius* his sonne did enuy it, and rauished from its restorer, the glory to haue named it, calling it *Anthonia*, by one of their names. But whatsoeuer hath a beginning in this World must haue an end: and the goodliest things paie tribute to change. In the yeere 1453. on Tuesday the seuen and twentieth of *May*, it was after a long siege made a prey to the victorious Turke: *Mahomet* the Second of that name, and the eleuenth Emperour of the Turks entred it by force, spoyled it, and sackt it: The Emperour *Constantine Paliologo* lost his life, with a great number of men of quality, and all the Christian men were subiect to the Sword, or to the rigour of bondage: the women were a sport to the lubricity of the Turkes, and their goods subiect to their spoyle, in reuenge (some say) of the sacke and burning which the Grecians made of Troy, from whom they will haue the Turkes to be descended: but rather for a punishment of the impiety of the Grecians, who blaspheming against Heauen, deny that the Holy Ghost proceeds from Iesus Christ the second Person in the ineffable Trinity. *Mahomet* the Second of that name, was the first that sealed the *Othoman* Throne there. They changed the name among them, and called it *Stamboll*, that is to say, the great, the Royall, and the abundant. Her goodly places suffer the like inconstancie, and are called *Bastans*, the stately *Hippodrome*, is called the place of Horses, *Atmaydan*, and the wonderfull Temple of *Sainta Sophia*, is become the chiefe Mosquee of *Mahomets* superstition.

The situation of Constantinople, and its forme.

This Citie is situated vpon a point of firme Land aduanced into the channell which comes from *Pontus Euxinus*, or the blacke Sea, which Geographers call the *Bosphorus* of Thrace. It is watred of three parts by the Sea: towards the North by a Gulfe or Arme of the Sea, called the Horne, which the Bospho-

Bosphorus thrusts into Europe, and make the Hauen of Constantinople the goodliest, the deepest, and the most commodious in Europe: Towards the East it is watred by the extremitie of the channell or Bosphorus; on the South by the waues of the Propontique Sea; and vpon the South it hath the firme Land of Thrace. The forme is Triangular, whereof the largest side is that towards the Serrail, which lookes to the Sea towards the seuen Towers, and its vast circuit containes about fiue leagues: The wals are of an extraordinary height, with two false Brayes towards the Land; and inclose seuen Hils within it. The first serues as a Theatre to the Imperiall Palace of the Prince, where it is commodiously and proudly seated: The last lookes vpon the extremity of the farthest parts of the Towne opposite to this, and vpon the way which leads to Andrinopolis by Land. But betwixt the third and the fourth, where a Valley doth extend it selfe called the great, is an Aqueduct of rare structure, which *Constantine* caused to be drawne seuen leagues from the City, and *Solyman* the Second aduanced it two Leagues beyond, and increased the current of water in so great abundance, as they doe serue seuen hundred and forty Fountaines for the publique, not reckoning those which are drawne into diuers parts to furnish the great number of Bathes which serue for delights, and the Turkes superstition.

Vpon the last of the seuen Hils are yet to be seene the ancient buildings of a Fort strengthened with seuen Towres in the midst of the situation; the Turkes call it *Giedicula*, that is to say, the Fort of the seuen Towres, in the which the wonders of Art was so great in old time, as what was spoken in the one was heard in all the rest, not all at one instant, but successiuely and in order. Two hundred and fifty Souldiers are in guard, commanded by a Captaine who hath the charge, who may not goe forth without the leaue of the Grand *Vizir*, except it be on two dayes in the yeare, when they celebrate their Feasts of *Bayrans*, or Easter. The first Turkish Emperour which possest Constantinople lodged their treasure in these Towres: The one was full of Ingots, and coyned gold; two of them

con-

contained the siluer that was coyned and in Ingots; another had diuers armes and ornaments for Souldiers, and the Caparisons for Horses, enricht with gold, siluer and precious stones: the fift serued for ancient Armes, Medales, and other precious remaynders of Antiquity: the sixt contained the Engines for Warre: and the seuenth, the Rols and Records of the Empire; accompanied with a goodly gallery, in the which were placed the rich spoyles which *Selym* the first brought from Tauris, when he triumphed ouer Persia. All these treasures were carefully kept, vntill the Reigne of *Selym* the Second. But it is in estates as with priuate Families: In these some gather together with much toyle that which their heires waste prodigally; and some Kings heape vp treasure which serue as a subiect of prodigality to their Successors. For this Prince base and effeminate, who it seemes, was not borne but for the ruine of his Empire (if Christians could haue imbraced the occasions) wasted in the expences of the Nauall Army, which the battaile of *Lepantho* made subiect to the Christians, and before in the warre of Cyprus, the best part of the immense treasure which his Father had heaped vpin these Towres: the rest serued for his lasciuious and disordered passions with his Concubines. Since *Amurath* his Sonne changed the place of the treasures of the Empire, and from the Towres transferred them into his Serrail: so they draw vnto him that which he loues, and seeing that money doth possesse the hearts of Men, it is reason they should haue a lodging in their Palace. This alteration hath since appointed these places of the treasure, to be Prisons for the great Men of the Port or Court, whom the *Sultans* will not put to death: For the Fortresse being of a great extent, such Captiues haue the more libertie. They shut vp in the Towres of the blacke Sea, which is a Castle vpon Europe side ioyning to the Sea, Christian Prisoners of qualitie, where in the yeare 1617. Duke *Koreski* a Prince of Moldauia was lodged.

Constantinople hath within the inclosure of the wals aboue two thousand Mosques, or Turkish Temples built by their Emperors: for we will make no further relation of the rarities of that Imperiall City, but such as are at this day. Wee may read the wonders of that ancient City in other Authours; and particularly in the Bookes which *P. Gillius* hath written. The chiefe of all these Mosquees is that which hath beene erected in the ancient Temple of *Sancta Sophia*, called by the Turkes *Ayasophia*; it hath sixe goodly and sumptuous Forefronts, the walls are of bricke, couered in old time both within and without with white Marble, Porphyry, and other rich stones; they are now of Lead. The open Porches about it haue six doores which augment the beauty; foure doores of the Church open at the entry; the height of the Vault couered with Lead, shewes the magnificence of the worke: sixteene great Pillars support it, foure are Iasper of the Ile of Cyprus, foure are of white Marble, foure of Porphyry, and foure of another stone as rich: forty eight other Pillars of lesse bignesse, but of the same matter serues to support this great Fabrique, and a lesser and lower Vault is supported by foure and twenty Columnes of the same Marble and Porphyry. The rare Statues and rich Images wherewith *Constantine* had adorned it, are no more to be seene: *Mahomet* the Second had vowed them to the sack of the City when he tooke it: only an Image of the Virgin who bare the Sonne of God, remaynes whole and vntouched in the midst of the Vault, not without a particular prouidence of Heauen: Yet the Turkes draw a vaile crosse to prohibit the sight; but this doth not hinder the Christians by creeping vp by ladders to satisfie their deuotion, when as at lawfull houres they may enter into the Mosquee: Now the Turkes haue white-cast the Vault in diuers parts, to write the Name of God in the Arabique tongue. The breadth and length of this Church may be well comprehended by the height, the which is limited by the shot of a Harquebusse: vnder it is a Vault full of Altars and Sepulchres, in respect whereof the Turkes haue caused the doores to be walled vp. In a place neere vnto it are found ten great Piles full of Oyle since the time of *Constantine*, which haue continued vnto this day free (by reason of the low vault) from the fire which consumed the first beauties of this Temple, the long continuance of yeares hath made this Oyle white like Milke: It now serues for Physique which the Apothecaries vse for the Grand Seigneur.

By these vaulted places they descended into two hollow Caues which goe vnder the streets of the City, the one leads to the Grand Serraill, and the other goes farre vnder *Constantinople*, vnprofitable at this day, except the one which hath receiued light by some breaches which time hath made, serues only to winde silke, and brings vnto the Coffers of the *Shasna*, or Exchequer, three or foure hundred Zequins of yearely rent. But the goodly and ancient buildings which did adorne this admirable Temple, haue beene ruined by the Turkish Emperours, except those which serue for a dwelling to some Congregations of the Priests of the Alcoran.

Besides this great and admirable Mosquee, there are foure others of note, the durable markes of the magnificence of the Turkish Emperours. The first was built by *Mahomet* the Second, after that hee had triumphed ouer Constantinople: He caused it to be erected after the Modell of *Sancta Sophia*, but much lesse; he enricht it with threescore thousand Duckets of Reuenue; hee caused two hundred faire Chambers to be built about it couered with Lead, as well to lodge the Priests which did serue, as to receiue all strange Pilgrimes of what Nation or Religion soeuer they were, where they are entertained for three dayes: without the Cloyster are also built fiftie other Chambers for poore men. The second Mosque was made by *Baiazet* the second sonne to the said *Mahomet*. The third by *Selym* the first sonne to this man: and the fourth by *Solyman* second sonne to *Selym*. These three last Princes are euery one buried within the walls of his Mosquee in stately Tombes, vpon the which there are continually a great number of Lampes burning, and Turkish Priests mumbling of the Alcoran, who pray after their manner for the soules of these Monarches. The most stately of these foure Mosquees is that of *Solyman* the Second,: it exceeds in Marble and other rich stones the pompe of *Sancta Sophia*, but it yeelds to the wonders of the Architecture, whereunto few could yet attaine.

Selym the Second built his Mosquee in the City of Andrinopolis: *Achmat* the last employed excessiue summes of money in the Fabrique of that which he built of late yeares in *Constantinople*: the magnificency of the structure exceeds those which we haue mentioned, the Turks call it the new Mosquee, and their Priests the Incredulous: for that *Achmat* caused it to be built against the aduice which they gaue him, that such a worke would not profit his soules health, seeing that hee had made no conquests vpon the Enemies of his Law. The other Turkish Emperours could not build any, for that they had made no conquests to enlarge the Empire of their Predecessors. For the Law of the state conformable to that Religion, forbids Turkish Princes to build any Temples, if they haue not extended the limits of their Empire in the Territories of Christians, where they may cause their Alcoran to be preached: for such workes of piety cannot be vsefull to the health of their soules (the *Mufties* say) who are opposite to such designes, if their Emperours would vndertake it.

The Grecians which are Christians, haue within Constantinople forty Churches for their diuine Seruice; the Armenians haue foure, and the Latines (lesse fauoured then these) haue but two: It is true that most of them are lodged at Galata, now called Pera, which is on the other side of the channell, where they haue nine Churches for their Deuotions and holy Mysteries. The Iewes haue the credit to be within the City in nine seuerall quarters, and haue eight and thirty Synagogues. They haue gotten more libertie and power then they haue in Christendome, for that they obserue the formes of the Grand *Signior*, and moreouer they haue the managing of the Domestique Affaires of great Men and Officers of the Port, where they are the common giuers of aduice. The walls of this Imperiall City are yet firme and entire. They are double vpon the firme Land, except it be towards the Gate of *Aiachapezi*, that is to say, the holy Gate, by reason of the great number of Religious bodies which were in a Church neere vnto that Gate. *Mahomet* the Second entred thereby to defile the holinesse of the place: there are nineteene Gates aswell

C vpon

vpon the firme Land as towards the Sea, which serue for an entrance into this City. Many great places are extended for the commodity of the Publike, some haue preserued the ancient Pyramides, and the workes of Brasse erected by Christian Emperours, amongst others that which they call *Petrome*, where there are to be seene whole Obelisques; and three great Serpents of Marble creeping vpward wreathed one within the other: One of the which hath a breach in the throat, for *Mahomet* the Second entring into the City, had a conceit that they were the worke of some enchanting Sorcerer, and spurring on his Horse to be satisfied, hee made this breach with his Launce. There is euery day a publique Market in some one of these places. One Friday it is in three, and the most famous are of Wednesday, Thursday, and Friday. They call them *Schibazars*, that is to say, Markets of things necessary for vse. About these places are erected aboue two thousand shops for Broakers, who sell any thing wherewith to furnish the necessity of those which desire to repaire their want: The tole of this old trash is not so little but it yeilds yearely vnto the Princes Coffers six Charges of Mony, which is in value eleuen thousand Sequins, or foure thousand, foure hundred pounds sterling; for the Turkish exaction makes profit of euery thing. The shops for Merchants exceed the number of forty eight thousand; they are diuided according to the diuersity of trades or Merchandizes into diuers places; but euery trade hath his quarter, and in diuers parts for the commoditie of the Publique. Only Goldsmiths, Iewellers, and Merchants of cloth of gold are in one place called *Bayston*, that is to say Market; the others *Bazars*. This rich place is inuironed with wals sixe foot thicke; there are foure double Gates one before the other, like vnto a little Towne, vaulted round about. This rich Market place hath foure and twenty Pillars which support the vault, vnder the which there are many little shops like vnto boxes in the wall, or in the Pillars, euery one is sixe foote broad, and foure long: There they shew forth their rich Merchandizes vpon little Tables which are before them. Without doubt the gaine must be exceeding great,

great, and the sale ordinary, seeing they paid vnto the Prince yearly fiue hundred Sequins, or two hundred pounds sterling, to haue leaue to sell there. These are only Iewellers and Merchants of cloth of gold: The Goldsmithes are without about the wals of this place, and euery one payes yearely a hundred Sequins, or forty pounds sterling to the same end.

Besides the Bayſtan, there is another leſſe inuironed with a wall, and ſupported by ſixteene ſmall Pillars; in the incloſure whereof they ſell linnen cloth and ſilkes, but without it is the deteſtable Market where they ſell men and women; on the one ſide they buy ſlaues which are already inſtructed to ſerue, or to practiſe ſome trade, and on the other thoſe which know not any thing. Theſe places repreſent better then the former, the fearefull Image of the Turkiſh tyranny: It binds them to ſlauery which the God of the World hath created free: the Merchants viſit ſuch Merchandizes, and ſuch as haue an intent to buy, doe firſt ſee the perſons of either ſexe naked: they handle the parts of their bodies, to obſerue if they be ſound, and they vncouer that which Nature herſelfe hath laboured to hide. The women if they be faire are bought at a deare rate to ſerue the luſtfull paſſions of ſome hideous and fearefull Moore: they to whom Nature hath denied ſuch graces, are taken to empty the cloſe-ſtooles of great Turkiſh Ladies, and to waſh with water the parts of their body, which ſerue to diſcharge their bellies, as often as they haue need. We will relate the reſt of the miſeries of this ſeruitude in another place, diuiding them of purpoſe to make them the more ſupportable. For in truth they are in this worke the moſt tedious ſubject of this Hiſtory. Who could without ſighing ſee an infinite number of Chriſtians laden with the fetters of a violent ſlauery by the barbariſme of the Turks? And in a place neare vnto this the Infidels keepe another Market where they only ſell Nurſes: and from this vniuſt traffique the Princes vndertakers draw ſixteene thouſand Sequins for the toll, or ſixe thouſand foure hundred pounds ſterling.

Many other places of this ſtately Citie yeild vnto the treaſury the Reuenues of many good ſummes of money. The Tauernes xernes which sell wine publiquely to Christians, and to Iewes, but in secret to Turkes (being aboue fifteene hundred in number) pay thirtie fixe charges of monie, and euerie charge is valued at sixteene hundred thirtie three Sequins. The Sea shoare towards Pera, payes for the toll of fish which is sold there, eighteene hundred charges of siluer yearely. The Market whereas Corne, Meale and Pulse is sold, yeelds yearely fourteene charges of monie. That where the Merchandizes which comes from Caira is vented, is worth yearely to the *Chasna* or the Imperiall treasure, twentie foure charges of siluer. The great custome which is leuied from the Castle of *Gallipoli* vnto that of the blacke Sea, vpon Spices and other Merchandizes which comes by shipping is worth a hundred and fourescore charges of siluer. The great Shambles of Beeues and Muttons, which are without the Citie, and furnish it with necessarie meate, yeeld two and thirtie charges of monie; they are called *Chaanaris*, two hundred *Capsaplers*, or Butchers, serue them: A Superiour called *Capsabassa* commands them, who hath a charge they shall furnish fresh meates: And no man may kill an Oxe or a Sheepe without his permission, vnlesse it be for the Sacrifices of the Turkes. The Iewes purchase license from him to furnish their owne meate. Finally, if this *Capsabassa* should through couetousnesse raise the price of meate aboue the ordinarie taxe which is set downe, and that his corruption shall come to the knowledge of the *Grand Seignour*; there is nothing could free him from the rigour of cruell death: Hee is torne in peeces, and cut into foure quarters, which they send vnto the Shambles to be an example to others: So as feare keeping him in awe, hee preferres the publique vtilitie before his priuate profit. The impost which is raised in *September* and *October*, vpon the great number of Cattle which come from Hungarie to furnish Constantinople, is too great to be easily reckoned: For during this great Faire, whereas the people only and not the Butchers may buy, you shall see troupes of fiue and twentie thousand Oxen, and fortie thousand Sheepe. The treasure doth also receiue an inestimable reuenew by the sale of Houses, Ships, Vessels, and Barques at Sea: and the two in the hun-

hundred of all sorts of Merchandizes by Sea, amounts to great and inestimable summes. The taxe of those which imbarque themselues to trauaile, which is an *Aspre* for euery head if they be Turkes, and two if they be Christians or Iewes, is of no small importance. The Tribute called in Turkie *Charay*, which is leuied vpon the Iewes in Constantinople, after the rate of a Sequin for euerie male Childe, is worth eleuen Millions, three hundred Sequins yearely, although there be many of that Nation which are free from this Tribute. They doe also giue a present of three thousand Sequins euerie yeare, for the confirmation of their Priuiledges, and to haue a Rabbin to command their Synagogues, and twelue hundred Sequins to haue leaue to burie their Dead. The Christians, Grecians, within three miles or a league of Constantinople, pay for euery Male a Sequin, which amounts to the summe of aboue thirtie eight thousand Sequins: They doe also giue fiue and twentie thousand yearely for their priuiledge to haue a Patriarch, and to preserue the number of their Churches. The priuiledge of their Burials cost them aboue three thousand Sequins. The Imposition called of Virgins, helpes to fill the *Grand Seigneurs* Cofers, or his Treasurers Purse. There is raised vpon Maids which marrie (whereof they keepe a Register) if they be Turks, they giue two third parts of a Sequin, the Iewes pay a whole one, and the Christians a Sequin and a halfe. The Christians, Latines are for the most part freed from the violence and oppression of these vniust taxes, for they get their dependance from some Kings Embassadour, or from an inferiour Prince. The Albanois, they of Raguse, and the Geneuois, pay not any thing.

For the payment of so many Tributes wherewith the people is opprest by the Tyrant of the Easterne Regions, it is necessarie there should be many sorts of Coine minted. In Constantinople the great Imperiall Mint workes continually in Gold and Siluer, but no man can bee admitted to bea Farmer to these precious workes if hee be not a Grecian borne, by a speciall priuiledge of the *Grand Seigneur*, who hath conferred this grace vpon the Grecian, in consideration that the

C 3   Mines.

Mines of Gold and Siluer, are within the territories of Greece, where foure hundred men labour daily. And the Master of this rich Mint, is to furnish into the Serraile, the first day of euery moneth in the yeare, ten thousand Sequins of Gold, and twentie thousand of Siluer new coined, the *Grand Seigneur* hauing so appointed, that the monie which is employed in the Serrail shall bee new. The said Farmer hath power to make Proclamation, that whosoeuer hath any forraigne Coine, hee should bring it in within three dayes and receiue the iust price, vpon paine of Confiscation. He hath likewise power to take the Ingots from the Mines, so many as shall bee needfull for his worke.

The Mines which furnish most of the Gold and Siluer, which is minted in the Turkish Empire in Europe, are fiue in number. The one is digged in *Macedonia* vnder the Roots of a Hill called *Monte Sancto*, and this yeelds Gold: The other which is of the same substance is opened in Bulgaria, vpon the Confines of *Macedonia*: The three of Siluer are in *Greece*, rich and very plentifull. Out of all which they draw that which Nature had wisely hidden, to be conuersant among men: the which doth breed Quarrels, ingenders Contempts, dissolues Friendship, corrupts Concord, violates Chastitie, troubles Estates, obscures Mens wits, rauishes life, vnthrones reason from her seate, and robs man of himselfe:

But to returne to this great Citie of Constantinople, the Magnificences of the Princes which possesse it at this day, and the riches of some Bashawes, or great Men of the Court, haue caused aboue three hundred *Carranasserrails* to bee built: these are great and vast places to lodge Strangers. The number of the Hospitals for the poore and sicke, come to the number of fourescore: Nine of them are the principall; the Turkish Emperours which haue built those proud Mosquees, haue added them vnto their Fabrickes, where they are eternall markes of their Pietie. Moreouer, there are sixscore Colledges for the instruction of young Turkes, and the abode of the Schollers, which they call in their tongue *Softha*, that is to say wise Students, although they be nothing lesse. Either of them hath a

Cham-

Chamber for his Lodging, a Carpet for his Table, foure loaues by the day, a proportion of Pottage and a Candle: They giue them two suites of clothes yearely and they are paid out of Reuenewes of the Colledge, by the Masters and *Præceptors* which teach them, who are called *Sofchani*; that is for the first yeare when they enter into the Colledge: for to the second they adde to their entertainment an *Aspre* by the day, which is a fift part more then a pennie; afterwards they giue two, three, or foure *Aspres* by the day, according to the number of yeares they haue continued. With this poore pittance these Turks can keep no great ordinarie, vnlesse they receiue it from other places: But the gaine they make in writing of Bookes, (for the Turkes vse no printing) is not little but doth furnish their necessitie abundantly, yea, their Riots: they goe also to houses to teach the children of men of qualitie. But there is not in all Turkie more dissolute youthes then these Turkie Schollers: there is no kind of villanie but they commit with all impunitie. The priuiledges wherewith the Turkish Emperours haue honoured them, or rather the abuse of them hath drawne them into all sorts of impudencie: no man can apprehend them for any crime, vnlesse their Generall be present, to whom only this power is giuen. It is true that the Princes presence in *Constantinople* doth restrain the insolencie of their riots: But the Townes of Caramania and Natolia are wonderfully pestered. *Amurath* the third desirous (by reason of some troubles which happened) to know the number of such Gallants; they were found to bee aboue nine thousand, aswell in Greece as Natolia, not reckoning those which studied in Suria, Caire, Arabia and else-where.

Another great place inuironed with wall, and shut vp with good Gates, doth likewise beautifie the Citie of Constantinople, the Turkes call it *Seracyana*, that is to say, the Sellerie, or the place where they make Saddles, and rich Caparisons for Horses of Seruice and Pompe. It is an vnspeakable pleasure for those that loue Horsemanship, to see foure thousand workmen in this place, labouring in their shops, artificially vpon diuers Caparisons for Horses. Some set great round Pearles

vpon

vpon the Saddle of an Arabian Horse out of the *Grand Vizirs* stable: Others fasten a Bitt of Gold to Reines of rich red Leather of Russia; some doe fit stirrop Leathers to stirrops of Gold, enricht with a great number of Turkishes of the olde Rocke: Others fasten vpon a large Crouper a great number of precious stones: In another place you shall see a rich Saddle cast forth a thousand flames; the number of the Diamonds wherewith it is enricht make it inestimable: The Bitt and stirropes of Gold couered with Diamonds, the Tassels of Pearles which are at the Reines, and at the Trappers of the Crouper, and the other beauties of this royall Harnesse, rauish the eyes of such as looke of it with admiration of their wonders, and some silently perswade themselues that Fortune adorned with these precious things which depend on her, meanes to goe in triumph through Constantinople, to let the Turkes see that she dwels amongst them. In the midst of this place there is a Mosquee built for the deuotion of these workmen, and a goodly Fountaine in the same place which powres forth abundance of fresh water for their vse.

Two other great places likewise walled about, serue for the Lodgings of the Ianizaries, which are the best Footmen of the Turkish Armies: the one of these places is called *Eschiodolar*, that is to say the old habitations. It is of a square forme, and diuided into many small Lodgings, in the which the Corporals remaine, called *Ayabassa*, which signifies the chiefe of glorie: there are about a hundred and fiftie of this qualitie, and either of them commands two hundred Ianizaries, who dare not goe out of the place without leaue: the Gates are shut by night, and the keyes are kept by the Captaine.

The Arsenall is one of the goodliest and rarest things in Constantinople, it is vpon the Sea shoare, and containes a hundred and foure score Arches, vnder either of which enters a great Galley, yea, three may be safely lodged. The Officers which serue in this Arsenall, and receiue pay, are commonly fortie six thousand men: But its greatest force is the good order that is obserued by the which there are certaine Merchants which haue contracted to entertaine fourescore Gallies alwayes furnished

nished with all things necessary, and readie to put to Sea: the Munition of Powder is kept in diuers Towres in the walls of the Citie which looke towards Pera: they bring it from Grand *Caire*, where the Sultans cause it to be made.

The Garners in the which they keepe their prouision of Corne and other graine are built in a corner of the Citie towards Pera, the walls are very strong, and the Gates of Iron: there is sufficient to serue for many yeares, but euery third yeare they renew it: In the time of *Amurath* the third, there was found a great quantitie of Millet, the which had beene preserued sweet and vncorrupted for the space of foure score yeares.

But this great Imperiall Citie cannot bee happily gouerned without the execution of Iustice, which is the soule of the World, and the order of Reason; A Soueraigne Iudge is the chiefe, the Turkes call him *Stambolcadisi*, that is to say, the Iudge of Constantinople. He takes notice indifferently both of Ciuill and Criminall Causes, and no man is put to death in that place, if hee hath not condemned him. There are foure Lieutenants generall, distinguished into the foure principall Quarters of the Citie, and execute vnder him the same Iustice, but from their Sentences they appeale vnto the Iudge. Besides these there is a great Captaine of Iustice called *Soubassi*, who doth execute the greatest Function of his charge in Prisons, to heare the Causes, and to make report vnto the *Grand Vizir*: There are also foure Lieutenants vnder him, separated into the Quarters of the Citie, by the order of the Policies thereof, and a great number of inferiour Officers, as Sergeants, and other base persons which serue him. The Prisons of Constantinople are diuided into two, either of them is beautified (if there be any beautifull Prisons) with a great Medow in the midst and a pleasing Fountaine: It hath two stories, in that below are lodged criminall Offenders, in that aboue are such as are committed for ciuill causes. Heere the Iewes are separated from the Turkes, and the Turkes from the Christians, but in the lowest they are altogether, as Persons whom their Offences haue made common. The Almes deeds & good

D workes

workes which are exercised there by the Turkes, surpasse in few dayes those which are done in our Countries in many yeeres: The Turkish Charitie towardes his Neighbour surmounts ours, and it seemes, that for such good deeds, Heauen suffers them in the Empire of the World; for his equitie doth recompence the good, in any subiect whatsoeuer, aswell as it doth punish the euill. The Turkish Emperours themselues shew great compassion, they many times deliuer a great number of ciuill Prisoners, paying their debts for them. The other particularities which concerne the Turkes Iustice, shall bee handled in another Tract. In the meane time seeing wee are come neere vnto the Imperiall Pallace, which is the *Serrail*, let vs striue to enter, although the Gates bee carefully garded, and let vs see the rare beauties of this famous place.

Chap. II.
Of the Grand Seigneurs Serrail.

Description of the Serrail in generall.

THree *Serrails* doe augment the glorie of *Constantinople*, the one is called *Eschy Saray*, that is to say, the old *Serrail*, which was the first Royall House built within the Citie, after that the Turkes became Masters: It is scituated almost in the midst of it; the forme is square, and the Citcle containes an Italian mile and a halfe, or halfe a French League, such as are in *Languedoc*, or *Prouence*. The women which haue serued the deceased Emperours, their Sisters if they bee not married, & their Childrens Nurses, haue it for their Lodging, from whence they may not depart vnlesse they marry. A Dame whose age and discretion hath purchased merit, hath the care and conduct of the rest as Superiour; they call her *Chiara Cadun*, that is to say, Great Dame. The *Grand Seigneur* in his most solitarie humours retires himselfe sometimes into this place to seeke the consolation which he cannot find elsewhere. The other *Serrail* is of a lesse extent, it is scituated at the *Hippodrome*, and serues at this day for the solemnizing of Playes, Pompes, and Sports for the Turkish Princes: and for an Academie

demie to foure hundred of the *Grand Seigneurs* Pages, which are there instructed in the Turkish tongue, to manage Armes, and other Exercises fit for them, and they goe not forth vntill they be made *Espayn*, that is to say, Men at Armes : they are bred vp and taught at their Masters charge: this place is called *Ebrayn Bassa Saray*, that is to say, the *Serrail* of *Ibraim Bassa*, who was sonne in Law to *Sultan Solyman* the Second, and his Fauourite for a time. Hee caused it to bee built at his owne charge. The third is called *Boyuch Saray*, that is, the great *Serrail*, now the ordinary abode of the Turkish Emperours: It is of this which we meane to speake.

This great *Serrail* the Mansion of Turkish Emperours and of their Family, is pleasantly scituated in the same place, whereas *Byzance* was in old time, built vpon a pleasant point of firme Land, which lookes towards the mouth of the blacke Sea : Its forme is triangular, two sides thereof are watred by the waues of the *Egean* Sea : the third is supported by the Citie; it is inuironed with high walls, and fortified with many Towres which doth better the defence. It hath three miles in circuit, Many Gates serue for the entrie, aswell towardes the Sea as Land: one principall neere to *Sancta Sophia*, is vsually open, the others are not; but when it pleaseth the *Grand Seigneur*. This Gate is guarded day and night by Companies of *Capigis* who are Porters, which relieue one another, and in the night some Ianizaries which are without the Gate in little Cabins of wood mounted vpon wheeles are in Sentinell, and when need requires aduertise the *Corps de Gard* of *Capigis*. In the Towres which are vpon the *Serrail*, certaine *Azamoglans*, that is to say, Children without experience, or Rusticks, of those of the Tribute, to see if any one doth approach by Land, or any Vessels by Sea neere to this Imperiall House : And in that case they discharge certaine Peeces of Artillerie, which are ready charged to that effect, vpon a little platforme of fiue fathome broad, which is betwixt the wall of the *Serrail* and the Sea.

The Chambers and Royall Hals of the *Sultans* Lodging are disposed according to the diuers seasons of the yeare : Those whi-

whither hee retires in Winter are built vpon plaine and eeuen ground: The others where hee seekes after the coole and fresh aire during the importune heats of the Summer, are scituated vpon diuers naturall Hills: Some of them view the agitations of the Sea; and these are termed *Chiosehi*, that is to say, Cages, and places of goodly prospect. The *Sultan* goes sometimes to these places to take his pleasure alone in this goodly view, and sometimes he cals his women to mingle with this recreation the soft deligts of their lasciuious conuersation. Neere vnto this goodly place, is that where the Turkish Emperour giues Audience to Embassadours; receiues or dismisses those whom hee sends to gouernment of remoted Prouinces. It is scituated in the plaine of a Court vpon a little Island, enameled with many goodly flowres, and watred by some pleasing Fountaines, richly imbelished according to their custome. Within it, is seene a *Sopha*; that is to say, a Throne, couered with some rich cloth of Gold, where is also to bee seene one of Crimson Veluet, embroydered with great round Pearles: this Throne is called the Throne without, to distinguish it from that within the *Grand Seigneurs* Chamber; and in this, *Osman* the Second, did sit, when hee could not enioy the other which was within, where his Vncle *Mustapha* was shut vp in the yeare 1617. There the Turkish Emperours are set in such actions. The walls of his Chamber are lined with certaine white stones which are cast and burnt, and painted in diuers colours, which yeeld a pleasant sight. The Chamber which is ioyning to it hath the walles couered with Plates of Siluer, pourfiled with Gold, and the Planchen is couered with rich Tapestrie, after the *Persian* manner with Gold and Silke. The Quarter where as the Women and Virgins are lodged, which are destinated for the Emperours pleasure, is like vnto a great Monasterie of Religious Women: But they doe not obserue the Vow of Chastitie: There are Dormitors, or sleeping places, Refectuaries, Baths, Galleries, pleasing Gardens, and goodly Fountaines, in so great a number, as they abound in all the Allies, and of all sides powre forth the sweet noyse of their charming murmurs. The other Lodgings for the Domestiques

of

of the *Serrail*, haue with the beautie of their structures, the commodities of their scituation. Two great places are ioyned to these buildings, whereof the one serues for the *Chasna* without (for they haue another within more retired from the houshold) the Mosquees, Bathes, Schooles, Kitchins, places to run Horses, to wrastle, shoote, and to represent any action, augment the wonders of this Imperiall Pallace whereof we haue spoken in generall: Now let vs descend to the particular description of the places thereof, at the least to those which wee could yet see; for no man that liues abroad may enter into the *Serrail* vnlesse the Emperour bee absent; and yet hee must bee highly fauoured by some person of credit and authoritie in that place: For the Turkes would imagine they should offend the Maiestie of their Prince, to giue entrance into his Quarter of the *Serrail*, to any one be he stranger or other.

The first wall of the *Serrail* is neere vnto the first Mosquee of *Sancta Sophia*, with the great and chiefe Gate of that stately Pallace, adorned with a great Portall painted with letters of Gold, in branches and compartiments after the manner of *Iaua*; fiftie *Capigis* with their Armes (which are Harquebusses, Bowes, Arrowes, and Semiters) keepe the Guard: By it they enter into a great place or Court about threescore paces long, and a hundred paces broad, in the which vpon the right hand is the place for the sicke persons of the *Serrail*, kept by an Eunuch, who hath vnder him a great number of men employed in the seruice of sicke persons; on the otherside on the left hand there are seene a great number of Waggons, with a great quantitie of wood for the vse of the House: aboue it, is built a long Gallerie, in the which they keepe ancient Armes, as Morrions, Gauntlets, Coats of Maile, Pikes, and Harquebusses; wherewith they arme the Officers of the Arsenall, and some other troupes to goe out of *Constantinople* in pompe, when as the *Sultan* or some other powerfull *Bashaw* makes his entre. Into this Court the *Bashawes* and great men of the Port may entrie on horsebacke; but they must leaue their Horses and goe on foot into another great Court, which hath neere three hundred foot in square, made in fashion of a Cloyster, with a
low

low Gallerie round about it, supported by Pillars of Marble; it is more richly adorned then the other; the Gate is likewise guarded by *Capigis*, armed as the first. They passe on to a third Gate into a lesser Court, but more delicious; Many goodly Fountaines powring forth abundance of water, and some Alleyes drawne by a line, and shadowed with a great number of Cyprus Trees planted vpon the sides which beautifie the place: And there are many squares of Medow diapred with diuers sorts of flowres which augment the pleasures of the sight: No man passeth thorough this Court on horsebacke, but the Turkish Emperour, who descends at the third gate: On either side are many goodly Portals supported by rich Pillars of Marble: without these Portals are ranged in Battaile the Companies of Ianizaries, well apparelled and better armed, when as they are commanded to shew themselues at the entrie of the *Serrail*, when as some strange Embassadour goes to kisse his Robe.

The Kitchins.
In this Court are the Kitchins of the *Serrail*, the which are nine in number, separated in their buildings one from another, with their dependances, and serued by particular Officers: The first is that of the Emperour; The second, that of the *Sultana*, which is most esteemed for her graces or for her fruitfulnesse; The third, that of the other *Sultana's*: The fourth, that of the *Capiaga*, who is great Master of the *Serrail*: The fift, that of the *Diuan*, which is the Councell, whereas the Prince doth administer Iustice by the mouth of his Officers, of the which we will speake hereafter: The sixt, that of the *Agalaris*, which are the *Sultans* Familiars, many are Eunuches, the rest are vntoucht: The seuenth, is that of the lesser Officers of the *Serrail*: The eighth, is for the women which serue the *Sultana's*: The ninth, is for the Officers which attend the *Diuan*, as Guards, Porters, Vshers, and such like.

On the left hand in the same place, are the *Sultans* stables, to containe only fiue and twentie or thirtie goodly Horses, which are appointed for his Exercises with his greatest Familiars in the *Serrail*: Aboue these stables are many Chambers, in the which they keepe the Saddles, Bridles, and other Furniture for

Court of the Grand SEIGNEVR.

for these Horses of pleasure: But all so rich and so glistering with Pearle and stone, as the price is inestimable: There are some which the very Reines and Crouper, exceed the value of a hundred thousand pounds sterling: What must the Saddle and the rest of the Furniture amount vnto? Along the bankes of that Channell which doth water the walls of the *Serrail*, there are built seuenteene great stables, whereas the *Grand Seigneur* hath a great number of Horses of rare esteeme, whereon he mounts when hee goes to the Warre; or when to dazle the eyes of some forreine Embassadour, with the lustre of his greatnesse, hee makes a solemne and stately entrie into *Constantinople*.

A little beyond in the same Court is the Quarter for the publique *Diuan*, where as the *Grand Vizir* Lieutenant Generall of the Turkish Empire with a good number of Officers keepes the Audiences foure dayes in the Weeke: Neere vnto it is the Chamber of the *Chasna*, or Treasure without, where they lay vp the Rents and Reuenewes of diuers Prouinces, wherewith they pay the Officers: They likewise furnish the Chamber of Accompts, the rest is carried into the *Chasna*, or secret Treasure within, whereof the *Grand Seigneur* keepes the Keyes: The first is vsually sealed by the *Grand Vizir*. In the same Court on the left hand is the great Gate which enters into the *Sultana's* lodging; It is carefully kept by a troupe of blacke and hideous Eunuches, to whom the *Sultan* hath intrusted the Guard. And as hee hath lodged therein (by the number of goodly Women which are brought vnto him from all parts) the liuely Images of Loue and the Graces; so he hath set at the Gates those of Hatred and Terrour. He himselfe goes vnto them by another passage neere vnto his Chamber. The last part of this goodly Court makes the entrie to the Emperours Lodgings, the which is forbidden to any whatsoeuer, except the slaues that serue him. If any great *Bassa* pressed with some important businesse desires to enter, hee must first haue leaue from the Princes mouth.

The entrie of this Gate leads towards the Hall, whereas the *Sultan* sits, when hee will giue Audience, and suffer any forreine

Diuan.

Chasna.

reine Princes Embassadour to kisse his Robe. At their entrance they discouer the new beauties of this place more particularly: A goodly Court paued with fine Marble in Mosaike worke, serues for a passage for those which are entred, and the goodly Fountaines which beautifie it, will not suffer them to goe farre, without fixing their eyes vpon their pleasing structure: The Pauillions and stately Chambers which are within it, seeme to haue beene built and embellished by the hands of delight and pleasure: For in them the *Grand Seigneur* eats most commonly, and takes his Recreations. The Bathes, Hals, and Galleries of this place, surpasse in their Magnificence the force of imagination: Wee may only say of them, that they are the buildings of the most powerfull and rich Monarchs of the Earth.

The *Sultans* lodging in Summer.

In another part of the *Serrail*, vpon a little pleasing Hill is built a lodging for Summer, whither the *Sultan* retires himselfe during the Canicular dayes, to enioy the fresh aire which is found there, and the pleasures of his Gardens, vpon the which he hath one prospect, and the other lookes towards the Sea: The place is exceeding beautifull, but amidst this great diuersitie there is a Hall which opens towards the East, supported by rich Pillars of Marble like vnto the ordinarie Mansion of pleasure: It is enricht with the goodliest workes the Leuant can afford, and furnished after a royall manner: The windowes haue their prospect vpon a little Lake of a square forme, made with admirable art: Thirtie Fountaines diuided vpon a Platforme of fine Marble which doth enuiron it, furnish water to fill it, and pleasingly trouble the silence of the place by their continuall murmurie. The *Sultan* goes often vpon this Lake in a Brigantine, being followed by some Iesters, and Mutes, who minister occasion of delight, some by their pleasant encounters, the other by their ridiculous faces and gestures, and sometimes tumbling them into the water they giue him occasion of laughter: Hee himselfe is pleased to lay ambushes for them, to make them fall by the Platforme into the Lake.

The *Grand Seigneurs* Chamber.

From this Hall they passe into the *Grand Seigneurs* Chamber,

-ber, it is proportionable in greatnesse to those of the Royall Pallace: The walls are after their accustomed manner couered with fine stone, in which are grauen many flowres: the Portals are of cloth of Gold, some are of Crimson Veluce embroidered with Gold and rich Pearle. The Bed is not inferiour in riches, the posts are of massie Siluer, vpon which are set Lions of Chryssall of the Rocke: The Curtaines are of greene Cloth of Gold, the richest that are made at *Bursia* in *Asia*, without any fringes, but in their place there hangs certaine Bels made of great Orientall Pearle: The worke is excellent and the price inestimable. The Couering hanging to the ground, is also of rich Cloth of Gold, the Cushions and Pillowes are of the same stuffe. This Bed is rather a piece of the Turkish pompe then for any necessarie vse: For the Turkes doe not vse these kind of Beds, but sleepe on the ground vpon Mattresses, whereof we will speake in the sixt Chapter. The floore of this royall Chamber is couered with *Persian* Carpets of Gold and Silke: The *Sopha*, that is to say, the places where the *Sultanesses*, are about a foot and a halfe from the ground, and couered with the like Tapestrie, vpon the which are Cushions of Cloth of Gold. Ouer this seate is a Cloth of Estate, of Wood, couered with plates of Gold, enricht with stones, and supported by foure Pillars adorned in the same manner. In the midst of the floore of this Chamber, hangs a rich Candlesticke of a meane greatnesse, and of a round forme, the midst whereof is of excellent Chrystall, the other parts are of Siluer gilt, set with Turkeyes, Rubies, Emeralds, and Diamonds, whose diuersitie giue a pleasing lustre. In a corner of the said Chamber, vpon a Table of massie Siluer, is a little Bason to wash his hands, It is of pure Gold enricht with many Turkesses and Rubies, with Ewre of the same; Against the walls are set two Cupboards, whose doores are of Chrystall, which through their transparent light, shew about two dozen of Bookes richly couered, in the which the *Sultan* sometimes spends his time, and passeth away his time in reading. Sometimes one of their Histories, and sometimes the true examples which are mentioned in the Old Testament. Aboue these Cupboards there is one lesse, in-

E to

26   *The History of the Serrail, and of the*

to the which the Treasurer of the *Serrail* doth every Wednesday, put three purses filled: whereof the one is with Gold, and the other two are of Silver, which the *Sultan* employes in his almesdeeds, and the gratifications which hee giues to the slaues that serue him, and which are his ordinarie Companie. Doubtlesse this kinde of people doe much imbase the glory of so powerfull a Monarch, and the shame to haue none about him but base persons, causeth him to be disesteemed. Soueraigne Princes should admit none but the ablest men of their Estates about their Persons. For as God hath in Heauen the Ministerie of the Angels, and other intellectuall creatures: So Kings, who are his liuely Images, should haue about them Men whose vertue and rare qualities of the mind haue raised aboue others. What entertainment can a great Prince find, in such abiect persons and so ill bred; and what seruice can hee receiue from a man drawne from the stable, and from the profession of a Horse-keeper, or a Coachman, from a Huntsman, and the bawling of Hounds? What contentment from a brutish Faulkoner, whilst that Men of merit are in contempt? This disorder is sometimes seene in the World, yea, in the Courts of great Princes to their shame, and to the great preiudice of the publique. Neere vnto this Chamber is a goodly Librarie, where are many Bookes, rich for their stately couerings, and precious for their workes, the immortall markes of the glorie of their Authours. This is called the Secret Library; It is the most renowned of all the *Serrail*. There is another towards their Quarter which serue the Chamber, and the *Grand Seigneurs* Pages, filled with a great number of Bookes in all Languages; among the which there are to bee seene at this day sixe score Volumes of the ancient Librarie of Great *Constantine*, of an extraordinary bignesse: They are aboue a fathome broad and two in length: Their leaues are of such thinne Parchment, as they seeme rather to be of Silke then Skinnes; most part written in letters of Gold, especially those which containe the Old and New Testament; their couerings are of Siluer guilt after the antique manner, set with a great number of precious stones. The price (without doubt) hath preserued them from
spoile

margin notes:
Great Monarchs should haue able men about them, & not Groomes whom they aduance, and are entertained by Fooles and Ignorants.

Libraries.

spoile and ruine, where as the rest haue perished by the barbarousnesse of the Turkes, who sacke *Constantinople* in the time of *Mahomet* the Second: The *Sultan* holds them so precious as he will not allow any one to handle them.

The number of Gardens in the *Serrail* are not fewer in number, then are delightfull to looke on: The Prince hath his, the *Sultana's* theirs, and without this Imperiall House, there are eighteene planted towardes the Sea, whereof the fruites and reuenewes are by the Law of State employed for the entertainment of the Princes Table; whereof we will speake elsewhere. He which hath the chiefe charge is called *Bostangibassi*, that is to say, great *Gardiner*; and is one of the most eminent Dignities of the Empire, he is many times much affected by his Master, and feared by the other *Bassas*, to whom hee may doe good and bad Offices with the Prince, when hee gouernes him alone in his walkes, and entertaines him in affaires of Estate.

Two Mosques serue in the *Serraile*, for their Deuotion. The one is towardes that Quarter where the Prince and his Officers lodge; and the other is neere the Lodging of the women and their slaues. And although the Turkes will not admit of the vse of Bells; yet there are a great number of little Clockes in the *Serrail*, which strike the houres both by day and night. The *Grand Seigneur's* Pages are instructed to keepe them: and most part of the men of qualitie in the *Serrail*, and likewise the women haue little Watches, whereof they make vse. This is all that can be written of the *Grand Seigneurs Serrail*, at the least that can come vnto the knowledge of Christians, to whom the entrie (vnlesse it be vpon the dayes of *Diuan*) is expresly forbidden, and the inward parts of this Imperiall House, whereof wee haue spoken, may not be seene by them, vnlesse the Prince be absent; and yet hee must haue some particular friendship with the Officers of the *Serrail*, and mony in his hand, the which doth not only open them the closest Gates in *Turkie*, but doth facilitate the most difficult affaires, through the auarice of the Turkes, to the which all their other passions seeme to yeeld. Let vs come now to the *Grand Seig-*

E 2 *neurs*

neurs Exercises, to his manner of liuing, to the number of his Officers, and other particularities of his Crowne: But let vs begin by his Coronation.

Chap. III.

Of the Coronation of the Turkish Emperour.

After that death (who strikes with an equall hand, aswell the stately Pallaces of Kings, as poore Cottages couered with straw) hath taken out of this World some Turkish Emperour, he of his Children which is destinated to the succession of his Scepter, parts from the gouernment whither his Father had sent him (the which most commonly is *Magnesia* a Prouince in *Asia*) and comes secretly to *Constantinople*, and into the *Serrail* by that Port which lookes towards the Sea; for the passage whereof the *Bostangibassi*, which is the great Gardiner, goes to receiue him in the Imperiall Galley vpon the side of *Asia*, passeth the straight, conducts him into the *Serrail*, and leads him into his Fathers Throne, whither the great men of the Port, that is to say, of the Court (for so they call it) come to adore him, and to acknowledge him for their Prince. Presently the *Basha* which is Gouernour of *Constantinople* causeth Proclamation to be made in the Citie, & then throughout all the Empire: *That the Soule of the inuincible Emperour Sultan N. enioyes an immortall Glorie, and an eternall Peace; and that the Empire of Sultan N. may flourish and prosper in all felicitie for many yeares.* The third day after they hold the great *Diuan*, which is the generall Councell, whereas all the great Men of the Court and Officers of the Crowne assist, and resolue concerning the affaires of the Estate: The Emperour doth not assist; yet he is in a Chamber neere, and sees but is not seene, and heares through a Lattice window what they treat of, and what they say. At the end of the *Diuan* all these Officers, goe by foure and foure, or by sixe and sixe into the Chamber where the *Sultan* is, and there without speaking any
thing

thing make a low reuerence, and so passe on, going forth to another doore: They returne to the *Diuan*, where as Dinner attends them. The *Sultan* dines at the same time; and after halfe an houre, (which is all the time he spends at the Table) he mounts vpon a stately Horse, being followed by the chiefe Commanders of the Warre, hee shewes himselfe to his people of *Constantinople*, and receiues from them their cryes and acclamations of Ioy: which are, *Liue, and long may Sultan N. Raigne.* Hee goes to some Mosquee where his Predecessours haue beene buried; Hee makes his prayers, which being ended one of the twentie Preachers of his Court goes into the Pulpit, and by a short discourse giues him to vnderstand after the Turkish manner the greatnesse of the charge wherewith God hath called him, exhorts him to haue a care of his Estate, and especially to the maintenance and increase of *Mahomets* Law. The Sermon being ended, the same Priest doth blesse him seuen times, and at euery time the people answere *Amen.* At the same time the *Moufti*, or high Priest of the Law who is present, makes him to take the Oath vpon the *Alcoran*; Girds him with the Sword which in old time *Ottoman* did weare, and blessing him sayes these wordes, *God send you Ottomans Bountie*: They doe so much honour the vertues of this Prince, who raigned about three hundred and twentie two yeares since, as they wish them to his Successors. I haue heard a Prince of the Turkish Emperours house say, That the Learned in their Historie report, that *Ottoman* going thorough the Towne of *Prussia*, beeing the chiefe of his Empire, hee said aloud vnto the people, that whosoeuer were an hungrie, thirstie, or naked, let them come vnto his house, he had wherewithall to feed and cloathe the poore. After the *Mufti* the people blesse him with their loude cryes: Thus charged with all these blessings hee goes to horsebacke, and carries them backe to the *Serrail*; where he busies himselfe to cause his brethren to be strangled in his presence, whom hee had caused to come from the places where they were resident: For it is written in their custome, *One God in Heauen, one Emperour vpon Earth*: They beleeue this is the only meanes

E 3

30   *The History of the Serrail, and of the*

Nec Regna so-
cium ferre nec
tæda sciunt, Se-
nec.

to settle the Estate, and to divert the Ciuill Warre which the pluralitie of Princes might breed: They haue often this Prouerbe in their mouthes, *That a Kingdome and Loue, admit no Companion*: Their Errour makes them beleeue that the Princes of their bloud are such. This bloudie custome hath been rigorously obserued for three hundred yeares and more, vntill the Raigne of *Achmet*, who died in the yeare 1617. who gaue life vnto his brother *Mustapha*, and at his death left him his Scepter: But the Officers of his Crowne tooke it from him with his libertie, and kept him prisoner in the Serrail; to make *Osman* his Nephew Raigne in his place, who was afterward miserably massacred by the people, and the same *Mustapha* restored to the Throne, where the inconstancie of his Fortune suffered him but few dayes, after which the *Bassa's* shut him vp in his first Prison, and seated in his Throne *Amurath* the Fourth a young Prince brother to the vnfortunate *Osman*.

The *Sultans* bountie at his Coronation.

The Largesse which the *Sultan* makes at his comming to the Crowne, is distributed after this manner. He must giue vnto the great *Mufti* two thousand fiue hundred Sequins, as much to the *Grand Vizir*; the other of the *Vizirs* or *Bassa's* haue either of them two thousand, the *Cadilesquers* euery one two hundred and fiftie Sequins, the *Tefterdars* euery one of them as much; the *Capigibassi* euery one a hundred; the *Aga's* of the *Ianizaries* two hundred and fiftie, the *Iman* Royall hath but fiue and twentie: the most famous Doctours of the Law receiue threescore, the other which are inferiour haue euery one thirtie two Sequins. They giue fortie to the *Bascousnamogi*, that is to say Iournalists, comes to the *Curusmuasabagi*, or Comptrouler of the Royall Tribute; twentie to the *Mucatagis*, which keepes the Bookes of the *Diuan*; sixteene to euerie *Muasferagas*, which are men at Armes; eight to euerie *Spahi*, or light Horseman, and moreouer fiue *Aspres* by the day in augmentation of their pay. Euery Deputie of the *Tefterdar*, hath fiue and twentie Sequins: The chiefe of the Pauillions of the field, called by the Turkes *Athuir Eter Bassi*, are set downe in the Roll of this Royall distribution euery

one

Court of the Grand SEIGNEVR. 31

one for fiue and twentie Sequins; They that lead the Horses before the King, called *Sarrassis*, haue either of them eight: The *Serchai* haue as much; The *Meirery*, which beate the Drums before the Prince the like summe; the *Sardigis*, foure; the *Capigis*, eight; the *Casnadaris*, eight; and the *Snalaris*, who carrie water to the *Grand Seigneur*, the like summe. The *Emirs* haue a better portion, either of them hath a hundred. The *Ianizaries* by their violence haue broken the bounds of the Monarchs liberalitie to them, they giue them more or lesse according to the time and necessitie they haue of them; their pay is alwayes increased at the least an *Aspre* by the day. The Groomes of the Stable and Cookes haue equally eight Sequins a piece; and they which pray vnto God after the Turkish manner, in the Chappels where the *Sultans* are buried, haue no more. This largesse and distribution of *Sultanins*, or Turkish Sequins, amounts (by season of the great number of those which receiue the Portions) to great and immense summes of monie.

The fourth day following, he takes his Gallion, and goes by Sea to a Garden inuironed with a Parke neere vnto the *Arsenall*; the Turkes call it *Vseni*, that is to say, the house of Pleasure; and there he hunts some houres, and courseth what Beast he pleaseth; If he take any thing, the Turkish Superstition teacheth him to hold it for a good signe. From his sport he goes to affaires, he visits his *Arsenall*; and hauing neere him the Generall of the Sea, called Captaine *Bassa*, hee makes him to giue an account of the affaires of the Sea, what number of Vessels there are fit for the warre, what Men, what Armes, and what Munition is in them: Being thus informed of his Sea forces, he returnes to his Serrail. The next day which is the fift after his Coronation, the *Grand Vizir*, or according to the Turkes, *Vizirhazem*, that is to say, the Supreame *Vizir*, goes vnto him, and in few words yeelds him an account of the generall affaires of his Empire. And as the Turkes haue Almes in singular recommendation, these first dayes of Coronation, after the Prince hath giuen a Largesse vnto the people, in casting of money in the streets where hee passeth, hee
vseth

vſeth great Charitie to Hoſpitals and Priſons, in ſuch ſort as the charges of the pious Actions, were found to amount during the Raigne of *Amurath*, Father to *Mahomet* the third, who liued when as *Henrie* the Great made *France* happie by the felicities of his Raigne; to the ſumme of one hundred and threeſcore thouſand pounds ſterling, which is in their money foure hundred thouſand Sequins. Doubtleſſe, the preſages of their Raigne cannot bee but fortunate, when as they are accompanied with good Works; and Charitie is a powerfull ſupport to a Crowne. It were to bee deſired (ſaid a great Man) that Soueraignes had tried the condition of a priuate Man oppreſt with miſery, to learne compaſſion, for no Man is ſenſibly toucht with the eſtate of a miſerable Man, but he that hath beene ſo.

Gaspard Zeblick, Chancelour to three Emperours, Optareſe dicebat omnes Reges aliquando priuatos pauperesque fuiſſe. Neque enim ſatis miſeretur qui nunquam fuit miſer, Æneas Syluius lib. 1. Comment. de reb. geſt. Alph.

After the fift day, the Ladies of his bloud, be they Virgins or married to ſome *Baſha*, goe to viſit him: He receiues them very graciouſly, honours them with many rich Preſents of precious ſtones, and grants them what fauours they demand, be it for the aduancement of their Husbands, or for his bountie to ſome other perſon. But this new *Sultan* is no ſooner ſeated in the Imperiall Throne of the Turkes, but hee doth preſently imitate the proud arrogancie of his Predeceſſours, and takes with the Scepter the vanitie of the proud Title wherewith they are puft vp: the following Chapter will ſhew it.

CHAP. IV.

Of the Titles and Qualities which the Turkiſh Emperours take.

Secundæ res acrioribus ſtimulis animos explorant; quia miſeria toleratur, fœlicitate corrumpimur. Galba ſaid it to Plato in Tacitus, lib. 1. hiſt.

THe proſperities of the World are a triall of the force of the minde, rather then aduerſities: Theſe are more eaſie to beare, thoſe doe commonly puffe men vp to a dangerous inſolencie. But where are great proſperities found but with Princes? If they vſe them ſoberly, their modeſtie binds Heauen to the preſeruation of their Eſtates, and would force men

to

to cherish their memorie. The Turkish Emperours are neuer crowned with this merit; their breeding to the excesse of vices rather than to the continencie of vertue, doth not make them capable to know themselues, and the excesse of the prosperities of their Empire transports them to pride: So as if Heauen suffers them to continue in the Monarchie of the East, it is to punish our disorders. Their actions doe not only shew their Pride, but their Titles speake it more plainly. *Selym* the First of that Name stiled himselfe Master of all the Soueraignes of the World. Behold the Qualities which he did assume. *Sultan Selym, Othoman, King of Kings, Lord of all Lords, Prince of all Princes, Sonne and Nephew of God.* Hee caused it to be written vnder his Portraite, the which *Solyman* the Second his Sonne did vsually keepe by his bed side. This man was no modester then his Father, for if he hath not set downe in his Titles that hee would be the only Prince of the World, hee hath often deliuered it in his words, *By the Soule of my Father* (said he being in *Hungarie* at the siege of *Buda*) *seeing there is but one God Gouernour in Heauen, it is reasonable there should be but one Monarch to rule and gouerne the inferiour World.* The rest which haue followed in the Succession of the *Othoman* Estate haue vsed the same vnto our dayes. *Achmat* the First, who died in the yeare 1617, treating with the inuincible Monarch *Henry* the Great, by the meanes of the *Seigneur* of *Brenes* his Embassadour at *Constantinople*, causeth to be set downe in the beginning of the Articles which were sent into *France*, the Titles which follow: *In the name of God, a marke of the high Family of the* Othoman *Monarches, with the beautie, greatnesse, and splendour thereof, so many Countries are conquered and gouerned. I, who am by the infinite graces of the Iust, great, and all powerfull Creatour and by the abundance of Miracles of the chiefe of his Prophets, Emperour of victorious Emperours, Disposer of Crownes to the greatest Princes on the Earth, Seruant of two most sacred Townes,* Mequa *and* Medina, *Protector and Gouernour of the holy* Ierusalem, *Lord of the greatest part of* Europe, Asia, *and* Africa, *conquered by our victorious Sword, & terrible Lance:*

F   *That*

That is to say, of the Caramaines and Beglierbeis of Grecia, Tomisuuer, Bosnia, Sogherie, and of the Countries and Strainesse of Asia, and Natolia, of Caromania, of Egypt, and of all the Countries of the Parthians, of the Curdzes, Georgians, of the deserts of Tiflis, of Soruan; as also which are under the refuge of that Prince of the Tartarie, named Seida, and of the Companions of Cipulac, Cyprus, Diabback, Alep, Erzerum, Damas, Babylon, the feede of the Princes of the Gaudes, of Bazera, Egypt, Arabia the Happie, Abes, Adem, Thunis, Boultrie, Tripoli, Barbarie, and of so many other Countries, Islands, Straights, Passages, People, Families, Generations, and of so many hundred Millions of vallerous Souldiers, which Iiue vnder the obedience and iustice of those who are the Emperour Achmat, Sonne to the Emperour Mahomet, of the Emperour Amurath, of the Emperour Selim, of the Emperour Solymon, of the Emperour Selim, and by the grace of God the residue of the greatest Princes of the World, and other of the admirable Emperours. They adde to this pride the contempt of other Princes, whom they esteeme little better then their Vassals. Doubtlesse, such Emperours which haue nothing great but the extent of their Empire, are like vnto gilded Collosses, which outwardly represent a forme of some Diuinitie, and are within nothing but earth or Plaister. Prouinces, Riches, Robes of Purple, and a Diadem make not a King; but Vertue and Wisdome. A Monarch which commands his passions raignes doubly, and entring into himselfe, proues the effects of this veritie necessary for a Court: *That the Prince which knowes himselfe to be a Man, will neuer grow proud.*

Regem non faciunt opes;
Non vestis Tyria color,
Non frontis nota regia
Non auro nitidæ trabes.
Rex est qui posuit metus,
Et diri mala pectoris:
Quem non ambitio impotens,
Et numquam stabilis fauor
vulgi præcipitis mouet, Senec.
in Thyest.

CHAP. V.

Of the ordinarie attire of the Grand Seignenr, *and of his daily Exercises.*

THe Turkish Emperour doth not differ much from his Courtiers in his ordinary Apparell: Only hee weares them

them somewhat longer, and his shooes are without buckles, and cut in leaues. But when hee adornes himselfe to honour with his presence the solemnitie of some great day, at the Circumcision of the Princes his Children; or to make his entrie into *Constantinople*: his Robes of Cloth of Gold, set with Pearles and great Diamonds giue the Maiestie of his person a glorious lustre. This is the glory of such Princes: Maiestie consists in Vertue, and not in the pompe of Habits. A King should rather shew himselfe a King by his vertuous carriage and his authoritie, than by his Robes.

The *Sultana's* differ not much in their Habits from their Soueraigne Prince: They weare breeches like vnto his, and vnder them linings of fine Linnen; Their Robes are of the same stuffe, and their shooes in like manner: They sleepe like vnto him in their Linnen lynings, and little Cassocks of Silke pinckt, which goes little beneath the waste.

The Prince riseth with the Day, and the Morning sees him begin his Prayers after the Turkish manner, wherein hee spends halfe an houre: After this hee writes as much, during the which they bring him some cordiall thing, which hee takes presently: Then reading followes for a whole houre, but it is many times without fruit; for that hee entertaines the time with fabulous Bookes: It is true that some *Sultans* haue taken delight to read the life of Great *Alexander*, and some others haue caused *Aristotle* to be expounded vnto them. An ignorant Prince is a Pilot without Card or Compasse. *Alphonso* King of *Arragon*, called such Princes by a Name, which I forbeare to mention; for the reuerence I owe to Kings. Hauing read, if it be a day of *Diuan*, or of Counsell, hee giues Audience to the *Grand Vizir*, who comes to make report of that which hath beene done, and he receiues the veneration of other Officers. From thence he descends into his Gardens or Walkes, contents his eyes with the aspect of good-ly Fountaines, and pleasing Alleyes; and feeds his eares with the fooleries and scurrilities of his Iesters and Dwarffs which follow him. At his returne hee fals againe to reading, if hee haue any delight in it, or to some other exercise, vntill he call

for

for Dinner, the which is speedily serued: Hee neuer spends aboue halfe an houre at the Table; from the which hee goes to his Prayers at noone, where after his manner hee entertaines the Diuinitie. But how variable is humane inconstancie: from this pious exercise he passeth to the embracings of humanitie, and entertaines himselfe with his Women for some houres; vntill the time of Prayer at Night doth force him to leaue them: When that is done, hee makes another walke into his Gardens, and being followed by his Iesters and Dwarffs, hee entertaines himselfe with their fooleries. The last Office calls him to his Chamber; it is that which the Turkes say, when as the day is spent and in the obscuritie of the night, where hee imployes himselfe vntill Supper time. These are his imployments in generall: Let vs now speake of them in particular.

Chap. VI.

Of the Grand Seigneurs Table of his Meate, and of his sleepe.

THe *Grand Seigneur* eates three or foure times a day in Summer, but lesse in Winter: He sits crosse-legged after the Turkish manner: Most commonly his Table is low, made of massiue Siluer, with a little border about it two fingers high, like vnto a Table of Accomptants which tell money. There is another of pure Gold enricht with diuers precious stones, whereon he feeds three or foure times in the yeare: He hath a great Napkin to couer his knees, and another vpon his left arme; On the one side are many Loaues made of three sorts, very pure and delicate, whereof the Graine is gathered at *Burfia* in *Natalia*, and is reserued for his mouth: They knead it with Goats Milke, whereof they feed a great troupe to that end in the Wood of the *Serrail*. His Cookes are at worke before day, for hee himselfe rising with the Morning, they haue alwayes meate readie if hee should call for it: The

Essay

Essay is taken at the Kitchin in the presence of the *Capiaga*, or Master of the Houshold, and they serue it vp in dishes of gold couered: His *Agalaris*, or Familiars goe and receiue it at the hands of the *Capiaga* without: For there is another of the same Office within, who goes not into the Kitchin, hee carries them to him that serues at the Table, who is vpon his knee: They serue out thirtie Dishes, in the which are thirtie sorts of meates; the Table is round, and stands vpon a Vise which turnes as it pleases the Prince, for no man carues him, neither doth he himselfe vse any Knife; his bread is so tender as it will not endure any, he breakes it with his fingers without any trouble; so doth he his meate prepared with the like delicacie: They serue no Salt vnto him, and whatsoeuer hee eats is not seasoned with Spices, his Physicians forbidding it in the Kitchin. The daintiest meat for his royall mouth are roasted Pigeons, whereof they serue a dozen in a *Copson* or Platter: Pullets, Lambe, or Mutton, rosted & boyled are after the Pigeons, which hee loues best: Hee makes a signe (for at his Table no man speakes any thing) that they should carrie of this meat what he pleases to the *Sultana's* whom he affects most: Sometimes the dumbe men and the Iesters haue a part: His *Agallaries* or Familiars are highly gratified, when hee casts them one of his Loaues, they kisse it, and giue it vnto others for a testimonie of a singular fauour. In the silence which is strictly obserued at his Table, as well by himselfe as those which doe assist, there is an ordinary entertainment in a dumbe fashion by signes and the gestures of the Mutes, and the Iesters, which are instructed therein, practize the abilities of their wits. He doth vsually drinke a liquour made of many sorts of fruits mingled with the juice of Citrons and Sugar: He swallowes it in a spoone of wood, although they serue him with little Cups of Porcelaine and others of *Indian* Mute, set vpon a foot of gold enricht with stones. They do not serue any fruit before Dinner, his last coorse is a Tart, and if he eats any fruit, it is at his after-meales, and likewise Parmisant, whereof they make great esteeme in *Turkey*.

In the time of *Ramadan*, which is the Turkes Lent, they doe

doe not serue him in vessels of Gold, but in yellow Porcelaine which is most precious and hard to be recouered. Hee fasts from the Sun-rising vntill night, when it is lawfull for him to leaue his fast, and to eat what meate hee pleaseth: Fish comes seldome into the *Serrail*, but when the desire of the *Sultana*, or the Appetite of the *Agalaries* causeth it to be brought from the Sea.

The *Grand Seigneurs* Bed is not made while it is day, in the Chamber where hee lodgeth; they make it only when he goes to his rest: that whereof we haue spoken is only a Bed of State. The Groomes of his Chamber lay vpon the floore a Mat, and vpon it a fine Turkey Carpet, whereupon they lay a Matteresse and a Bed of Feathers; The sheets are of fine Linnen, and the couering of goodly Carpets: In Winter, they vse Couerings of white Wolues, or of Sables, which keepe the Prince from cold. After his Bed is thus made, they straine ouer it many strings of Silke, vpon the which they lay Cloth of Gold, or rich Tapestrie to make the Tester and Curtaines: This Couch being made, the same Groomes of the Chamber goe and fetch the Emperour, and bring him to his rest with a little Turbant on his head in stead of a Night-cap: Whilest hee sleepes they watch; one stands at the doore of the Chamber, another at his Beds side, to raise vp the Clothes and to couer him if it be needfull: Two others are at the Beds feete with two Torches, which they neuer put out vntill the *Sultan* bee risen. Their Guard continues three houres, after which they are relieued by their Companions. Thus he rests which troubles all *Europe*, disquiets *Asia*, and afflicts *Africa*, and the sheares of the *Mediterranean* Sea with his Fleets.

Chap. VII.

Of the grauitie of the Grand Seigneur, and of the dumbe discourses which are made in the Serrail.

THat Prince of the Iewes which made choice rather of the scourge of Pestilence then the rigour of Warre, had

reason

Court of the Grand SEIGNEVR. 39

wased to say that hee had rather fall into the hands of God, than to those of Man, for the one is a plentifull and inexhaustible Fountaine of all Mercie: The others are vnpittifull, although they be created after his Image. It is lawfull, yea, it is commended to speake vnto God, and to begge those things which are necessary; and in the World it is a crime to presume to speake vnto Men. The true Table of this humane Pride may be drawne from the *Serrail*, at this day the principall seat of the Arrogancie of Princes: for there it is not only forbidden to speake vnto the *Grand Seigneur*, but he that dares to lift vp his eyes to looke him in the face, is guiltie of a great crime: so as all the *Bassaes* of his Court, except the *Vizir*, the *Mufti*, and the Physician, going towards him to reuerence him, or rather to adore him, haue their hands ioyned and their eyes cast downe, and in this posture inclining themselues to the ground, they salute him without seeing him, although they be before him. When he goes into the Citie, they which present any Petitions vnto him, to haue Iustice from him, when they cannot obtaine it from his Officers, lift them vp vpon the end of a Reed, and themselues lie prostrate on the ground by humiliation. Other men which are of his Family, speake not vnto him but by signes, and this dumbe language is practised, and vnderstood as readily in the *Serrail*, as a distinct and articulate voice among vs. For which cause they vse the seruice of as many dumbe men as they can find; who hauing accustomed others to their signes and gestures make them to learne their Language. The *Sultana's* doe the like. The grauitie of his person, and the custome of the Empire forbids him to speake to any. The *Sultana's* his women practise it, they haue many dumbe slaues in their *Serrail*. *Sultan Mustapha* Vncle to *Osman*, who in the end of the yeare 1617. held the Scepter of the Turkish Empire, for that he could not accustome himselfe to this silent grauitie, gaue occasion to the Councell of State to complaint of him, and to say, that to speake freely vnto his people as *Mustapha* did, was more fit for a *Ianizarie* or a Turkish Merchant, then for their Emperour. They contemned him, and held his freedome and familiaritie

miliaritie vnworthy of the Empire. To play the *Sultan* in state, hee must not speake, but by an extraordinary grauitie make men to tremble with the twinkling of his eye: For the frowning arrogancie of the Turkish Princes is growne to that insolencie, as he liues amongst his Subiects as some diuine thing, adored by the dumbe admiration of his slaues. The Emperour of the *Abyssines*, whom they doe vulgarly call *Prete-Iean*, is also blamed for pride, although it differs from the Turke: He speakes, but he suffers none to see him, saying, that being the Image of God in the Soueraigntie of his Empire, he must imitate him in his answeres, wherein God speaks and is not seene. When as the Master of the Ceremonies brings any forreigne Embassadours vnto him, it is most commonly by night: His Halls and Chamber are full of Torches burning; and he himselfe is hidden in his *Mustabe*, or Royall Bed, before the which there are fiue Curtaines drawn, whereof that in the midst is of Cloth of Gold, the rest are of Silke. The Master of the Ceremonies speaks with a loud voice *Hunca, Hialebuchia abeson*: that is to say, I bring those vnto thee whom thou hast commanded me: Hee repeats it often, vntill he heare a voice from within which saith, *Cafacinele*, which signifies enter in: At this voice all they which heare it bow downe and make a low Reuerence: Then they aduance a little making stayes at euery six steps, repeating the same words, and being come neere vnto the Curtaines they heare the same voice *Cafacinelet*: Then they aduance a little farther, to heare the words of *Prete-Iean* who speakes and is not seene, and answeres the demands which they make vnto him. Some pettie Kings of the *Indies* keepe themselues so retired, as they neuer speake but to one man; and he receiues the demand, which they will make vnto the King, by the mouthes of fiftie others, who deliuer it from one to another, vntill it comes vnto him. The grauitie of a Prince should rather appeare in his manners then in his silence: and his wisdome should make him more venerable, than all the fantastique fashions of speaking and commanding. If the Prince will imitate God, as he is a liuing Image, let him know that three things shine in the diuine

In the description of Ethiopia by Don Francisco Aluarez, printed 1558.

Andrew Corsall a Florentine writes it to Iulian de Medicis, in a Letter from Cochin a Towne of the Indies.

uine Maiestie, Power, Wisdome, and Bountie. Let them adde vnto their Soueraigne power of Command, the effects of wisdome, and those of a Royall bountie. By these they shall raigne securely in their Estates; and shall be more cherished and honoured, then by the vaine gestures and signes of their puft-vp grauitie.

CHAP. VIII.
How the Grand SEIGNEVR *receiues the Embassadours of Forreine Princes, and the forme of his Oath in an Alliance.*

THere are two sorts of Embassadours which come to the Turkish Court; those of Kings, and others of inferiour Princes: The first who without contradiction haue the precedence, must likewise haue it in this Historie. We will speake of their Reception, and will take for a President that of the Embassadour of *France.* Being arriued at *Pera*, hee passeth within few dayes after to *Constantinople*, sees the *Mufti*, visits the *Grand Vizir*, salutes the *Bostangibassi*, or great Gardiner, vseth some complements to the *Testardar*, or high Treasurer, and performes some testimonies of honour and courtesie to the other great men of the Port, to make them fauourable vnto him vpon occasions. After this they aduertise him of the day, when he shall be receiued to kisse his hand; It is vsually vpon a day of *Diuan*, when as the *Sultan* giues audience to his principall Officers: The *Grand Vizir* cals the *Diuan* or assembly of the Councell, hee sends for all the *Chaoux*, the *Mutaferagas* which are those of the light Horse; the *Spahis* who are also of the Cauallerie, the *Ianizaries* which are Footmen: All which with their Leaders haue commandement to arme and attire themselues with as much state as may be, to let the Embassadour see with the curiositie of their Armes, the pompe of this great Court. They come into the *Serrail*, and ranke themselues in the second Court,

G (whereof

(whereof we haue formerly spoken) where all together make a bodie of stately troupes. The Embassadour aduertised of the houre appointed, parts from his lodging at *Pera* attired vpon his own Clothes with a Robe after the Turkish manner, of Cloth of Gold curled, and furred if the season require it with Sables: His Gentlemen and Secretaries are attired in the like Robes, but the stuffe is not so rich, wearing on their heads caps of blacke Veluet like vnto the Masters of the Accompts in *France*: He hath twenty seruants attired in Robes of Scarlet, which the Turkes call *Ferrages*: and vpon them other long Robes of the same stuffe, and on their heads caps of blacke Taffatae: The foure *Dragomans*, or the Kings Interpreters are of the number, the Captaines, Masters of Ships, and other Frenchmen doe accompany him. Being thus followed, hee passeth the Channell of the Sea, which separates *Pera* from *Constantinople*, being twice as broad, as the Riuer of *Seine* is at *Paris* before the *Louver*: Being come vnto the other shoare, hee findes many goodly horses for him and his followers, which the Turkes that are friends to *France*, send him to carry him to the Citie. At the entry whereof hee finds many *Chaux* and *Ianizaries* which attend him to conduct him to the *Serrail*: Two *Choux Bassi* goe of either side of him, the other Turkes goe before: In this order hee comes to the Imperiall Pallace, at the Gate whereof he finds two *Capigis Bassis* who receiue him, and lead him to the *Grand Vizir* in the Hall of the *Diuan*, (that day they dispatch little businesse) he sits right against the *Grand Vizir* vpon a forme without backe or supporter, couered with Cloth of Gold. Therefor a little time by the helpe of his Interpreter or *Dragoman*, they entertaine themselues with discourse, vntill that the *Grand Vizir* commands Dinner to bee brought: The Steward of the Diuan serues it presently, where some other *Bashaes* doe assist: Their fare is more delicate then vsuall, and in greater abundance, for the which the Chamber of Accompts in the *Serrail* sets downe a thousand Crownes. There is a *Dragoman* which doth assist the Embassador to entertain the *Bashaes*. In the meane time his traine is carried to dinner

in

Court of the Grand SEIGNEVR.

in a low Gallerie, where a Table is prepared in this manner: A great Tapestrie is laid vpon the ground, and some dishes are set very thinne and sparingly: Their Meates are *Panade* made with Sugar, and some broths with Pullets, two men carrying as in a Scarfe a certain vessell of boiled Leather, like vnto a Bagipe, in the which they carrie *Cerbet*, (the which is a Drinke made of the juice of Citrons, water, and Sugar) They giue to euery one drinke in his turne, in a Cup of Copper tinned, and they goe betwixt the Dishes to serue them more commodiously. The Embassadour and his people hauing dined in this manner, hee retires to a certaine place neere vnto the Gate of the *Sultans* Quarter, where they attend vntill the Officers of the *Diuan* haue had Audience of their Master; after which they all retire, except such *Bashaes* as remaine about his person: Then the Master of the Ceremonies goes for the Embassadour, and brings him to the Emperours lodging; The *Capiaga* assisted by many Eunuches receiues them at the Gate, and conducts them into the Imperiall Chamber, whose walls are within couered with great plates of Gold and Siluer, enricht with stones and Pearle: At the entry thereof two *Capigis*, or Porters, take him vnder the Armes, not to kisse the Emperours hand, but his Robe. This vnworthy custome to lead the Embassadors of forreine Princes by the Armes, growes from the treacherie of the Turkes themselues. *Baiazet* the Second, sonne to him that tooke *Constantinople* going one day to a Monasterie, hee found in his way a Religious man of his Law of the order of the *Deruis*. This Monke of the *Alcoran* seeing the Emperour, ran towards him to execute his detestable designe: comming neere vnto him he demands an Almes: and in saying his *Ailahithi*, that is to say in the Name of God, hee drew a Semiter from vnder his Robe of Felt, with the which *Baiazet* had beene murthered, if his Horse in bounding had not receiued the greatest violence of the blow; yet hee was hurt, and this wretched Parricide had alreadie lifted vp his arme to double the blow, if *Bassa Schender* had not suddenly beaten him downe with his *Bosdagnen*, or Poll-axe: After which it was

G 2 or-

ordained, that whosoeuer should come to salute the *Grand Seigneur*, should be led vnder the Armes by *Capigis*; And this custome hath hee carefully obserued. Wee doe not read that there was euer any stranger but suffered this Rigour, except an Embassadour of *France*, named *Monsieur Nouailles* Bishop of *Aix*, who was sent to *Selim* the Second, by King *Charles* the Ninth, to mediate some accommodation for the *Venetians* affaires: comming into the Chamber, when as the *Capigis* had laid hold of his Arme he scattered them with his Elbowes, and spake aloud, that the libertie of a Frenchman, and the dignitie of a Bishop could not endure to be led like a slaue: And so leauing the *Sultan* and those that were in the Chamber amazed, he went freely to his Reuerence, and would not cast himselfe at his feet, as others doe; but inclined a little to kisse his Robe.

When the Embassadour had kist the *Sultans* Robe, who sits vpon Cushions of Cloth of Gold curled, he retires backward with his face alwayes towards the Prince, and plants himselfe against the wall of the Chamber, to giue way to the Gentlemen of his Traine, who goe likewise to kisse his Robe: And then he presents the Letter which the King sends written in the Turkish Tongue. The *Grand Seigneur* answeres nothing for the present; his *Grand Vizir* doth only speake some wordes to dismisse the Embassadour, who goes out of the Chamber hauing made a Reuerence in bending downe his head, but doth not vncouer it. But you must obserue that no man comes to kisse his Robe, vnlesse hee be attired in Robes after the Turkish manner, giuen him by the *Sultan*, the which is the Present of a Soueraigne to a subiect or slaue: For this cause the *Grand Vizir* forgets not to send vnto the Embassadour such Robes as are set downe by the Ordinance of the Custome of the Empire, that is to say, two that are rich for the Embassadours person, and one for either of his followers. Moreouer euery Embassadour must haue a Present for the *Grand Seigneur*, the which he sees first before him thorow a Lattice window, whither he is carried by *Capigis*: There he busies himselfe to looke on it, whilest the Embassadour and

his

his Gentlemen doe their Reuerence; so as they can see but halfe his face. To this purpose a generous action performed by the said *Monsieur Nouailles* Embassadour to *Charles* the Ninth is worthy to bee related. *Mahomet* Grand *Vizir* to *Selim* the Second prest him much not to forget a stately Present for his *Sultan*, and sent him word that if he had none readie bee would furnish him. This Embassadour went, of purpose, to kisse his Robe without any Present. The *Basha* reproacht him; and imputed it to contempt that hee had not giuen any. The *Seigneur* of *Nouailles* made answere that the King his Master, who was the first and greatest Monarch of Christendome, hearing that *Selim* demanded it as a Tribute, had forbidden him to present any. Thus in giuing none, he serued his Master profitably and honourably; leauing among the Turkes a great admiration of his generous dexteritie, and carried backe into *France* the glorie which those Embassadours deserue, whom vertue and not fauour haue aduanced to such Charges.

Other Embassadours of inferiour Qualitie to a Royaltie, receiue Robes in like manner to goe and salute him: But they enter not into the *Serrail* with so much Pompe, neither are they feasted, nor haue so much familiaritie with the Grand *Vizir*, yea, there are some which sit not in his presence. Thus the Turks can measure the honour which they doe vnto men, according to the Qualitie of the Princes which send them, whose persons the Embassadours represent. They haue long hands and portatiue eyes, to see into the Realmes that are most remote to their Estates:

The forme which the Turkish Monarches vse to sweare a League or Alliance with any Forreigne Prince, is no lesse specious than fraudulent; for most commonly they hold nothing that they promise, and their Oaths are as false as those of Louers; thus they Court all the Estates of *Europe*. When as *Marin C*——*us* a Man doubly famous aswell for the lustre of his Birth a—— knowledge, was at *Constantinople* Embassadour for the —— netian to renew the League with the Turke, *Selim* sware i—— his manner: *I sweare and promise by the*

G 3 *great*

great God which hath created Heauen and Earth, by the soules of seuentie Prophets, by mine owne, and by that of my Ancestors, to obserue with the Seigneurie of Venice, all the points and rights of the League and Friendship which hath beene entertained to this day, and to hold them for sacred and inuiolable, as they are declared by my Signature. But he brake it suddainly; for Iean Mique a Spanish Iew, chased out of Spaine by King Ferdinand, as a dangerous Spie, to Europe, who had runne thorow all the Prouinces, hauing related vnto him that the Arsenall of Venice had beene burnt, and that there was want of victuals in that State and Seigneurie, he perswaded him to the warre of Cyprus, which he said did belong vnto him as Sultan of Egypt, and King of Palestina, whereon Cyprus aswell as Rhodes depended, as Homagers. Selim vndertooke it without any other subiect, and made himselfe Master thereof in short time, taking this Realme from the Venetians, who had kept it long : So to be a Turke and to keep his faith, are incompatible things.

Chap. IX.

Of some Manuall Workes of the Turkish Emperours, and of the Religious custome which they obserue, to liue of the labour of their hands.

THe Authour of the Alcoran, hath deckt the deformities of his Law, and couered the falshoods thereof with some lustre of truth, to make them passe the better amongst his followers : Among the many Rules which hee prescribes them, he enioynes them to labour and doth assure them that hee is not worthy to liue, that doth not labour with his hands. The people doe not only obserue it, but the respect of this precept is crept into the Imperiall Throne of the Turkes; The Sultans embrace it, and of twentie Emperours which haue

swayed

swayed the *Othoman* Scepter, yee shall hardly find one which hath not laboured for his liuing. *Mahomet* the Second manured his Gardens, and of the reuenew of the Fruites which were sold, he caused meate to be bought for his mouth. But as the actions of such men, how religious soeuer they be, haue not true Charitie for their Guide, they doe easily incline to vice. This Prince added to his Manuall labour so horrible a crueltie, as it was to be wished his hands had beene idle. We haue written in the Historie of his Empire, that visiting one day, (being followed by his Pages) the Squares of his Gardens which he did manure himselfe; one of the young Boyes seeing hastie Cowcumbers, gathered one and eate it: *Mahomet* returning that way found it wanting, his choler enflamed him to crueltie, hee saw by the stalke that it was newly gathered, and hee knew that hee had no company but his Pages, and therefore some one of them had done the deed, the which he would know at what price soeuer: Hee calleth the *Bastangies* or Gardiners, puts sharpe Kniues into their hands, and commands them to open the stomacks of his Pages: They take them one by one and open fourteene, finding the Cowcumber not yet disgested in the stomacke of the fourteenth: Such was the rigour of this Prince, who for a light offence, caused fourteene of the goodliest young Boyes (the flowre and choice of all the youth of his *Serrail*) to be murthered. *Solyman* the Second, hee which tooke *Rhodes*, spent his idle houres in making of Shooes, the which he sent to the *Bazar* or Market to sell, and with the money he caused victuals to be bought for his Table. *Selim* the Second who lost the battaile of *Lepantho*, made little Crescents or halfe Moones, which the Turkish Pilgrimes carrie vpon their staues, when they goe the Voyage to *Meque*. *Amurath* his Sonne made Arrowes, and others made little Kniues, all which is sold at a deare rate, in regard of the grossenesse of the worke: Hee thinkes himselfe happie that can recouer any for monie. They ground this Custome of labouring for their liuing, not only vpon the rules of their Alcoran, but also vpon that passage of

Ge-

In sudore vultus tui vesceris panem donec revertaris in terram de qua sumptus es, quia puluis es, & in puluerem reuerteris, Gen. 3.19

Genesis: Their Schoolmasters make them learne it by heart: *In the sweat of thy browes thou shalt eat thy bread, untill thou returne to earth, whereon thou went made.* It is only in the time of peace; for in the time of warre the Prince must liue vpon the charges of the people, for whose defence and increase hee takes Armes. But in another season if the *Sultan* should employ the Money which he leuies of his people in his delights, the Law and the custome of the Empire would hold it a crime. They call their Taxe and Subsidie, *Aarum Agemini Cani*, that is to say, *The prohibited blood of the people*: And for that the labour of their hands cannot furnish the expences of their diet to keepe a Table worthy of their Qualitie, they adde vnto it the reuenewes of their Gardens, which in truth is great, and almost incredible. I haue learned from some Turkes, that they yeeld two hundred thousand Crownes a yeare rent: some others say a hundred thousand pounds sterling. Besides those which he hath in the *Serrail*, hee hath along the Sea side, and towards the *Arsenall*, great Gardens which are very fruitfull. Foure Leagues from *Constantinople*, and further at *Andrinopolis*, and vpon the side of *Asia*, at *Scutary* (where the Citie of *Chalcedonia* did sometimes stand) there are the goodliest Gardens in the East. The fruits which are gathered are sold at *Constantinople*, and elsewhere in so great abundance, as they furnish all the Countrie. The *Bostangibassi* or great Gardiner, who is an Officer of the Crown: hath a care of this Reuenew, causeth it to bee brought to the *Serrail*, and the *Sultans* hold it for their true Patrimonie and Demesnes, wherewith they may feed themselues without any oppression.

To these Manuall workes of the Turkish Emperours, wee must adde their Religious custome to plough the Land, when as they come from their Gouernment to *Constantinople* to take possession of the Empire, they are bound to hold the Plough and to make some furrowes. *Amurath* the Third Grandfather to *Achmat* obserued it; after the decease of *Selim* his Father, when as comming from *Magnesia* (where he was

was Gouernour) to goe and take possession of his Scepter, he met with an Husbandman in the fields, where lighting from his horse he laid hold on the Plough, and made three or foure furrowes: After which he drew a handfull of Gold out of his pocket, and gaue it in charitie to this Labourer: and withall he put off his Robe, which was of rich Cloth of Gold, furred with Sables, and gaue it him. The Law which makes him to obserue this Ceremony is mentioned in the Glosses of the *Alcoran*, in these termes: *That the Emperour comming to the Empire and going to the Imperiall Citie to take possession, hee must manure the Land to banish sterrilitie from his Countrie, and to make it fruitfull.* It is nothing the more for all this: For the Prince employing so great a number of his Subiects in his warres, much good Land lies waste, for want of men to till it. Thus doe the Turkish *Sultans* employ themselues, and yet they doe not flie idlenesse, to the which they many times abandon themselues: Wee shall see something in the following Chapter.

Chap. X.

Of the Grand Seigneurs *Loues*.

AMong all the passions which rule the affections of Princes, Loue (as the most powerfull) triumphes more ouer great men, then all the rest together, for they obtaine no victories, but to encrease its glory: Couetousnesse heaps vp to furnish the charges, Ambition aspires to make it great. So we see the most powerfull Princes after they had subdued all other passions, were vanquished by Loue. *Alexander* laid the honour of so many victories in *Persia* at the feet of his Captiue *Roxana*. *Cæsar* being in *Alexandria*, submitted all his triumphs to the beautie of *Cleopatra*, who afterward was friend to *Anthonie*. And the Turkish Monarches make subiect vnto the allurements of their *Sultana's*, the glory and lustre of that Soueraigne power, whereby they are Masters

H of

of the best parts of the World. But behold how these singular beauties enter into their *Serrail*, and the bonds wherewith Loue doth captiuate their wils.

After that the Rights of birth haue brought a Turkish Prince to the Imperiall Throne of his Ancestors, the women which his Predecessor did honour in the *Serrail*, are put forth, and conducted to a place called in their Language *Eschy Saray*, that is to say the old *Serrail*, as a man would say the old place: for *Saray* in the Persian Tongue, signifies a place or Hostell: There they are shut vp, vntill they be married to some great Men of the Port. In the meane time others must supply their roome, to bee new subiects of Loue to the new Emperour. Then the *Bashaes* which are at the Port, and others which represent the Soueraigntie of their Master in remote Prouinces, imploy all their care to find out Virgins, in the Leuant or else-where, the rarest in beautie, and of the sweetest perfections of their sex; whether that the greatnesse of their treasurs force the necessitie of miserable Mothers to deliuer them for money, or that the chance of warre hath made them Captiues at the taking of some Towne, and so fall into their hands: They cause them to bee instructed after the Turkish manner in all gentile Qualities fit for their sex (if they be not alreadie:) they learne to sing, to play of the Lute, and the Gittern, and to dance, & hauing had a speciall care for the keeping of their Virginity, they bring them to the *Sultan*, and present them vnto him: The Princes Mother, & his Sisters which are married labour in the same designe, and make him the like presents: for the law of Poligamy or pluralitie of women, allowed by the *Alcoran* and receiued in Turkey, giues them leaue to keepe as many as they will, so as they bee able to feed them. The *Sultan* doth recompence their care that bring them such gifts, with some rich present to buy (saith he) these Virgins which they bring, that they may bee his slaues: But hee will be soone fettered in their beautie. The *Serrail* of women being thus furnished, hee passeth thither when he pleaseth, and is not seene by any man, by a doore right against his Chamber, whereof he hath one Key, and the

the *Chiſſar Aga* or great Eunuch of the *Sultana's* another: He doth aduertiſe the *Cheyachadun*, which is an ancient woman their Gouerneſſe, to ranke them in a Gallerie, in the which he paſſeth and repaſſeth often, beholding their allurements or elſe he cauſeth them to dance in a round, in a goodly Hall, where he doth aſſiſt and place himſelfe in the midſt, like vnto a Butterflie in the midſt of many gliſtering fires, where he loſeth himſelfe: For feeling his heart ſuddenly enflamed by the eyes of ſome one of them, which pleaſeth him beſt, he caſts her his handkercher, for a ſigne that he is vanquiſhed: ſhe receiues it with great demonſtrations of humilitie, kiſſes it and layes it on her head; preſently the *Cheyachadun* or Mother of the Maids, takes this faire ſlaue, which comes to triumph ouer her Maſters libertie, ſhe leads her into a Chamber appointed for the ſports of loue, decks her with the goodlieſt Ornaments ſhe can deuiſe, perfumes her, and addes to her naturall beautie the cunning of her Art: This is while the Sun ſhines; for imitating his courſe aſwell as his luſtre, this faire Creature lies downe as ſoone as this Planet ſets: The *Chadun* conducts her into the ſame Chamber where the *Sultan* is lodged, layes her in the ſame Bed, where ſhee enters by the feet for the greater reuerence, and during the night ſeaſon many old Mooriſh women watch and ſtand ſentinell, one at the Beds feet, another in the midſt of the Chamber, and a third at the doore: They are relieued euery third houre by others of the ſame hue, vntill it bee day. There is one ſtands at the Beds head, with two Torches burning, and doth carefully obſerue on what ſide the Prince doth turne leaſt the light ſhould offend his eyes. I haue learned from a Iew, a learned Phyſician which had ſerued the *Grand Seigneur*, that the *Chadun* watcheth at the Beds feet, and doth ſometimes ſpeake ſome words to encourage the young Maide, giuing her to vnderſtand that this night would be the cauſe of her good fortune, and that ſhe would attaine to the dignitie of a Princeſſe. It is the cuſtome in Turkey that on the Marriage night, an olde woman doth aſſiſt in the Chamber of the married couple, and imployes the experience of her time paſt, to encourage the woman. Day being come they bring new Garments to the *Sultan*: for those which he had the day before, with the Money that was in his purse, belongs vnto her which hath kept him company: He riseth, returnes to his Quarter, and sends by his Eunuches vnto his new Loue a Present of Robes of Cloth of Gold, Iewels and Money, the greatnesse whereof is measured according to the pleasure which hee receiued that night. Then they prepare a lodging for her distinct from the rest, and draw her from the common sleeping place, whereof wee will speake in the Chapter following: They giue her foure white slaues to serue her in the Chamber, two others to labour in her Kitchin, a blacke Eunuch for a Groome, three thousand Sequins in a Purse, and as much apparell as shall be needfull for her person and her slaues. Moreouer, they enter her name among the Entertainments of the *Serrail*, for two Charges of Money yearely. Thus the Turkish Princes purchase the losse of their libertie with the Treasure of their Cofers: to verifie in their affection the effects of this veritie, that loue is to Louers a pleasing wound, a sweet bitternesse, a sauourie poyson, a disease which contents them, a punishment which they imbrace, and a death which they hunt after.

Est enim amor gratum vulnus, sapidum venenum, dulcis amaritudo, detestabilis morbus, iucundum supplicium, blā· 1· mors, Franciscus Petrarcha Dialog. 69.

If the vaine pleasure of loue hath so charmed his senses as he sees this new Mistris the second time, he increaseth her felicities. The next day Morning they augment her traine with two women of her Chamber, one Eunuch and two Cookes: They bring her ten thousand Sequins in a Purse, her Pension is encreased by two other Charges of Money, and the Emperour causeth her to carrie the name of *Sultana*. But if this loue be constant vnto the third time, the brute of this womans happinesse flies throughout all the *Serrail* of the *Sultana's*, and makes others to conceiue a passionate desire to equall her, and shee her selfe reapes the benefit; shee is honoured for the second time with the qualitie of *Sultana*, and that name is then confirmed vnto her, the which shee cannot lose but with her life. The Emperour augments her Traine vnto sixteene Women for her Chamber, two Eunuches more, and

and her Pension is made sixteene Charges of Money. The rest of the *Serrail* which are yet Virgins, or haue had the Princes company but once, imploy all their allurements to please him, and finding their cunning deuices too feeble, they adde the help of Charmes and Sorcerie, which they purchase at any rate whatsoeuer. But if any one of these women be deliuered first of a Sonne, which is to succeed in the Empire, shee is called Queene, the *Grand Seigneur* honours her with a Crowne of pretious stones; hee causeth a cloth of Estate to be carried into her Chamber of Presence, inlargeth her Lodging, and giues her a Family fit for a Queene, or Empresse of Turkey: Shee hath a sufficient Reuenew to supply her necessities and her bounties. If shee be deliuered of a Daughter, they send her a Nurse, three thousand Sequins and Slaues to serue her, the honour is the lesse; but the joy which shee conceiueth (if there be Male Children formerly borne) is incomparable, for shee is assured that the young Princesse shall be bred vp with her, and that shee shall be one day married to a *Grand Vizir*, or to some other *Bassa* of the most powerfull in the Empire, who will honour her, and fill her old age with all contentments. On the other side, if shee had beene deliuered of a younger Sonne, he should be taken from her at the age of twelue yeares or thereabouts, and put into the hands of Schoolemasters to instruct him, where shee might not see him but foure times in the yeare, and in the end hee should bee sacrificed to the safetie of his elder Brothers Raigne, and soone strangled by Mutes. This is that which makes them desire to haue Daughters, when there is alreadie a Sonne liuing.

All these women although they bring forth the true Successours of the Empire, yet they are but the Emperours Concubines; he neuer marries any, vnlesse he be wonderfully surprized with her loue, which hath first brought him a Sonne, then he followes the blind motions of his passion. And doubtlesse when as loue makes him to feele in this sort the rigour of his flames, it is iustice that one Tyrant should torment another: for if the one doth captiuate their mindes, the other tor-

ments

ments their bodies with a cruell seruitude. This Tyrant loue doth force him to marry his *Sultana*, and causeth him to dispatch letters of *Chebin*, which containes a declaration of her libertie, and an assurance of her Dowrie, in the presence of the *Mufti*, or High Priest of his Law, and he receiues her for his married wife. Besides the ordinary expences of this new Empresse, they assigne her aboue fifteene hundred thousand Liuers to furnish her liberalities, or to make a stocke sufficient in some yeares to build a Moschee, or to rent some Hospitall according to her deuotion. These Marriages as wee haue said are made by the violence of loue, for the Princes Councel oppose themselues, for that they would not giue their Master a Companion in the Empire, nor be answerable to two Commanders. The Law which was setled in the same Councell, ordaining that the *Sultan* should not marrie, tooke its beginning from the Raigne of *Baiazet* the first, who hauing married a Wife of the Family of the *Paliologa's* Emperours of *Constantinople*, saw her by the disaster of the Warre Captiue with him in the hands of *Tamberlaine* Emperour of the *Tartars*, and intreated with so much contempt, that one day this *Scythian* causing them to eat at his Table, he commanded this Princesse to rise and to fetch him drinke from the Cupboord; then the Turkes aduised that their Emperours hauing none but slaues would be lesse offended, when they should be contemned by the Victor. But Loue which admits no Law but from it selfe, refused to obey, and commanded *Solyman* the Second to marrie *Roxilana* one of the Women of his *Serrail*, who was the Delights of his affections: Hee made her Companion of his Scepter, and gaue her so great authority in his House, as shee chased away the Children of another Woman which were elder to hers, and armed the Fathers hand against them to ruine: For *Solyman* caused *Mustafa* the eldest and the most generous of all his Children to bee strangled in his Tent by foure Mutes, and gaue occasion to *Giangir* the younger to kill himselfe vpon the body of his dead Brother. This affliction was not alone, *Roxilana* stirred vp others, shee deuided *Baiazet* and *Selim* her owne Children, to aduance the

A hundred & fiftie thousand pounds sterling.

Quis legem det amantibus? Maior lex amor est sibi. Boet. de Consolat. Philophiæ lib. 3. metr. 12.

one

one to the succession of the Empire, brings him to ruine, and makes him to end his dayes miserably by the Sword. *Solyman* hath beene the only Prince since *Baiazet* the First vnto this day, whereof there hath beene fifteene Emperours, & twenty in all, by a direct succession from Father to Sonne, which hath married a Wife. *Amurath* the Third his Grandchild being charmed with the beauty of *Asachi*, being enformed of the practices of *Roxilana* in the *Serrail*, by the power of her infranchisement, and the authoritie of the Princes Wife, refused the Letters of *Sebyn* although he had had fourteene children by her, and loued her aboue all his Women. Yet they say that *Osman* which died last, had married the Daughter of the *Muftie* of *Constantinople*.

But the History of the extraordinary Marriage of the Turkish Prince, hath made vs abandon the relation of his loues with his Concubines: But let vs returne and follow him into his Garden, where hee is in the midst of his lasciuious imbracements. It is dangerous to see him: but no feare of danger should deterre vs from seruing of the publique. He goes often out of his Lodging to goe and dally with his women in the goodly Alleys of his delightfull Gardens, the blacke Eunuches which serue the Women, are the only Men which accompany him, all the rest retire as farre from him as they can: The *Bostangies* or Gardiners goe out at a Gate towards the Sea, the other slaues flie farre from the sight of their Master. For if there should any man whatsoeuer be found in the *Serrail*, that should attempt to see these women when they walke with the *Sultan*, they should be put to death without delay. Thus the contagion of these faire creatures is dangerous: some die for that they haue beene seene, and others for that they haue seene them. So as when they say the Emperour is in the Garden with his women euery one flies as farre as hee can. If in these places of pleasure he can play the Prince and Louer both together, it is hard to beleeue, seeing that Maiestie and loue agree not well in one Throne. The particularities of his entertainment are vnknowne vnto vs: for the rigour

which

which he obserues against those which would see him, forbids to reueale the secret: Only wee know that in the effeminate delights wherewith the women charme him, hee is pleased with the ridiculous encounters of his Iesters and Dwarffes, and shewes that Loue is an entertainment of Men that are Birds.

Diogenes speaks it in Laertius, lib. 6.

A curious person which hath had authority in the *Leuant*, enformed me that in these places there many times happens light riots of Loue betwixt the *Sultan* and his Women: Hee vnderstood it from a blacke Eunuch of the womens *Serrail*: and he told him that if the iealousie of these faire creatures did raise them, they were suppreft by the discretion of the *Chadun*, which is their old Gouernesse, and by her humilitie which is interessed in the Quarrell. Thus the giddie Quarrels of Louers, are the winds which kindle and enflame their foolish passion. And the Pigeons bils, which were the armes of their choller, are the sweet instruments of their loue.

Amantium ira amoris redintegratio est, Terent.
Quæ modo pugnarunt iungunt sua rostra columbæ; Quarum blanditias, verbaq́, murmur habes, Ouid. 2. de Art.

That which we haue formerly written of the entertainment of the Turkish Prince with his women, is not the most blameable of his affections. The greatnesse of his power, which makes all mens wils obey him, and the contagious example of his Courtiers, carries him to the detestable excesse of an vnnaturall passion. Hee burnes many times for the loue of men, and the youngest Boyes which are in the *Leuant*, the flowre of beautie and the allurement of graces, are destinated to the filthinesse of his abominable pleasures. The *Bashaes* bring them from remote Prouinces, and present them vnto him. This disorder is so inueterate in the *Serrail*, as of twenty Emperours which haue carried the Turkish Scepter, you shall hardly find two that were free from this vice. *Achmat* the last which died, abandoned it a little before his death, by the wise aduice of the *Mufti*, and his Sonne *Amurath* the Fourth who raignes at this present 1626. is yet so young, as hee may be easily diuerted from this excesse, and framed to vertue, eschewing the Rockes, where his Predecessours haue suffered shipwracke. What doth it auaile such great and redoubted

Court of the Grand SEIGNEUR. 57

doubted Monarchs to be the glorious vanquishers of so many Nations if they themselues be captiues to vices? The Prince is the Physicion of the State; but how can hee cure it if hee himselfe bee sicke? Hee is the heart, but what meanes is there to giue it life, if it hath weaknesse and faintings? Hee is the eye, and how can he see and lead others, if it be troubled and darkened with passions? Euery Prince that loues his Throne, his Scepter, and his Estate, must flie vice and cherish wisdome: For a wise Prince is the assurance of these, and the support of his people.

Terrenæ potestas vult esse victrix gentium, cum se captiua vitiorum, D. Aug. *lib. 15. de ciuit. Dei, c. 8.*
Si delectamini in sedibus & sceptris, ô Reges populi, diligite sapientiam, Salom. *cap. 6.*

CHAP. XI.

Of the Grand Seigneurs Women, of their Lodging, their Liues, their Gouernment, and their Fortune.

THe precedent Chapter hath related the fire of the Grand Seigneurs Loues, this will shew you in particular the manners and life of all those which cause it. Faire women are to vnstaid spirits, flames which burne afarre off. Those of the Serrail which make the greatest shew by the lustre of their graces are most commonly strangers taken in the warre, or rauished by force: But bred vp with an incredible care, to make them learne Ciuilitie, to play of some Instruments of Musique, to Sing, and to worke with their Needles, most decent for Maids of Qualitie: These good parts added to their naturall perfection, make them the more commendable: They are for the most part Christians; but their disaster causing the beauty of their bodies to serue the dishonest pleasures of Turkes, prostitute their soules to the false worship of their Law. They are no sooner come into the Serrail, whither some Basha sends them as a Present to the Sultan, and sometimes the great Cham of Tartaria, but they cause them to make profession of the Turkish Faith, by lifting vp the second fin-

I ger

ger of the hand, in signe that they beleeue but one God only in one only Person, and they speake this word *Mahemet*: There are old women which haue the charge to instruct them in the rest of the Turkish beliefe. And thus the *Princes Serrail* is furnished with women.

They are of two sorts, the one haue had his company and are women, and the others are yet Virgins. The women lodge a part and more at large, they are better serued, and haue greater libertie in the royall Pallace. The Virgins eate by troupes in the common refectory, they retire by day into Chambers, vnder the guard and gouernment of old women, who gouerne them by tens, to labour in some workes; and in the night they lie like religious women (but not very chast) in long Dorters, where their Beds are made of soft Mattresses and Couerings (for the Women in Turkey as wel as the Men lie clothed) and are ranckt of either side; there is a passage in the midst and many Lamps burning in the night time: And euery ten Maids haue one of the Gouernesses lie by them. They which know not the Turkish Tongue, goe to learne it in Schooles appointed to that end in the same *Serrail*. These see not the Prince but when they first arriue, and conuerse not with him, but when he will make vse of them. They are furnished with all things necessary for their Entertainment, with that abundance which is found continually in the *Sultans Serrail*.

The Eunuches which bring them their meat obserue the same order which wee haue described in the *Sultans* seruice. But the Queene who is Mother to the Prince, Successour to the Empire, is serued in her Quarter (where she is stately lodged) by her owne Officers. Her vessell is not of Gold like the Emperours, but of excellent porcelane artificially wrought: In her Lodging are the most sumptuous Feasts of the Womens *Serrail*, whereas many *Sultana's* meet, to shew themselues vnto the Emperour, who is of the Party, to glut the disordered appetits of all his senses in their company. There hee makes a dangerous triall, that Beauty wounds deeper then a Dart, and the respect which all these women yeeld him, carrying

Court of the Grand SEIGNEVR. 59

rying themselues towards him with a singular Modesty, and a sweet pleasing, exempts him from making that troublesome experience: that a bad Wife is the shipwracke of her Husband, the tempest of the House, a trouble-rest, a slauery of Life, a Quotidian Euill, a voluntary Combat, a Chargeable warre, a Sauage Beast which we nourish, a Lionesse wee imbrace, a Rocke adorned, a malicious Beast, and finally a necessary Euill.

The Ladies, the Subiects of the *Sultans* delights, liue deliciously neare vnto him: Their *Serrail* containes so great a space, as there are within it foure and twenty great Courts, most of them paued with polished Marble, beautified with their Fountaines, inuironed with stones and baths, very commodiously, where these Nymphes wash themselues, and plunge their fires, but doe not quench them. A stately Mosquee is in the same place for the exercise of their deuotion. The number of the Chambers and goodly Halls are fourescore, adorned with precious moueables, the Planchers are guilt, the walls are painted in flowres of rare Art: The floore is couered with rich *Persian* Carpets of Gold and Silke, with a great number of Cushions of Tinsell: the Bedsteeds are of Iuory, or of Aloes-wood, and of great pieces of Corall, whereof one of them cost in the time of *Amurath* the Second ninetie thousand *Sultanins*, or three hundred and sixtie thousand *Liuers*. They are garnished with rich stuffes of Cloth of Gold. The Gardens in great number are the places where as Nature assisted by Art, sets forth the beauties of the Spring: The Bird-cages and Fountaines adorne them, and the Alleys by their shadows defends the beauties of the *Sultana's* from the heat of the Sunne. Seeing that in this stately Pallace the most powerfull Monarches of the Earth serue the beauties of their Loues, it is fitting that others should serue their persons: So they haue many women that doe that office: Some are Moores, others are white. But the Men that serue them are blacke Eunuches, from whom they haue taken all. They were boldly articulated of the Inferiour parts which serue for generation: But *Solyman* the Second, who ended his

Secundus Philosophus interrogatus, Quid esset mulier mala, respondit, viri naufragium, domus tempestas, quietis impedimentum, vitæ captiuitas, quotidianum malum, voluntaria pugna, sumptuosum bellum, bellua cominua leæna complectens, exornata scylla, animal malitiosum, malum necessarium, Max. Seuerus.

36. thousand pounds sterling.

Raigne, whereas *Charles* the Ninth gouerned *France*, seeing a Gelding leape vpon a Mare, he iudged thereby that the Eunuches which kept his women might busie their lasciuious passions, and then he caused all to be cut off; the which hath continued euer since. These Eunuches are all blacke, to distinguish them from those of the *Sultanas Serrail*: and their perfection consists in their deformitie, for the most hideous are the fairest: For being neare vnto those beauties so perfectly accomplished, they serue for a lustre. They bring them from the *Grand Caire*, the chiefe Citie of *Egypt*, instructed to serue in this Court, by the care of the *Bassa* who is Viceroy there: If they be not, there are Men in the *Serrail* appointed to teach them what they should know: From this Schoole they passe vnto the Ladies, they giue them names fitter for their handsomenesse than for their *Moorish* deformity. For to some Boyes which haue flat Noses, wide Mouthes, thicke Lips, Eyes almost out of their heads, great Eares, their Haire curled like Wooll, and their Face fearefully blacke, so as there is no white to be seene but their Eyes, and Teeth: They call them *Hyacinthe*, *Narcissus*, Rose and Gilliflowre. Doubtlesse such flowres are soone withered and vnable to fructifie. They assigne them a hundred *Aspres* by the day (an *Aspre* is about a penny of our sterling Money), two Robes of Silke, a piece of linnen cloth, and some other thing for their meaner necessities: They are vnder the obedience of an old wretched Eunuch, blacke like themselues, who is their Commander, called *Chissar Agassi*, that is to say, the chiefe of the Virgins. Hee is, as it were, the Chiefe and Superintendent of this Pallace of Women, speakes when hee pleaseth to the Emperour, and hath most commonly a share in the fauours of the Court: For the Prince being inclined to Women, he is the *Mercurie* of his affections: the other inferiour blacke Eunuches passe many times to the *Grand Seigneurs Serrail*, to carrie the secrets of the *Sultana's* in some note to the *Capiaga*, who presents it to the Emperour: Their Office honours them with this priuiledge, aboue the white Eunuches which serue the Prince, who neuer enter into the Womens lodging, neither

doe

Court of the Grand SEIGNEVR.   61

doe they see them. The blacke goe not out of the *Serrail*, without the leaue of the *Sultana* Queene, Mother to the eldest of the *Sultans* Children. In other places they would make some difficultie to giue vnto Queenes, yea, to women of an inferiour condition, *Moores* to serue them, for feare that comming to conceiue, their imagination should make an impression in their Children, of the complexion and forme of such Groomes: But the Turkes doe not insist vpon that. And I haue neuer heard that any *Sultana* hath beene deliuered of a *Moore*, although I know this may be done: Histories furnish vs with examples of such accidents, women haue borne children like vnto the pictures which were in their chambers. There are fiue hundred of these blacke Men, from the age of twelue yeares to fiue and twenty, and at the most thirty. The women are vsually three hundred or thereabouts, as well of the *Sultana*'s as of those that serue them: To tell the number of the *Sultana*'s directly, it is difficult: For they daily present Maidens vnto the *Grand Seigneur*, who seeing his Pallace sufficiently furnished, sends them to the old *Serrail*. The women slaues which serue them haue fiue or six *Aspres* by day, two Robes of Searge, and one of Silke yearely, a piece of fine Cloth of twenty Ells or more, and many gifts from the *Sultana*'s their Mistresses, who reward their fidelitie and diligence with many Presents of Money and other things: For they abound in all sorts of Presents, as Bodkins set with precious Stones, Earings, Iewels, Plumes of Feathers, Cloth of Gold, rich Furres, and other Moueables which the King sends the more willingly for that they cost him nothing. The *Bashaes* at the returne from their gouernments present him. The Embassadours of the Prince of *Tartary*, & other Soueraignes in *Asia*, bring vnto him and fill his Wardrobe with rich diuersitie of Presents. But aboue all things these Ladies loue to make prouision of Money; for their beautie doth not hinder them to participate with the defects of their Sex, which is subiect to Auarice.

Mulierum genus est auarum, Cic. Rhet. li. 1.

This is the cause why they draw into their *Serrail*, some cunning female Iew, with the Emperours permission, whom they

they giue to vnderstand that it is to teach them new workes with the Needle, or to make triall of some excellent Receipts in Physicke for the cure of their infirmities, or the preseruation of their healths: Thus the Iew being entred into the Serrail, she gaines affection of the Eunuch which commands at the Gate, in giuing him Money and other rich Commodities, and in a short time she gets the loue of the Sultana's; yea, she hath a transcendent power ouer their wils, bringing vnto them from abroad whatsoeuer they desire to buy, and receiuing from them what they are willing to sell. This trade is kept secret; for the Sultan would not take it well that they should sell that which he giues them: But these women desirous to make prouision of Money, which hath alwayes beene the most precious of their Moueables, to the end that if their Soueraigne dyes, being conducted to the old Serrail, they may get forth in being married to some great men of the Port: The which is easie to effect in gaining the friendship of the Chadun their Gouernesse by great gifts: They giue vnto this Iew rich Diamonds, great round Pearles, great Turquoises, and most precious Iewels for a base price: For they which haue no conuersation out of the Serrail, know not the worth of things, and part with them as it pleaseth the Iew: she sels them to strangers, and buyes such things as shee brings vnto the Ladies at a deare rate: So as the great wealth which they

Male parta,
male dilabuntur, vetus poeta.

enioy in a short time, doth shew that they frequent the Serrail of women. But goods euill gotten are many times wasted, in the same manner. The Iew is sometimes stript, and for a punishment of her frauds, leaues her life comming out of the Serrail. The Bashaws aduertised of this deceitfull trade, caused it to ceaie, and the Tefterdars or Treasurers, when their Cofers are emptie, seeke to fill them with the gaine of these Brokers.

If the Emperour be a child, and that his Mother hath any part in the administration of affaires, the trafique of these Iewish women mounts higher, and from precious Stones they passe to the Offices of State: They which affect them rather by the power of their purse, then by the merit of their ver-

tue

the addresse themselues vnto them, and their affections being bought, they doe easily purchase the fauour of the *Sultana* Mother: we haue obserued a famous example in the seuenteenth Booke of our Turkish History, which will not be vnfitting to make a briefe description, for the commodity of such as haue not that first Volume.

Cheira Chedun a Iewish woman being crept into the *Serrail* of women, by the meanes which we haue mentioned, enioyed the friendship of the *Sultana* Queene by the cunning of her industrious trade, and the sweetnesse of her pleasing humour: Soone after *Mahomet* the Third left his life in his *Serrail*, and his Scepter to *Achmet* his eldest Sonne, being about fourteene or fifteene yeares old: The *Sultana Valida* or the *Sultan* Mother, is called by her Sonne to assist in the Gouernment of the State. *Cheira* was in fauor with this Princesse, who in short time purchased him that of the Emperour: For this Prince falling sick of the small Poxe, the Iew did visit him with his Mother, attended him in his Bed, as she was cunning and indued with a good wit, she did ease the importunities of his Feuer by telling of pleasant tales, and sometimes repaired his forces with a little wine, which shee brought out of the Citie, and made him to drinke contrary to the prohibition of his Law: The *Sultan* recouered his health, he remembers the Iewes good seruices, and giues her no lesse share in his affection, then she had in his Mothers: Thus she growes doubly powerfull, and she deales no more in selling the goodly trash of the womens *Serrail*: The most eminent dignities of the Empire are her Trafficque. The great *Visir* buyes the Seale at her hands, and the Dignitie of Lieutenant Generall of the Turkish Empire. The *Mufti* mounts to that supreame Ecclesiasticall Dignitie by her meanes; and the other great Men of Portfollow in the currant of their Fortunes, the minde of her desires: Money and the Iew does all things in *Constantinople*. And he which before durst not thinke of Offices in Court but to admire them, doth now enioy them by these two meanes: Auarice calls all disorders into the State, and leaues valour, and the rare vertues of Men of merit to contempt, if they were

not

not furnished with Money: And the Prince did not only suffer them, but commanded it, for that the Iew said it must bee so. This must not continue long, and the Qualities of *Chiera* being of the Nature of those of the Court are found passable and perishable. The Ianizaries who are the force of *Constantinople*, and many times the violent reformers of the Turkish State, deale in it, and to this insupportable mischief they bring the rigour of their remedie: They goe to the *Serrail* in armes, demand the Iew, and they refuse her, they threaten to breake the Gates, and to dragge her, with many others, into the midst of the place, to reuenge vpon them the disorders of the State: They were ready to execute their words by effects, when as of many Mischiefes they made choice of the least, and thrust the Iew out of the *Serrail*, to the mercy of their rage: There were none grieued in the *Serrail*, Nouelties are pleasing, when they happen they loue them, and Enuie swimmes in ioy and pleasure when as they see any Fauourite fall. And what could they doe in this case? What meanes were there to calme the spirits of Men that are armed, and the force of the Empire, who at that time did not acknowledge any other Master but their passion? Moreouer, the people followed their motion, and demanded Iustice of this Horseleech who suckt all, swallowed all, and left others to suffer: Thus they abandoned her to force and to the rigour of the Sword. An example which tels vs that the fauour of the Court which doth not aduance any to dignity but such as are incapable, which contemnes vertuous Men, and builds the continuance of his fortune in the heaping vp of perishing wealth, runs headlong to his owne ruine, and makes himselfe fat to bee an oblation which they will offer vp vpon the first sedition. The Ianizaries take *Chirra*, they strip her, whip her, and put a burning Candle into her priuie parts, and so drag her laid all along thorow the Citie of *Constantinople*, to serue for a spectacle vnto the people: In the end they teare her in pieces, and naile the principall parts of her body, to the Gates of the greatest Officers of the Empire: That of the *Mufti* or High Priest of their Law, had the hand with this writing. *Behold the*

hand

Court of the Grand SEIGNEVR.

hand which hath sold thee thy Office, & the favours of the Port: The Head was set vpon the *Grand Vizirs* Gate, & these words vnderneath it. *This is the head which hath given thee counsell to the preiudice of the State.* They did hang her Tongue at the House of the *Cadi* or chiefe Iudge of *Constantinople*, with this reproch in writing: *Receiue the tongue which hath taught thee iniustice.* Thus in the year 1604. ended the Iew which practised in the *Serrail* of women: & the rest haue as bad an end: if not so exemplary, which is for that they attain not to the like fauour.

This is the successe of the Iewes couetousnesse which frequent the *Sultanaes Serrail*: But none of them enter, before the Eunuch of the Gate vnuailes her, and sees what shee is; left that some man vnder the habit and trade of such Brokers, should enter into this Pallace, to make traffique of his amorous passion. The order which they obserue in guarding these faire creatures is exact: They doe not only search the women which enter, and the Eunuches at their returne from the Citie: But moreouer they haue a care of beasts: They will not allow the *Sultanaes* to keepe any Apes, nor Dogges of any stature. Fruits are sent vnto them with Circumspection: If their Appetites demand any Pompeons which are somewhat long, or Cowcumbers, and such other fruits they cut them at the Gate in slices, not suffering to passe among them any slight occasion of doing euill; so bad an opinion they haue of their continencie. It is (without doubt) a signe of the Turks violent jealousie: for who can in the like case hinder a vicious woman from doing euill? She is too industrious in her Designes; and hee which had his body couered with eyes alwayes watching was deceiued. In the meane time if any woman in the *Serrail* be discouered in the effects of her lasciuiousnesse, the Law long since established for them by the *Sultan*, condemnes her to die, the which is executed without remission: she is put into a Sack, and in the night cast into the Sea; where she doth quench her flames with her life. This seuere punishment doth follow the enormitie of their Crimes: for lesse faults they suffer lighter correction: Their Superiours beat them, and if they continue obstinate, the *Sultan* causeth them to be put out of his Pallace, and sends them to

The exact guard of the women.

Their punishment.

K the

the old *Serrail*. At their departure the *Cheira Chadun* strips them of their goodliest commodities, and addes to their misfortune the losse of their most pretious things, and most necessary for the comfort of their liues in that sad and troublesome abode.

The others which enioy a better fortune in the Royall Pallace, doe sometimes try that beauty is a fraile good; The violence of an infirmitie, and the burning of a Feauer makes the Roses which adorne their Cheekes to fade, and the Lillies of their countenances to wither. When there is question to seeke for remedie for their diseases, they labour after an extraordinary manner. If the sicke person be one of the *Sultana's*, whom the Emperour doth most affect, the old women which gouerne them, goe downe vnto the Apothecaries shop without the inner Gate of the *Serrail*, and shewing the Physician her Vrine, she relates the estate of the sicke person. He prescribes without seeing her, vpon the report that is made, so as many die for want of helpe. But if the Queene who hath giuen a Successor to the Empire, or some other whom the *Sultan* loues with passion, falls sicke, they aduertise the *Lochin Bassi*, which is the chiefe Physician, who hauing obtained leaue from the Prince to goe and visit her, hee enters into the womens *Serrail*, where the Eunuchos receiue him; for all the women retire at his comming. They lead him into the Chamber of the sicke party, who hath her face couered with her couerings, for they vse no Linnen; to the end the Physician should not see her; shee hath her arme only out of the Bed, couered with fine Cypresse; vpon the which hee feeles her pulse, and knowes the Qualitie of the Feuer, but it is not lawfull for him to speake, whilest hee is before the sicke person. After this he retires backward for that hee may not turne his backe towards her. The remedies which hee doth prescribe are most commonly solutiue potions, all other Physique is in a manner neglected in that Court: For the Turkes beleeue that from the day of their birth, the time and continuance of their liues is written vpon their foreheads, by an ineuitable destinie, which no kind of Physicke can change.

Their diseases.
Forma bonum
fragile est,
quantumq; ac-
cedit ad annos,
Fit minor, &
spacio carpitur
illa suo, Ouid.
de Art. lib. 2.

If

If it were necessary for the sicke person to change the aire, this remedie would be very difficult. For the women neuer goe out of the *Serrail*, but in the *Sultans* company, and they goe to no other places but to the old *Serrail*, and to his houses of pleasure, and are not seene by any Man. The Black Eunuches which guard them, helpe them into their Coaches, which they shut vp close before they goe out of the *Serrail*: The streets of *Constantinople* by the which they are to passe, are made cleane and hanged with cloth, to the end that no man should violate by his lookes the absolute content which the Prince hath of these goodly creatures, who seeme to be only borne for him: Hee alone doth see them, hee alone doth conuerse with them, and he only doth enioy them. But seeing the relation of the liues of the women of this great *Serrail*, hath brought vs to the Gates of the old *Serrail*, let vs enter into it, and finish the History of their Fortune.

<small>Their going out of the *Serrail*.</small>

This Imperiall Pallace was sometimes the stately designe of *Sultan Mahomet* the Second, whom the Turkes call Conqueror, who after he had taken *Constantinople*, caused it to be built for his Mansion, in that part of the Citie, which his Architects did hold to be the most beautifull and the most commodious. It is spacious enough to lodge a great Prince, with all the Officers of his House. Its circuit containes aboue halfe a French League or a good English mile, the walles are high and strong, there is but one Gate guarded by a Company of white Eunuches, by the which no man enters but the Emperour: If the necessitie of his house drawes him thither, they cause the women to retire into a priuate place vntill that he be gone. It hath aswell as other Royall Houses beautifyings and commodities; delightfull Gardens, pleasing Fountaines, commodious Bathes, and a Moschee for their deuotions. The three strange Harbingers, but all three allied, haue lodged many faire women in it, that is to say, Death, Inconstancy, and Contempt: Death hath sent a great number thither, when shee hath taken away the Prince, which cherish their beauties; and amongst those are the *Sultana's*, Mothers to the Princes Children, his Daughters and his Sisters, and the

<small>The old *Serrail*.</small>

Mo-

Monarches Aunts, which is newly seated in the Throne of his Predecessour Inconstancie; when as the *Sultan* wearied with the lasciuious imbracements of the women which haue beene the Idoll of his affections suffered himselfe to be perswaded to a new Loue, that they haue abused his fauours, and that they haue made themselues vnworthy to continue in his Pallace. Contempt, when as some of these Virgins which are presented vnto him, haue not in his judgement, allurements sufficient to captiuate him: Or when as yeares (an Enemy to beauty) doth blemish them with wrinckles, and doth ranish the honour of their delicate complexions, and the glory of their countenances. These vnfortunate Ladies which haue beene that which they are no more, haue no other consolation, in this kind of exile but the hope to be married to some *Basha*, or some other great Man of the Port, at the least such as had no children by the *Sultan*: For the condition of others which are Mothers binds them to a perpetuall widdowhood, yet they may easily attaine vnto it if the *Sultan* giues way, if the *Chadun* or Gouernesse be pleased, and if they haue money: Of this last the other two depends, by it they gaine the *Chadun*, and she perswades the Prince that they are worthy: Thus Gold may doe any thing in all places, and the darts which loue imployes in such places, haue golden heads. This is the reason why they gather together all the Money they can, partly by the sparing of their Pensions, and partly by the sale of their most rich Commodities brought from the other *Serrail* in secret, and without the priuitie of the Gouernesse, who strips them at their going forth (but vnjustly) of the pearles, pretious stones and other rich gifts, which their graces haue in their season deserued from the Princes bountie: This seuere old woman restores them to the *Sultan*, but most commonly she keeps a share to her selfe. A strange alteration of humane things, they which formerly had possest the Empire in Mastering its Monarches, suffer the disgrace to be shut out of his Pallace, and to lose their moueables: They which are more politique, which haue foreseene their putting out, and haue secretly conueyed their richest stuffe, they haue the aduantage to be rich: They winne the Lady which commands them, and by Eunuches let the *Baſſaes*, vnderſtand the number of their *Sultanins* & wealth: Theſe without any further bruit demand them in Marriage, and promiſe the Prince to make them a rich Dowrie. Others which by their fruitfulneſſe are depriued of this ſearch, liue in ſtately Lodgings in this Pallace, with abundance of all ſorts of commoditie for life, with the which they enjoy the Qualities of *Sultanaes* and Queenes: But thoſe which haue had Fortune aduerſe vnto them, which hath depriued them both of the fauour of the Court, & of their goods, liue in care with a ſmall allowance in this *Serrail*, and if they can make any delicate Workes, they haue the gaine by the Traffique of the Iewes which viſit them, and therewith they doe in ſome ſort eaſe their diſcommodities.

In this old *Serrail* there is a quarter where as no body lodgeth, royally furniſhed, and reſerued for the Prince when he goes to viſit his Kinſwomen, or practizeth the commerce of his Loues. Carrying with him cloſe Coaches full of his faire *Sultana's*, as we haue ſaid elſe-where, with whom he ſpends the beſt of his dayes, and abandons all noble exerciſes, more worthy of a Prince, to enjoy their charming company. Thus theſe women detaine him, poſſeſſe him, and diuert him from vertue. In this ſenſe an Ancient had reaſon to ſay, *That if the World were without Women, Men ſhould conuerſe with the Gods.* This muſt be vnderſtood of vitious women, and not of thoſe that loue vertue, the which is to be eſteemed and embraced in what ſubiect ſoeuer it be found. *Cato Vticenſs. in Plutarch.*

Chap. XII.

Of the Grand Seigneurs Siſters, and his other Kinſwomen, and of the Marriages of his Daughters.

THe Turkiſh Emperours Siſters lodge and liue in the old *Serrail*: their Quarters are diſtinct from the other women

Emperour to be *Sageis*, or Father to the Bride, in rich Robes mounted vpon a Horſe with a royall Capariſon, hauing about him twelue Footmen, he conducted theſe precious Moueables, or this Royall bundle, which had in the head of it Muſique on horſebacke of Hoboies and Drummes after the Turkiſh manner: It was diſtinguiſhed into ſeuen and twenty Preſents, diuerſly carried by ſeuen and twenty Men.

The firſt was a little Hatte of maſſiue Gold couered with rich ſtones. The ſecond was a paire of Pattins after the Turkiſh manner alſo of pure Gold, enricht with Turquoiſes and Rubies. The third a Booke of *Mahomets* Law, the couering whereof was of maſſiue Gold ſet with Diamonds. The fourth vnto the ſixt was three paire of Bracelets of Gold and precious ſtones. The ſeuenth and eighth two great Bodkins of Diamonds. The ninth a little Cofer of Chryſtall of the Rocke, with the corners of Gold halfe a yard high, and halfe as broad, in the which were ſeene great Diamonds, and huge Pearles of the value of eight hundred thouſand Liuers. The tenth vnto the fifteenth, were ſix Smocks imbroydered with Gold and ſtones. The ſixteenth to the one and twentieth, were ſix head-bands for her forehead of the ſame ſtuffe and as rich. The two and twentieth vnto the ſeuen and twentieth, were ſixe ſtately Robes of Cloth of Gold, richly ſet with Pearles and Diamonds.

Foureſcore thouſand pounds ſterling.

After theſe Preſents followed eleuen Chariots full of young Virgins-ſlaues to ſerue the Bride; they were couered and cloſe, and either of them accompanied or rather guarded by two blacke Eunuches: Twentie other Virgins ſlaues followed on horſebacke, and ſo many blacke Eunuches richly attired and mounted in like manner accompanied them. After all this marched a hundred and forty Moyles laden with Tapeſtrie hangings of Cloth of Gold, of Sattin, of Veluet, with the ground of Gold, and a great number of Cuſhions of Veluet and of Cloth of Gold, which are the Chaires of the Turkiſh Ladies, with great ſtore of other rich and ſumptuous Moueables. All theſe things made the Spouſes Bundle, giuen by the Emperour her Father: Not comprehending the

the Presents and Moueables which the Bridegroome gaue her.

The next day which was the day of the marriage, this Princesse was conducted to her husbands lodging, with no lesse pompe and state then her moueables. The *Ianizaries* made the front of this royall Conuoie: The great Prouost and the great Surueyor followed as before. The *Emirs* or *Cerifes*, which are the cursed remainders of the race of *Mahomet* the Impostor, and only carry among the Turkes a greene Turbant (the marke of their sottishnesse, and of the foolery of their predecessor) came after with a graue march of their vaine holinesse; The Priests, *Santons, Talismans*, and about two hundred schollers in the *Alcoran* diuinitie, came after. The *Vizirs* or chiefe Iudges of Turkey, shewed themselues in this pompe, and before the *Grand Vizir* who came in his rank, hauing on his left hand (which is the most honourable in Turkey) the *Mufti*, or high Priests of the Law, thirty men on horsebacke with Drums and hobois made the musique after the Turkish manner; seuen or eight Egyptians shewing of apish tricks following them, made it knowne that foolery had a ranke in the geratnesse of the World: forty Musitians marcht two and two playing on Lutes, Harpes, and Gitterns; A foole musled with a Cap and a Cloake couered with sheepes bones, and held for a Saint by the Turkes (for folly is esteemed in the Court and is reuerenced for holy) danced alone, and shewed tricks. Fiftie of the principall Officers of the *Arsenall* well attired did honour this Solemnitie, or rather were honoured. Thirtie men followed them with Hammers and other instruments to breake downe the houses which aduanced too farre vpon the streete, and might hinder the passage of two great trees of a wonderfull height, laden with diuers sorts of fruits, wherein Art did imitate nature; They were carried by many men, and supported in the midst by many Ropes; vnder the shaddow of these trees marcht twenty Officers of the *Testardar* or Treasurer *Amet Bassa Seguia* or Father to the Bride. Hee himselfe came after richly attired and royally mounted. Two great torches light carried by many slaues fol-

L lowed

lowed him: Another Torch of a wonderfull great proportion, burning likewise was carried a part; It was couered with plates of Gould: A man would say in seeing it, that this precious Metal had beene moulded into a Torch, and kindled by a new flame, to giue light in this *Celebritie* as well to the eyes of the body, as it did dazle, yea, blind those of the minde. Moreouer, this Torch was more glistering with precious stones, then with the flame which burnt it. The *Raisser Aga* with fiftie of the Princesses Officers followed these stately Lights. After these, there was carried a great Canopie of Crimson Veluet, where no man was couered. Another came after richer than the first, all couered with plates of pure gold, with great Curtaines like vnto a bed hanging downe to the ground, and close of all sides: Vnder it the young Princesse was on horsebacke, being the only subiect of this ioy: Some of her blacke Eunuches were about her: her Coach couered with Cloth of Gold, drawne by foure goodly white horses followed emptie: Eight other Caroaches came after this, in like which were set among the blacke Eunuches many faire Virgins belonging to the Bride, as glistering starres amidst darke and blacke Clouds: In the number of these Gentlewomen slaues they had made choise of fiue and twenty of those whose beautie seemed most accomplished: They were on horseback richly attired, their haire confusedly dispersed waued with the motion of the Westerne winde, like waues of Gold in a Sea of Loue vpon their delicate shoulders: They made the pleasing end of this pompous shew, it may be artificially, but it was cunningly enough for Turkes, to the end the spectators of this Royall Solemnitie, should for the last obiects of their eyes see the Images of beautie, which might frame in their imagination the durable Marks of pleasure, and of the greatnesse of this pompe.

Yet it doth not promise to the Children that shall be borne of this Marriage, a fortune equall to the Qualitie of the Emperours Grandchildren: the fundamentall Lawes of the Turkes Estate, (which supports it by all the meanes they can, and sometimes cements it with bloud) prohibits them euer to
haue

haue any charge, or gouernment which may make them eminent in the Court: The highest degree they can attain vnto, is to be a *Saniac*; which is the Gouernour of a Borough or little Town; or to haue the charge of *Capigibaffi*, which is the chief of the Porters of the *Serrail*, as in *France* the Captaine of the Port at the *Louvre*. Thus they keep them vnder to the end they may neuer trouble the Estate by their authority, and Birth, which makes them Kinsmen to the Crowne. Contrariwise, if the *Bassa* their Father hath children borne of his slaues before the Marriage, these shall precede them, and without contradiction may attaine, if they deserue it, or be fauoured, to the greatest Offices of the Empire.

The *Sultans* Vncles by his Wiues and his other Kinsmen, haue not in regard of this proximitie of bloud, any freer accesse into his Pallace, and neere vnto his person, then that which their places giue them. They carry themselues towards him with the same basenesse and submission as others doe, with the which they are equally his slaues. The reason hereof is, that the Turkes make no great esteeme of women, and they doe not beleeue that they giuing them to base slaues, or to great *Bashaes* do dishonour or honour their Family: The Alliance which comes by their meanes is little regarded: Moreouer the preseruation of Maiestie is so recommended vnto them, as for this reason they keepe in subiection all the men of their Empire, and in like manner those which might aduance themselues by the rights of their birth, the which makes them allied to the Prince:

Chap. XIII.

Of the Grand Seigneurs *Male Children, of their Education, and of the solemne Pompe at their Circumcision.*

THe *Sultans* Male Children are after their birth, lodged and bred vp together in the *Serrail*, if they be borne of

L 2 one

one woman, but if they haue diuers Mothers they are separated into diuers Lodgings. Their Mothers see them bred vp to the age of sixe yeares, with the iealousie and enuie which raignes proudly among the women of diuers beds. After this time the Emperour causeth the Nurses to bee recompenced, and sends them to the old *Serrail*, if they be not married nor haue any houses in *Constantinople*. These young Princes from the age of fiue yeares, vnto eleuen or thirteene which they are with the women, haue their Schoolemasters called *Cosas*, whom the Father giues them: These enter daily into the *Serrail* of women, and are led by blacke Eunuches without seeing any of the Ladies, into a Chamber where these young Princes remaine: They instruct them in the presence of two old Moorish women as long as it is allowed them to continue, after which they returne with the same guides, who bring them to the Gate of the *Serrail*. This exercise is continued vntill the Prince comes to the age of thirteene yeares, which is the ordinary tearme of the Turkes Circumcision, after the imitation of *Ismael*, from whom they glory to be descended, who was circumcised at the same age: Sometimes the Father seeing him grow great and neare him, stayes not so long: He causeth him to be cut at eleuen yeares, to send him out of the *Serrail*, and to remooue him from him into some Gouernment of *Asia*. The Ceremony of the Circumcision is in Turkey the most famous of their Pompe; they call it Marriage, but a Marriage of the Soule: And for that the Soule is more excellent then the Bodie, so the solemnitie of these Marriages doe farre exceed those of Corporall Marriage. We will succinctly describe the particularities, and will take for a Table of this royall Magnificence, the Presents, Playes, Feasts, and gallant Showes, which were made at the Circumcision of *Mahomet* the Third, Grandfather to him that now raignes: Some dayes before he was cut: For the Circumcision followes the Feast; which was celebrated vpon his occasion.

The place of pompes and showes.

The *Hippodrome* is a great place in *Constantinople*, about fourescore fathome long and fortie broad, artificially built vpon a great number of Pillars and Arches which support it

strong-

Court of the Grand SEIGNEVR.

strongly, and keepe it from drowning by the waters of the Sea, which run vnder it, by certaine Channels which giue it entry: It was the ancient mannage and courſe for Horſes as the word doth ſignifie, where the Greeke Emperours cauſed their Horſes to be ridden, and gaue vnto the eyes of the people which beheld them from a goodly Theater built at the end, the pleaſure of their ſtately courſes. The Theater is now ruined, and the goodly ſtones wherewith it was built haue ſerued for the proud Pallaces of *Baſhaes*, which they haue raiſed thereabouts: This place is called at this day *Atmeiden*, that is to ſay Mannage; There the Magnificences of the Circumciſion of the Turkiſh Princes are performed.

The day being come when they are to begin the Feaſt, the Emperour goes on horſebacke from the *Serrail*, to come to the *Hippodrome*; the young Prince his Sonne is on the right hand, (which is the leſſe honourable among them) attired in a rich Robe of Cloth of Gold, couered with an infinite number of Diamonds, and great round Pearles of ineſtimable value: The point of his Turbant gliſtered with precious ſtones: He was mounted vpon a goodly Horſe, with the richeſt Cariſon that could be found in the *Sultans Serrail*: The Bitt was of maſſiue Gold ſet with many Diamonds, the Stirrops of the ſame mettall couered with Turquoiſes, the Buckles were alſo of Gold enricht with Rubies, and the reſt of the ſtately Furniture accordingly: The *Grand Vizir*, the *Beglierbeys* of *Aſia*, and *Europe*, with other *Baſha's* of the Port follow their Lords, the *Ianizaries*, *Solaquis*, *Spahis*, *Capigis*, and the other Guards and Officers of the Court accompany them, all of them attired with ſo great luſtre and pompe, as it ſeemed that all the wealth not only of the Eaſt, but of the whole World had beene transported to *Conſtantinople*, to adorne the Men which ſhewed themſelues in this Solemnitie. Being come to the *Hippodrome*, they were receiued with a double harmony: The firſt conſiſted of Hoboyes, Fifes, Drums, and Trumpets, with ſuch a noyſe as the Ayre and Earth ecchoed againe: The ſecond, the acclamations of the the people, who cried with a loud voice, Liue *Sultan Amurath*,

In what Equipage the Turkiſh Princes goe to the Hippodrome.

78   *The History of the* Serrail, *and of the*

rath, and liue *Sultan Mahomet* his Sonne. Hee to let the people know, how much he did cherish their affection, gaue them a Largesse, and cast many great handfuls of Gold and Siluer amongst them. Whilst the Princes crosse the place, they caused to march before them fiue great Tapers of waxe kindled and enricht with *Clinquant*, and beautified with all sorts of flowres: They were for their proportion of bignesse and height rather like vnto great Oakes than Torches: They carried fortie foot in height.

The places for the *Sultans.*

The *Sultans* hauing crost the place entred the Pallace of *Hibraim Bassa*, where the pauement of the Court was all couered with Cloth of Gold, whereon they marched, and went to take their Places, to be the Subiects and Spectators of this Royall Pompe. The Father entred into a Pauillion which was prepared for him, hauing a Portall adioyned beautified with rich pictures of *Arabia*, which looked towards the place: The Sonne went into a Chamber vpon the left hand, where his seate was prepared. The *Sultannes* place was ioyning to the Pauillion; In the which were only the Mother of the young Prince and Wife to the Emperour, his Sister the young Princesse, and the women of their Traine: Their Robes and glorious lustre of pearles and precious stones which they carried were worthy of the wife & Daughter of the most powerfull and rich Monarch of the Earth. All the *Agaes* and Captaines of the Port were in a Gallery neere vnto them: At the end of the same lodging were other Galleries erected of three stories: They had diuided them into little Lodgings like vnto Cabinets; In the first and highest was the *Grand Vizir*, and the other *Vizirs*, with the *Beglierbeys* of *Asia* and *Europe* were placed next, and the *Bassa Occhiali* Captaine of the Sea, or Generall of the Galley, and of all the Fleets of the Empire, whom Fortune had drawne from the Trade of a base Fisherman of *Calabria*, and aduanced to that degree. In the second story were many Lords & Courtiers of the Port. In the third and lowest they had made places for the Embassadours of Kings and Christian Princes: That of the French Embassadour was in the first Ranke, the Emperours had the second,

The place of the *Sultana's.*

Those of the *Bashaes.*

Those of the Christian Embassadour.

the

Court of the Grand SEIGNEVR. 79

the Polonians the third, the Bailiffe of *Venice* the fourth, and he of *Raguse* the fift: They were all in Cloth of Gold, and their Gentlemen in like manner. He of *France* did not assist, holding it vnseemely for the Embassadour of a most Christian King and eldest Sonne of the Church to be spectator of a superstition, contrary to the Law of his Religion, yet his lodgings were kept void, aboue those of the Imperiall Embassadour, and no man held it during the Feast.

On the other side of the place there were Theaters and Lodgings erected for the Embassadours of *Mahometan* Princes, who would not haue their places neere vnto the Christians. The first place was giuen to him of *Persia*, who was stately attired in those goodly Robes of Cloth of Gold after the Persian manner, buttoned about him bandrick-wise; The Gentlemen of his Traine did equall in pompe and gallantnesse any other of their condition whatsoeuer. The top of their Turbants couered with goodly Turquoises, whereof their Country abounds, made a goodly shew: They had brought their wiues with them, who were wonderfull faire, and attired with great aduantage to grace them: They couer their heads with many little Bands of Silke and Gold wreathed with their haire which they suffer to hang downe vnto their girdles, and they artificially make two little hornes of haire enricht with Pearle and precious stones, the which fall vpon their faire fore-heads: They made the *Sultana's* to enuy them, who beheld them and admired their grace thorow their lattice windowes. *Persia* hath alwayes had the glorie to haue had the fairest women in the World. The Daughters of *Cyrus*, and the Wife of King *Darius*, had so many allurements in their beautifull countenances as *Alexander* durst not looke on them, fearing to be vanquished, and *Roxana* although of base condition, was found so beautifull, as she deserued the honour to be wife vnto this great Prince. The Turkish women enter not into comparison with the Persians for beautie; to whom they yeeld it; and they say that their Propher *Mahomet* would neuer goe into *Persia*, and when they demanded the reason, his answere was that the women were so beautifull

Those of the Mahometan Embassadours.

as they were able to moue the Angels to loue: But this Counterfeit was nothing the chafter. The Embaſſadour of Tartarie was Ranck't next vnto the Perſian; hee was bruitiſhly attyred, and followed as by Leaders of Beares, or of wild beaſts. For his Men were couered with the skinnes of Beares, Foxes, Wolues, and ſuch like, whereof the haire was outward, they had Caps of the ſame, and hee himſelfe was clad in Sables. So as they which beheld him in this manner might well conceiue that the wild Beaſts had left their Dens and Caues, to ſee the ſtately Pompe of this royall ſpectacle. The Embaſſadours of *Feſſe*, *Morocco*, *Tranſilvania* and *Moldavia* were next vnto him. Hee of *Polonia*, was accidentally on their ſide in a lodging apart which was ſuddainly built. For ariuing late and ſeeing his place held, hee would not ſit after the other Chriſtians. The Players of Inſtruments, and the Turkiſh Muſique were neare vnto them, being ſix ſcore in number, with Kettle-drums, Fifes, Flutes, Tymbrels, Cymbals, and other Inſtruments, *A La Moreſco*, playing confuſedly altogether, and making a Melodious harmony able to make Aſſes dance. For they neuer change their Note. There were fiue hundred Ianizaries appointed for the place, to preuent all diſorder: and with them were three hundred Men fantaſtically attired, couered with Bells, holding in their hands bladders blowne, with the which they ſtrooke thoſe that did not make way. This did baniſh all confuſion and tumult, whereby euery Man might eaſily ſee the wonders that are in that place.

The Embaſſadours preſents

The Rançkes thus diſtributed, and the order carefully obſerued, the Embaſſadours went to the *Baiſemain* of the *Sultan*, or to kiſſe his Robe, and made him rich Preſents: For they neuer goe vnto him emptie handed. This cuſtome hath made me often remember, in reading it, the miſerable condition of thoſe which plead in *France*, which goe not but with full hands. Hee was preſented by the Embaſſadours in this manner. He of *France* deliuered his in priuate, and not publiquely like vnto the others. To the end this Prince might know, and the people ſee that our Kings giue in the way of courtesie and friendship, that which the others brought for tribute: Hee gaue him a stately Clocke of rare Art which strooke the houres melodiously in Musique, by eight and twentie Bels of siluer, and with it thirtie peeces of Scarlet. The Bailiffe of *Venice* presented a Cupboord of siluer plate, the one halfe gilt, and the other white, sixe great Payles of siluer to draw water, ten peeces of Cloth of Gold, ten of Silke, Sattin, and Veluet, and twentie of Scarlet. The *Polonian* brought a Semiter, whose hilt and scabberd was all couered with precious stones. Hee of *Ragusa* gaue fifteene goodly Cups of siluer, many Tapers of white Waxe, which the Turkes esteeme, and some peeces of Scarlet. The Persian presented two Alcorans, and some other Bookes of *Mahomets* Law, couered with massiue Gold, many Persian Carpets of Gold and Silke, and a good number of great Pearles: The Embassadour of *Tartarie* gaue many skins of Sables and other exquisite Furres of great price. All the rest made their Presents according to the order and rancke of the Princes which sent them.

They whom the Lawes of seuere loue, and the rigours of Iealousie, had restrained from the publique sight of the wonders of this solemnitie, yet they did celebrate the Feast, in those goodly places where they are kept: For the *Sultana's* & the *Grand Seigneurs* Côcubines made Playes & Feasts in their *Serrail*, where the Prince did visit them, honoured them with rich Presents, and gaue at that time vnto the *Sultana Asachi*, that is to say crowned, whom we haue lodged neere vnto him in the Pallace of *Hibraim Bassa*, a Crowne of precious stones of the value of a hundred thousand Crownes. He caused to be brought vnto them a great number of beasts of diuers sorts, all made of Sugar presented to the life, of the greatnesse and proportion they ought to be of, as Camels, Lions, Elephants, Tygres, and many others: The Embassadours had their part: six peeces were sent vnto him of *France*. This was performed some dayes before the Pompe of *Hippodrome*, which was celebrated in this manner.

Feasts of the Sultanaes that were shut vp.

M The

82 The History of the Serrail, and of the

Mahomets Clergie.

The *Mufti* who is the high Priest of the Turkish Law, opened the beginning; he appeared first in the place, being Maiestically set in a Tabernacle carried vpon a Camels backe: He had a Booke in his hands which hee turned alwayes ouer: About him were on foot a great number of Priests, and religious *Mahometans*, who held Bookes in like manner. But their fantasticke attire did shew plainely the humours of their brutish spirits: Some had their heads couered with hoods, others with Mitres, some with Crownes, Many had Robes of beasts skinnes. They were no sooner come vnto the place, but they made shew of their Religious modestie, in whistling, howling, beating vpon Pans and Basons, ringing of little bels which they carried in their hands, as a man would say that these testimonies of their zealous deuotion, were an insolent iangling; at the sound whereof they did leape & friske without ceasing. In this posture they made three turnes about the place, after which they stayed before the *Grand Seigneurs* window, who looked vpon their fooleries. There they made their prayers, during the which some religious Men of the troupe drew out great Kniues, and cut their flesh in diuers parts of their bodies, for the loue of the Prophet, and of their *Sultan*. The *Mufti* descended from his Tabernacle, entred into the Pallace, and made his Presents, which consisted in some Bookes of the Law. After which he retired with the brutish company of this monstrous Clergie.

The Patriarchs of the Christians.

And for that this first troupe was ridiculous, that which followed was lamentable: They were the two Christian Patriarches, the one of the *Grecians*, the other of the *Armenians*, attired in long blacke Copes, which are their Patriarchall Robes; the true colours of their seruitude and heauinesse: They were followed by some Christian Priests: Their Gate was pittifull, hauing their heads hanging downe, in such sort, as the Christians that were come thither to laugh, found a worthy subiect of weeping, seeing the Church captiuated to the cruelty of Turkes, and the Reuerend Pastors thereof forced to goe and humble themselues at the feet of their Tyrant, and Ene-

Court of the Grand SEIGNEVR.   83

Enemy of their Law, in a superstitious Ceremony, and contrary to their Religion: to lift their sacred hands vpon him, and prostitute vpon his person the grace of their blessings: This is the estate whereunto the Diuision of Christians hath reduced them. When they came before the *Sultan*, they prayed vnto God with a loud voice to blesse him, they presented him with a great Bason of siluer full of peeces of Gold, and so returned poorer than they came.

   The Merchants followed, to vent without profit the most precious of their Merchandize: They were a thousand in a troupe, Turkes, Christians, or Iewes, all attired in Robes of Gold, and followed by a pleasing band of young men attired like maidens, hauing Bowes in their hands, and Quiuers at their backes full of golden Arrowes. A childish troope of daintie young Boyes like to many *Cupids* crowned with flowers, and holding Darts in their hands, drew without any difficultie a Chariot which followed them, whereon was set and opened a shop full of Cloth of Gold and Silke, with Tapestries of all sorts, which they presented to the *Sultan*, and cryed; Liue *Sultan Amurath*.   *The Merchants.*

   The Goldsmiths followed after; their decking did shew that they traded in precious Wares: They were all couered with precious stones: Some of their number drew a rich shop full of Vessels of Gold and Siluer which they gaue vnto the *Grand Seigneur*. A small troupe of other Goldsmiths made a band a part: They were those of *Baiestan*, whereof we haue spoken before, stately attired: The stones and pearles which were vpon their Garments, were valued at a Million of gold. The Presents which they made were great and rich.   *The Goldsmiths.*

   All the other Tradesmen came in their order, and all laboured in their profession. The makers of Cloth of gold and silke, to the number of fiue hundred men well attired, caused two Loomes to match with them, whereon they made a peece of cloth of gold, and another of silke before they had gone thrice about the place. The Lace-makers did the like in their kind; They were in the midst of many sorts of beasts made of silke,   *Tradesmen of diuers sorts.*

M 2   which

which marched with them by Art: The Linnen Weauers, Tapestrie men, and Cotton makers, laboured also in their Vocation. The Feather-makers fed the curiositie of the spectators with Feathers and winde: They made many artificiall Birds, which did flie in the Aire, as if they had beene naturall. Tailors made Garments in passing vpon the place; Smiths did worke in Iron, Potters made Pots, Cutlers made Kniues, and Sadlers Saddles, Masons did build, and Glasse-makers did blow their Glasses, Bakers did bake; and that which was not pleasing, the sluttish Butchers did kill and flay Beasts, and gaue the flesh to the people. The Gardiners were there laden with Flowres, the Ploughmen with their Ploughes tilled the Sand: The Shepheards with their fat troups made their three turnes: The Keepers of Moiles, Asses, and Carters, brought their Moiles, their Horses, and their Asses: Their grosse speeches did not greatly tickle the *Sultans* eares: Nor their Presents did not draw his eyes to the contemplation of their beautie: He had nothing but Wood, Stone, and Water: and that which he did, as I conceiue, suffering their foolery to entertaine his leisure, was only to represent vnto his ambition the fabricke of the World, to the gouernment whereof he aspires, in receiuing such homages as these men could yeeld. The Iewes were the last which gaue Presents: They were three hundred young men separated into three bands, disguised in diuers Nations: The one was attired and armed like French, the other represented Spaniards, and the third seemed to bee *Swissers* with their great Cod-peeces: They had for their traine an infinite number of Dragons, Sirens, and Tortoyses of the Sea, which marched artificially: And with this pleasant Antiques, as women which had resigned their Distaffes vnto their husbands, and made them to spin: They were gotten vpon their shoulders to shew their Empire, and so let them see the miseries of these Coxcombes, charged with such importune burthens.

Artificiall Combats.   These Homages and Presents being thus ended, the Combats of warre, did shew the force of their art, and the sports

the

the pleasure of their brauerie: The *Grand Vizir* would haue the honour to expose vnto his Masters eyes, the representation of his victories against the Christians. He caused to be drawne into the place two great Castles of Wood, diuersly painted, mounted vpon Wheeles, garnished with Towres, fortified with Rampiers, and furnished with Artillerie: The one was kept by Turkes, who had planted vpon their Tower, many Red, White, and Greene Ensignes: The other was defended by Men, attired and armed after the French manner, who seemed Christians: Their Ensignes carried white Crosses, without doubt they had beene taken in some encounter, or at the sacke of some Towne of the Christians: either of these Castles had thirtie Horse, which made diuers sallies: The Turkes forced the others to make their last retreate into their Fort, where they shut them vp, besieged them, battered their walls, made a breach, sent to discouer it, and marched to the assault with their vsuall cries and howlings: The little resistance they found made them soone Masters and vanquishers, although they were themselues vanquished; for they fought against themselues: If they had had to deale with Christians, they had not preuailed so easily. As soone as they were entred, they abandoned the place to their cruelty, put all to the sword, cutting off the heads of the principall, and lifting counterfeit heads aboue the walls. The contempt which they make of vs ended the triumh; They let slip into the place about thirty Hogs which they had shut into a Fort, and ranne after them crying and howling in mockerie: Thus the Turkes doe not sport but in contemning the Christians, nor labour seriously but in ruining them. And they by a fatall diuision prepare their victories, and dispose the triumphs which they obtaine of them with great facilitie.

Occhiali Bassa great Admirall of the Sea, exceeded by his industrie, the *Vizir* diuertisement. Hee caused to come rowling into the place, a great Iland, admirably well made of boords and pastboord, which represented *Cypres*: Two powerfull Armies held it besieged, the one by Sea and the other by Land:

A representation of the taking of Cypres.

Land: There was artificially seene their descent into the Iſland, the siege of *Famagouſte*, the ſallies, skirmishes, batteries, counter-batteries, mines, counter-mines, breaches, aſſaults vpon aſſault, fire-workes, and whatſoeuer the furie of Warre could inuent. Sometimes the Turkes were Maſters of the Wals, and ſuddainly the generoſitie of the Cypriots repulſed them: But time, force, and the want of ſuccours made them receiue the compoſition which they offered them; yet the diſloyaltie of the Turks did not obſerue it, for ſome they made ſlaues, and the reſt they put to the Sword: All this was ſeene in the place. When as the ſound of Trumpets, the noiſe of Drums, the howling of Turkes and the thundering of the Canons ſeemed to be at the taking of another Iſland at *Cyprus*. The wonder of this artificiall repreſentation did much pleaſe the *Sultan*, reioyced the people, and reuiued in the Chriſtians minds the griefe of their loſſe: Heauen would haue it ſo to puniſh their great curioſitie, for aſſiſting with theſe infamous *Mahometans*, and to be ſpectators with them at the Pompes of their Superſtition. But he did not ſuffer their inſolencie to be vnpuniſhed; Hee made it knowne that if his Iuſtice ſuffers them to bee a ſcourge to the Chriſtians, yet hee doth not alwayes ſuffer them, to haue them in deriſion: The Cannonadors, where there was nothing but Powder, flue many of theſe takers of the Iſland in Picture vpon the place, & wounded a great number.

Artificial Caſtles. Some other artificiall Caſtles appeared after, ſhewing the like thing to that of the *Grand Vizir*: One among the reſt, the leaſt of all, carried two Towers, in the which there were two men armed, which fought one againſt the other with their Semiters, they did manage greene Enſignes, and Battle-axes of glaſſe without breaking them. The *Rovvelievs* and *Albanois*, whom the Turkes hold for the beſt men at Armes, came after with their Launces and their Targets vpon their leſt armes; they haue no Reſidence, it likewiſe the *Erkrytes*, it *That is to ſay, Italians, French Spaniſh, &c.* is onely tied to their Saddles by a leathed thong, ſome haue no Cuyraſſes: Many of their Horſes were ſlaine there in com-

combating. After the Encounter, they did runne at the Ring after their manner, which is to set a little rod of Iron on the ground, on the end whereof they put a Ring somewhat bigger than those which they vse in *France*. They which tooke it, carrying the Ring on the end of their Launce being on foot, went to present it vnto the *Sultan* before his window, who threw him out a Ring of Gold in recompence; the manner of receiuing it was not without a Mysterie: In raising it from the ground, the Caualliers kist it, laid it vpon his head, and bending downe very low made a Reuerence and so retired. When these men had voided the place, they brought in thirtie Christian Souldiers, lately taken in the Wars of *Hungarie*: They followed with their Irons the triumph of certaine Turkish Captaines which had taken them; some Ensignes and Drums of their Companies made vp the Trophie of these *Barbarians*.

A goodly troupe of Archers on horsebacke arriued soone after with a more generall joy: The Actiuities which they shewed are admirable. After they had finished their courses, with a Target in the left hand, and a long Dart or halfe Pike in the right, sometimes ranged in battaile, sometimes disbanded, casting them one at another, and taking them vp from the ground in running: They ranne their Horses with their full speed, and in the swiftnesse of their course, drew their Semiters thrice out of their Scabbords, and put them vp as often without any stay: In like manner they shot thrice with their Bowes, with the first they hit an Iron on the hinder part of the horse; with the second they strooke an Apple of Gold, which was vpon the top of a great Mast of a Ship set vp in the midst of the place: with the last they hit the Ring at which the *Albanois* had runne: Then standing vpright in their Saddles, they did run their Horses with full speed, and did mannage their Armes as before. Some of their Troupe did things which were admirable: There was one who tooke the Saddle from his horsebacke, laid it vpon his necke, and set it in its place againe all with running. The same men

Archers on horseback and their description.

set

set an Orange vpon the Turbant of his slaue, and in running pierced it diuers times with his Arrowes, and neuer hurt his slaue; Hee pierced a great brazen Morter with an Arrow; Moreouer, hee tied two Horses together, set a foot vpon either of them, and standing vpright, supported a young Boy who shot with his Bow as the Horses galloped. Another of the same Archers ran with all speed his head in the Saddle, and his feet vpwards betwixt foure Semiters, which had their points set against him: Two men of their troupe put themselues into one Saddle, and vaulted before and behinde while the horse did run, lighting and remounting againe without stay. An *Arabian* which was amongst them added the force of his jawes to their dexteritie: He did set a packe Saddle on a horse with his teeth, hauing his hands bound, hee put on the panniers, and then set on his Boy to load it, hee did also saddle his horse after the same manner, and leapt vpon him; doubtlesse the biting of such a Gallant would be dangerous.

This day (for all these wonders were not one dayes worke) ended by some actions of piety after the Turkish manner, which the *Sultan* caused to be performed at the Gate, by the which they goe to *Andrinopolis*: Thither he went going from the place with the young Prince *Mahomet* his Sonne, and all the great Men of his Court, where being ariued he caused foure thousand sheepe to be sacrificed, and a great number of Beeues which he caused to be rosted whole, in either of which they put a whole sheepe, and in the sheepe a hen, and in the hen egges, and caused all to be distributed to the poore. Hee then receiued newes of the defeat of his Army in *Persia*; for the pleasure of humane Pompe is neuer so absolute, but it is accompanied with some cares and crosses: The feeling of this Rout fell vpon the Embassadour of *Persia*. The Turke offers violence to his person, and commits him to Prison, and in the open day, and in the view of the people, and of other Embassadours, caused his Lodging to be sackt and spoiled.

But this was no hinderance, but the day following the Feast was continued. A troupe of excellent Tumblers and
Moun-

Court of the Grand SEIGNEUR.

Mountebankes (whereof Turkey abounds aboue all the Regions of the Earth) did to the common amazement of all the Spectators, these things which follow. The first which shewed himselfe in the place, shut a young Boy naked into a Hogshead, with fiue and twenty or thirty great Serpents, and rowled it about the place, and then drew out the Boy whole and sound: The same Serpents stinging and biting others which came neere them. After this they buried a young Boy deepe in a Ditch, and couered him with Earth as if hee had beene dead, and yet he answered as distinctly and intelligibly to that which they demanded of him, as if hee had beene out of the ground. Another presented himselfe naked without shame, but not without more than humane force, hee layed himselfe flat on his backe vpon the edge of two Semiters; being in this posture, they laid vpon his Belly a great Anuile of Iron, whereon foure men did beate with great Hammers, and moreouer they did riue many great pieces of wood without any offence to him. When this man was retired, a troupe of other naked men exposed themselues to the view of the World all couered with wounds, their bodies being yet larded with the same armes which had made them, some with Arrowes, others with Kniues and Swords; But before these mad men had gone thrice about the place, two of the troupe fell downe dead, which shewed that their wounds were rather markes of their folly than inchantments. Another shewed the force of his iawes and his hands: he held a horse-shooe betwixt his teeth, and puld it in pieces with his hands; He brake a Plough-share, with three blowes with his fist; and hee caused a piece of Iron to be made red hot, the which hee tooke in his hand licked it with his tongue, rubbed it on his face, and yet was not burnt: Afterward hee caused a Goat to dance pleasantly vpon his shoulders, and neuer tought it, causing it to passe from one shoulder to the other without mouing. A headie-brain'd fellow followed this man, vpon whose head they did breake with Hammers a great stone, which a man could hardly lift from the ground. Hee caused them to couer him with so great a heape of stones as he could

N not

not besides, and yet for all this hee felt no discommoditie. Another band came after, whose feet were so hardned, as they trod vnbare vpon a Harrow full of sharpe Pikes and cutting Kniues: There was one followed them, who with a cord, tied to his haire without the helpe of his hands, did lift vp a stone of a hundred and fifty pound weight. Many Beasts instructed in this Art of tumbling augmented the pleasure of the Assistants: little Birds, went to fetch a piece of siluer as farre as they directed them, and brought it to their Masters, Asses danced, Dogges and Apes shewed a thousand pleasant tricks. The *Grand Seigneurs* Wrestlers, came to shew their force and actiuitie, being oyled and greased to auoid the surprize of their Enemies: These are the most continent men in Turkey, they keepe their Virginity pure and vntouchte, and say with reason that it doth entertaine and preserue the force of their bodies: The *Speichs*, which are the *Sultans* Footmen, would also be of the partie, they came vnto the place with their feet shod, running and leaping with admirable swiftnesse and disposition. These men haue the skin of their feet so hard as a Smith can hardly make a naile to enter, they doe harden them for pleasure. The Dancers vpon Ropes shewed strange Feats of Actiuity: In those places they exceed all others whatsoeuer for their Agility.

Elephants and Giraffe.

Two Elephants, and a *Giraffe*, were brought into the Hippodrome, to augment the *Sultans* delight by this nouelty. The Elephants differed in forme: One was great and the other little. The great one was thrice as high, and bigger than a Buffle, or small Steere; hee carried vpon his back a little Castle of light wood, in the which might stand fiue or sixe Souldiers without crowding: The head in comparison of the rest of the body was little: From the end of the vpper part of the Muscle, there did hang a long trumpe, whereof this beast makes vse as readily as a man doth his hands, takes what his appetite doth aduise him, carries his meate to his mouth, vseth it for a defence with incomparable force; his eyes are small like to those of a Bore, his neather chap is like vnto the same beast: Hee hath two great teeth, about fiue foot long, his eares are round

Looke *Lipsius* Epist. in his Centuries where hee speakes of this Beast.

Court of the Grand SEIGNEUR.

round and great, lying vpon his backe: hee sometimes raises them vp: his legs are euen like vnto pillars, in the which there appeares no joynts, yet this Beast hath some, he doth but halfe bend them, and therefore hee suffers himselfe to fall vpon his side: his feet are round, and haue fiue nailes, his skin is blacke, and hath little haire. The Naturalists obserue, and experience doth confirme, that this beast hath so powerfull an instinct, as it seemes, hee is indowed with judgement: Examples are familiar in Histories: This beast being brought before the *Grand Seigneurs* window, lifted vp his head to looke on him, then he bowed it downe very low in signe of reuerence. They cast vpon the ground a handfull of *Aspres*, which is a little Coine like vnto the French *Carolus*; the which hee gathered vp with his heauy trunpe as handsomely as any man could haue done with his hand: Eight strong Turkes held a long Pole in their hands, and gaue him the end; as soone as he had seized on it with his trunpe, hee made them to turne about as easily as if they had beene feathers: Afterwards hee lifted vp the Pole, and strooke it so hard against the ground, as those men were forced to abandon it: Being Master of it, hee did flourish with it like a two hand-sword with admirable dexterittie. Wherefore the *Indians* haue reason in their warres to make vse of the force and addresse of these beasts. They carrie many men, and when they tie a Semiter to the trumpe, one of them kils more then a company of Foot could doe.

Trunck.

The Giraffe.

The *Giraffe*, whereof the portraite is here represented, was at the same time brought into the *Hippodrome*. This beast for that it is little knowne in *Europe* was much admired. It is not only beautifull of it selfe, but it is also gentle and very tractable: It hath a head like a Stagge, armed with two little hornes halfe a foot long, couered with haire; the eares, the feet and the tailes to like vnto a Cow: It hath a neck like vnto a Camell; it hath hard knobs vpon the hams, and brest; The skin is speckled like vnto a Leopard; and some beleeue that it

is

as that Camelopardalis of the Ancients; his legs before are
foure of five times longer then those behind, so as his naturall
posture represents a Goat standing vpright against a Tree to
browse the buds: The which makes him to feed with discommoditie: for in this action hee is forced to open his legges to
make passage for his head. If we had not vndoubted proofes
of the wisdome of Nature in the wonders of her workes, wee
might say that this beast alwayes standing vpright is one of
her fantasticke Creatures. Being led about the place, they
were carried backe, passing thorough the Citie; the *Giraffe*
had such aduantage in the forepart, as his head looked Into
the windowes of their houses.

Such were the pomps of the day, the night wanted not hers,
if there were any night during the solemnity of this royall
Circumcision: For at such time as the Sunne did not shine in
their Hemisphere, they had raised a ship Mast in the *Hippodrome*, whereon there was a great Circle like a Crowne furnished with burning Lamps: and neere vnto the Obelisque
which is the ancient ornament of this place, there was a huge
wheele set vp, the which did turne continually, and made
twelue other smaller to moue, all which were invironed with
lights, which remayning firme, seemed notwithstanding to
follow the motion of the wheeles, not without a wonderfull
content to the eyes of those which beheld them. Besides this
there were many ship Masts with their ropes and tacklings, all
couered with lamps, which gaue so cleer a light, as in the dark
night they made an artificiall day: by the fauour of which
light, most of those goodly things which had appeared in the
day, came after Supper to giue contentment to the company
by their shew. After this, many artificiall Fire-workes, some
drawn by Satyres, others by Dragons, which did vomit forth
flames, filled the aire with agreeable flashes, and pleasing
thunderings, and the spirits of the spectatours with contentment: But their flames quenched, their thundering ended,
and there remained nothing to those which did behold it, but
the sent and smoake of powder, to teach them (if they could
comprehend it) that humane pomps, and the shewes of the

great-

greatnesse of the World, diffolue in the end into winde and smoake. The most stately of these nocturnall sports was the representation of a nauall fight so artificially exprest, as it made the Christians that were present see, that the recompence of labour, and the reward of merit, hauing drawne into Turkey the goodliest inuentions of men, haue made them to lose the name of barbarous to send it vnto vs, whereas vertue is not acknowledged. There they saw many Shippes and Gallies vnder sailes, furnished with Artillerie, adorned with their flags, the Trumpets sounding, fight, inuest, leape from one beak-head to another, kill, cast into the Sea, burne, and sinke the Enemies Vessels, with admirable dexteritie. The battailes at Land, Sieges, and taking of Townes, were represented with no lesse art.

But if the description of this Royall Feast hath beene a pleasing diuersion vnto vs in the toile of this Historie, let vs end it according to the naturall course of pleasure, by the griefe which followes. Doubtlesse it will be great enough to impart it to those which shall read the issue of this Chapter, where we obserue that during the spectacles of this solemnity, the wretched Grecians ran by troupes in this place to make themselues *Mahometans:* Some abandoned Christianitie to auoid the oppression of the Turkes, others for the hope of priuate profit: The youngest and most beautifull were sent into the *Serrail*, with the *Ichioglans*, and the rest among the *Azamoglans*. This hope of better fortune drew the Idlenesse of many young men, so as they could hardly find Masters enough to cut them: This detestable troupe of Rascals, went to shew themselues before the *Grand Seigneur*, their Bonnets vnder their feet, in signe that they did tread their law and honour vnder foot: There a Turkish Priest did cause them to lift vp the demonstratiue finger of the right hand, in signe that they did not beleeue but one God in one person, & to say with a loud voice, *La illa eʒ lula alla* Mehemet *rasoul jalla*: Then they led them into certaine Pauillions, which were erected expresly at the end of the place where they were circumcised.

The

The number of these cast-awayes was found to bee aboue foure thousand soules.

These sports and triumphs being thus miserably ended, the young Prince for whom they had beene made, was brought into his Fathers Chamber, where hee was circumcised by one of the great Men of the Court in the presence of all the *Basha's*. His wound being cured within few dayes, hee goes to take his last leaue of the *Sultana* his Mother, whom she shall see no more vntill hee comes to take possession of the Empire, after the death of his Father, if hee be the eldest, or to end his life with a halter if hee be a younger brother, when his elder shall Raigne. She giues him presents: and the other *Sultana's* doe the like: All the *Basha's* present him, and the Emperour his Father appoints his Family, giues him a *Praeceptor*, an Eunuch for Gouernour, with many other men to serue him, and sends him into *Asia, Samaque* only of the Citie of the *Magnesia*, the chiefe of *Mysia*, or Lieutenant in that Region vnder the authoritie of a *Basha* who is Gouernour: whilest he carries the Title, hee must gouerne his Actions with prudence and modestie; for if he should haue any designes of Innouation by the Counsailes of some discontented seditious persons, he should worke his owne ruine by his owne hands: The Eunuch which is the most apparant man about him, hee is bound to aduertise the *Sultan* his Father, and the principall *Basha'es*, of all his carriage.

Chap. XIV.

Of the Presents they make vnto the Grand Seigneur, *and of those which hee himselfe giues.*

THe custome to giue Presents vnto the Prince hath beene so practized in the Turkish Monarchie, as it is past for a Law of State, so as it is written in the great custome of the

Em-

Empire, that all the Bassa's and great men of the Port shall at certaine seasons of the yeare, and at the Circumcision of the Emperours Children, giue him Presents, and likewise when they returne from the Gouernment of Prouinces, where they haue continued some yeares in the administration of their Charges of Viceroy. The Generals of Armies at the returne from their victories, are bound to present gifts to the *Sultan*: They doe it vsually in a great quantity of Vessels of gold and siluer, Swords and Daggers enricht with precious stones, and bowes of the like manner, Plumes of Feathers with precious Iewels, rich Girdles, exquisite Furres, and sometimes pieces of cloth of gold, with Tapestries of silke and gold: whereof the Princes Wardrobe is commonly well stored, to supply his bounty to his *Sultana's* & slaues, and to send to forreine Princes: All these men being slaues to their Master, and as it were forced to these liberalities, cannot when they please follow their good aduice which say, that *It is a noble folly to giue vnto great Men, for they beleeue they oblige a man much when they receiue that which he presents.* The *Bassa's* which returne from the gouernment of Egypt, parting from *Cairo*, dispose the value of the Presents into ready money, and arriuing at the *Serrail*, they sometimes present vnto the *Sultan* foure or fiue Millions of *Liuers*, which is foure or fiue hundred thousand Pounds sterling. The Generals of Armies doe many times practise the same liberality, they are the better receiued by their Master, and the glory of their magnificence flyes into the mouth of the people, and they find by their great gifts, that the offering of Presents, pacifie both Men and Gods, (as they said in old time) These notable summes enter into the inward *Chasna*, which is the Princes secret treasure. The Christian Patriarch giues vnto the *Sultan* newly crowned an honourable present, which the *Greekes* call *Pesquesian*, or when the Patriarch enters into his charge, by the death or deposition of another. Besides this the Turkes giue vnto the Eunuches which are familiar to the Prince many rich Presents, to make them speake from them vpon all necessary occasions: for the ballance doth alwayes decline on that side which is

hea—

Et vna noble necedad dar à los Reyes, por que creen hazer merced, quando reciben, Anth. Perez en las cartas segundas.

Munera crede mihi placant hominesq̃; Deósque, Placatur donis Iupiter ipse datis, Ouid. de Arte.

heauiest, and the only meanes to gaine the affection of these gelded men, is to glut their auarice, which is no small labour. *Nassuf Bassa*, who ended his fortune and his life in the yeere 1614, did often say that the Eunuches of the *Serrail* were insatiable: They doe also hold, and they practize this Maxime in the Turkish Court, the which is generally receiued by all men, that *The sweetest action of men is, To take*, although in truth it be more generous to giue, for him that is able.

Omnium est dulcissimum accipere, Senec.

As pleasure and griefe are naturally ioyned together, haue one Temple, and their Offerings are vpon the same Altar: The *Othoman* Monarch who takes a great delight to see himselfe glutted with Presents; not only by his owne subiects, but also by strangers, yet he sometimes finds a distaste in it: As it happened to *Selym* the First, whose example shall suffice in this Chapter, that by its breuity wee may ease the long descriptions of the former, This Prince hauing taken the *Othoman* Scepter, his hands being yet bloudy by the death of his Brethren and Nephewes, and the chiefe of his *Bassaes*, thinking to be honoured according to the ordinary custome of his Predecessors, with Presents which forreine Princes make, hee saw his cruelty taxed, by that which the *Persian* Embassadour presented vnto him, who gaue him in his Masters name, a great furious Lyon, inaccessible, alwayes foaming for rage, and neuer made tame by any Man. This present being brought, *Selym* fell into a rage, stampt with his foote, complained that hee was wronged, and sware that hee would be reuenged, and demanded satisfaction from the Embassadour, who being aduised and cunning, couered the part which hee had played with many goodly words: He told *Selym* that this Lion did rather represent the greatnesse of his courage, and that of his generosity rather than any other thing; but this did not pacifie him, he chased him out of his Territories, and gaue him to present vnto his Master many great Dogges with bloudie mussels, as if hee would say, they had torne his Lion in pieces, and that in the assaults of Warre hee would intreat him in like manner.

Seeing then the Turkish Prince doth continually receiue

Presents from others, it is fitting he should likewise giue: For it is more seemly for a King to giue then to take, so his Wardrobe is vsually open to giue. The *Sultana's* are enricht by his Presents; The *Mufti* and his *Præceptor* are honoured, and the *Bashaes* receiue: and all this consists in precious stones, Purses full of gold coyned, Robes of cloth of Gold, Plumes of Feathers, Iewels, rich Armes, and other things of value. The *Chasnadar Bassi*, who is the high Treasurer, hath the charge to buy what is needfull for Presents, hee imployes yearely in cloth of gold, for Robes which they giue, the which is made at *Bursia* in *Asia*, foure Millions of *Liuers*; besides that which comes into the royall Wardrobe, by the Presents of *Basha's* and other great Men: but as all Riuers come from the Sea and returne vnto it, so all the *Grand Seignears* Presents returne backe in the end to his owne Cofers: The *Sultana's* die, and their goodly stuffe comes to him; The *Bashaes* end their liues, he takes all as the Master doth of his slaues: Sometimes hee leaues a part for the execution of the Will which he hath made. So as he doth not giue but lends for a time, seeing that the fundamentall Law of his Estate, which makes all men his slaues, restores that vnto him which he had giuen, and moreouer, all the wealth of his Subjects.

Foure hundred thousand pounds sterling.

But all the Presents of the Turkish Emperour are not pleasing to them which receiue them, they are sometimes fatall fore-tellings of death to him to whom hee giues them: For when hee sends for any great Man of the Port into the *Serrail*, to feast him, or to speake with him, after the Feast or at the end of his discourse, meaning to take away his life in his presence, he giues him a blacke Robe wrought with gold and silke: as *Baiazet* the Second did to *Bassa Achomat*, who had supt in the *Serrail* with the other *Bashaes* at his Masters Table, amidst the delights and pleasures of a royall Feast, whereas Wine, forbidden by the Law of their Religion, was poured forth as plentifully, as in any part of the World. Supper being ended and the Table taken away, the *Bashaes* humble themselues before their Prince, some kisse the ground in his presence, to obtaine pardon for that they had drunke Wine,

O and

The History of the Serrail, and of the

and so returned to their houses. The *Sultan* stayed *Achomat*, with their sweete Words, *Milalah* (that is to say my Protectour) tarrie here with mee. When the others were gone, hee caused a rich Robe of blacke silke wrought with Gold to be brought vnto him. At the sight hereof *Achomat* entred into furie, hee knew well what it meant, and assured himselfe of his ruine, hee accuseth *Baiazeth* of injustice and crueltie, and tells him in his rage, Why didst thou Sonne of a Whore suffer mee to drinke wine against the holy constitutions of my Law, if thou wilt presently put mee to death? Hee ended his rage with the rest of the discourse which his passion had dictated. But his life was freed from the present danger: his Sonne seeing him not returne with the other *Bashaes*, informed himselfe from them what was become of his Father. They tell him in what a pittifull estate hee was, whereupon hee flyes to the *Serail*, moues the *Ianizaries* to compassion, who loued *Achomat* for his valour, as he whom they had followed in the Warres, in Battailes, and assaults of Towns, they filled the *Serrail* with the horrour of their cryes, *Br'e, Br'e*, that is to say Arme, Arme. They beate at the Gate of the Emperours lodging, threaten him, raile on him, called him drunkard, and force him to restore *Achomat* who was pale and wanne, hauing the halter about his necke, with the which the Princes dumbe Men were ready to strangle him. In this manner force hindred the effect of this fatall Present of a blacke Gowne wrought with Gold. But besides these accidents hee that receiues it must expect his infallible Ruine. This Present is not giuen by the *Othoman* Monarch to any but to his owne subiects, but hee sometimes sends others, which shew the contempt which hee makes of forreigne Princes, as when hee sends a Robe how rich soeuer vnto a soueraigne Prince. For a Robe is the Present of a superiour to his inferiour. So *Baiazeth* the first intreated *Themir*, or *Tamberlan*, Emperour of the *Tartars*, when hee sent him a Robe in disgrace to contemne him. *Themir* was much offended, and answered those which brought the Present from the Turke, that he should not intreate those of his sort in

that

Court of the Grand SEIGNEVR.

that manner: but hee soone had his reuenge. Hee entred *Baiazets* Countrey in *Asia*, (*Constantinople* was then held by the Christians) and with eight hundred thousand fighting men, tooke *Sebaste* the Seate of his Empire, slue his Sonne *Orthogules*, defeated his Armie in Battaile, tooke himselfe Prisoner, reuenged this contempt by many others, and afflicted him so in following him, as hee died of griefe, sorrow, and paine: to be an example to Princes, not to contemne those which are Soueraignes like themselues, and therein Images of the Soueraigne God. But thus they giue Presents of Death and contempt in Turkey, the one is of crueltie, and the other of offences and not Presents, for the Presents of Enemies are no Presents.

The *Sultana* Queene that is crowned, and Mother to the young Prince Successour of the Empire, giues many Presents: Shee receiues daily from the Great Men of the Port which send vnto her, and therefore shee is bound to giue; to this end the Emperour doth furnish her with much goodly stuffe, and peeces of price which are giuen vnto him, and with great summes of money to buy others. The *Grand Vizir* doth also giue many Presents both within *Constantinople* and without: Hee sends many Roabes of Cloth of Gold and Silke, to Embassadours which arriue at the Port: and when hee is in the Armie, performing the the Charge of Lieutenant Generall to the *Sultan*, hee giues to draw strangers vnto him that may be vsefull, or to recompence the generositie of some valiant Captaine. And for that all these Presents are giuen in the *Sultans* name, he doth furnish those things which he giues. And to this end the *Testardar* deliuers him Money, pieces of Cloth of Gold, of Silke and many other Stuffes. This is all that can be spoken of the *Sultans* Presents.

CHAP. XV.

Of the Treasures of the Serrail.

Iulius Cæsar potentiam duabus rebus, pecunia scilicet, & militibus parari, conseruari, augeri dicere solebat, Ciphilinus in Cæsario

THe *Othoman* Monarch hath his Treasures: what Soueraigne Prince can preserue and maintaine his power and estate without their force: It is gotten by Armes and Money, preserued and maintained by the same meanes. Hee doth lodge it in his *Serrail,* one part in the Court which is without his Quarter: and the other within it: In the Treasurie without is layed the money for the ordinary and extraordinary expences, which is leuied vpon all the Renewes of the Empire. The *Grand Vizir* and the great *Testardar,* or Superintendent of the Treasure keepe the Keyes, but it is sealed onely by the *Grand Vizir.* The other place for the Treasure is more important: it is within the Quarter of the *Sultans* lodging, or most commonly vnder the Chamber where he sleeps, taking his rest vpon the subject of his disquiet. This is vnder the charge and care of the *Chasnadar Bassi,* who is a white Eunuch, and a Fauourite to the Prince; hee hath one Key and the Emperour another: The Treasure which is laid vp yearely there, is that which hee spares out of the Renewes of *Egypt:* When they haue paid the *Ianizaries* of *Caire,* their Commanders, and others which are the force and defence of that rich Kingdome, there remaines vsually six hundred thousand *Sultanins,* which makes two Millions foure hundred thousand *Liures* of French money. Besides this Treasure the jealousie of Turkish Emperours hath built another in the *Serrail* of the *Sultana's,* in that Quarter where as the *Sultan* Queene doth lodge, to the end that no man of his *Serrail* should enter into it: The doores are of Iron; and they wall it vp as often as they put any Treasure into it, and they which carry it are Mutes, to whose silence the *Sultan* confides the secret: They carrie it in great sacks of Leather like vnto Purses, and let it downe into Cisternes, which are made of purpose to keepe it: Thus the Money which is gotten with paine, is kept

Two hundred and forty thousand pounds sterling.

with

with feare, and if it be lost it is with griefe. The Prince which doth waste it by his prodigalities, weakens his Estate, and exposeth himselfe to the dangers of many violent necessities. That Turkish Monarch which first made the place for the secret Treasure in the *Sultanaes Serrail*, was *Selym* the First, who hauing drawne together all the coyned Gold which hee receiued of the Reuenewes of *Caire* and other places, hee caused it to be moulten, and made a great Ball, which his dumbe Men did roll to put into the Cisternes of this Treasurie. Doubtlesse, it must needs be very painfull to roll it, seeing the weight of this precious metall is so cumbersome, as it drawes all the World after it. Hee himselfe had the Key of this secret place, making vse of his dumbe Men, to the end they should not reueale the rich treasure which he had drawne together. *Amurath* the Third did afterwards seeke a more secret place, vnder the Chamber of the *Sultana Asachi*, (that is to say the crowned) where he caused Cisternes to be digged to that end : He entred into it foure times in the yeere, and at euery time he put into it aboue two Millions of Gold : This Prince drew together more Treasure than any of the rest, hauing in few yeares filled those Cisternes with coyned Gold. Wherefore we must not wonder if the Turkes Armies be so strong, seeing they furnish them with so many sinewes; if they vanquish and triumph, seeing they haue both Men and Money in abundance: But rather wee haue cause to wonder that they doe not get all the rest of the World : For what is there in it that is not to be sold for Money ? The King of the *Numidians* had reason to say in beholding that Citie which was the seat of the most powerfull Monarchie of the Earth : *A Citie that is to be sold, is neere its ruine, if it find a buyer:* Men haue giuen the Turkish Emperours that fearefull greatnesse which they enjoy, but Money hath bought the men.

Iugurtha Roma egressus, eam sæpe tacitus respiciens, postremo dixisse fertur ; urbem venalem, & maturè perituram, si emptorem inuenerit, Salust. de bello Iugurth.

CHAP.

Chap. XVI.

Of the Reuenewes of the Turkish Emperour in generall and in particular, and of the extent thereof.

THe greatnesse of Monarchies consists chiefly in three things, in the number of men, in the extent of Countries, and in the abundance of his annuall Reuenewes. Which three things are found in Eminencie, aboue all other Estates of the World, in the Turkes Empire: His Armies are many times 400000. fighting men or more; the Townes and Champion Countrey are inhabited and abundantly peopled, by the Law of their Religion and State, which forceth Men to marrie being fiue and twenty yeares olde, and they haue libertie to keepe as many Concubines as they are able to feed. The yearely Reuenew is proportionable to this abundance: Wee may comprehend it in two sorts; In the ordinary Reuenew which is alwayes equall, and doth not alter; and in the extraordinary and casuall. The ordinary amounts yearely to twenty Millions of Gold; the extraordinary is not lesse, but more vncertaine, for it is not raised but vpon Escheates and casuall things; as when the Turkes die without Heires, all their goods come vnto the Prince; If they leaue any Children, he takes only ten in the hundred; most of the rich *Bashaes*, and wealthy men of the Court, leaue the best of their Estates to their Prince, although they haue Children: For being all slaues by the fundamentall Law of the State, the *Sultan* seizes vpon their Pallaces of their most precious moueables, and doth not suffer that the great summes of Money which they leaue should be otherwise imployed, but to fill the Cofers of his *Chasna*, or Treasury. Besides all this hee is the first and chiefe principall Steward of the Benefices of his Empire: For if any pious person according to his Religion, leaues any great Legacies to the Priests of his Law, to read the *Alcoran, tan*, or to performe some other deuotion after their manner, hee lookes what is necessary for the nourishment and entertainment of a number of Priests, which are appointed, not according to the Lawes of Excesse, but in termes of modesty and Ecclesiasticall Sobrietie: He causeth it be deliuered vnto them, and puts the rest into his Cofers. So as he that could justly calculate the Reuenewes of the Turkish Empire, without doubt he should find it to exceed forty Millions yearely, aswell the Ordinary as the Casuall: whereunto no Monarch of the Earth doth come neere.

They which haue seene the Turkes Court, dwelt in *Constantinople*, and conuerst with the naturall Citizens thereof, vnderstand the greatnesse of the Annuall Reuenewes of this spacious Empire. And others who haue not trauelled so farre, to attaine vnto this particular knowledge, will not call this truth in question, if they consider the vast extent of the *Othoman* Empire; for the Soueraigne Princes thereof are Lords of *Africke*; they possesse a part of *Barbary*, they rule beyond *Thunis* and *Argier*; they draw Tributes from the Crownes of *Fesse* and *Morocco*. They are Kings of high and low *Egypt*: they force obedience in *Asia*: The three *Arabiaes*, that is to say, the Stony, the Desart, and the Happy, acknowledge no other Lord: The Holy Land suffers the rigour of their command, which is absolute in *Syria*, *Mesopotamia*, and *Chaldæa*, a part of *Persia* doth acknowledge them: *Media* and *Assiria* are theirs: *Armenia* the lesse bowes vnder their Lawes, and a part of the greater, with the Countrey of *Mengrelia*: All *Asia* the lesser obey them, and In it the Prouinces of *Caramania*, *Cilicia*, *Cappadocia*, *Pamphylia*, *Paphlagonia*, *Gallacia*, *Phrygia*, *Bithynia*, *Lydia*, *Caria*, and *Magnesia*: The Emperour of *Trebisonde* acknowledgeth them for Masters: Their power is not lesse in *Europe*, which is the goodliest, the most flourishing and the ciuillest part in the World: All *Greece*, as *Thrace*, *Macedonia*, *Bulgaria*, *Peloponesus* now called *Morea*, *Bosna*, and *Seruia*, doe what they command: *Slauonia* is subject vnto them: A part of *Sarmatia*, *Dasia*, *Hungaria*, and *Valachia* are peopled by

them:

them: The Prouinces which lie vpon the blacke Sea and the *Archipelagus*, belong wholy vnto the Turkes: and the Ilands of the *Mediterranean* Sea, which make the greatest number yeeld vnto their yoake. They haue wrested from the *Venetians* the Crowne of *Cypres*, and from the Knights of *Ierusalem* that goodly Island of *Rhodes*, leauing nothing in that Sea vnder the obedience of the Christians, but *Candie*, *Sicely*, *Corfou* and *Malta*. Thus the extent of that great and redoubted Turkish Empire, ends towards the North at the Riuer *Tanais*, the most famous bounds betwixt *Asia* and *Europe*: Towards the South it ioynes with the Countries of *Preste-Iean*, or the greater *Negus* of *Æthiopia*: Towards the East it extends its limits to the *Persian* Gulfe, yea, it passeth beyond *Balsara*: And on the West they are neere Neighbours to *Ragousa* a Citie not farre from *Venice*. And if God did not restraine the course of their great prosperities, they would adde vnto their Monarchy many other Prouinces of Christendome, which the discord of Christian Princes, and the carelesse neglect of their subjects seeme to expose to their Ambition: For if the *Sultans* doe what they can to inlarge their Estates, these furnish them occasions by their diuisions.

Chap. XVII.

Of the Grand Seigneurs *going forth of* Constantinople *by Land, and his returne in* Pompe, *where he displayes to the view of Strangers, the greatnesse of his Magnificence.*

THe *Othoman* Emperour hath a Custome, to goe once a moneth at the least out of his *Serrail*, to shew himselfe vnto his Subjects, and to free them from all sinister opinions which they might conceiue of him, and to preuent the dangerous effects of any Tumult or Sedition: He takes occasion on the Friday (which is with the Turkes as Sunday is with vs)
to

to goe vnto the Mosquee to performe his deuotion, and to sheare himselfe in publique. When he goes forth in this manner it is vsually by the great Gate of his *Serrail*: Hee is alwayes on Horsebacke, simply attired, and in the same manner as he is in his Pallace: His head is couered with a little Turbant, to be more at his ease: Few *Basha's* accompany him, the most part of his traine are the men of his Family. The *Soubassi*, who is Captaine of the Iustice, or as the Knight of the Watch at *Paris*, goes a little before with fiftie Souldiers of his troupe, to free the streets from all incumbrances, which might hinder the Princes passage, and to keepe euery man in awe while hee passeth. His most familiars accompany him, the Eunuches of his Chamber, his Pages and the rest which attend his person follow him: The Captaine of the Pages, hee of the *Capigis*, and the foure Captaines of the *Ianizaries* of his guard goe before him well mounted, and at his horse head there march foure *Capigis* on foot, and foure *Solachis* at his stirrops; These men most commonly are very tall, for being on foot, and the Prince on horsebacke, their heads must bee equall with his eares: They haue charge to receiue the instructions and petitions, which are presented to the *Sultan*, the which containe complaints of the insolencies of *Basha's*, the iniustices of *Cadis* or Iudges; the theft of *Testerdars* or Treasurers, and the other bad behauiour of his Officers. The *Sultan* hath a speciall care to haue these papers collected, which many times poore miserable men, lying flat on their bellies in signe of humilitie, and lifting vp their hands offer vnto him, the which they present vpon the end of a Reede: Being returned vnto his *Serrail*, hee causeth them to bee read, and findes that which flattery had concealed from him, and learnes those thinges which the timorousnesse of the most sincere men durst not reueale: Presently hee giues order, and loseth no time in the search of long information, which giues an oportunity to the wicked to euade and slip away, or to quench by the power of their purses, the fire that is kindled against them: Presently they see the effects of this Royall care: Many Officers are dismist

P from

from their places, which they terme to be made *Manſuls*, and some others are put to death: Such is the vertue of theſe flying Notes and Petitions; yet they vſe prudence and diſcretion, and cauſe the crime to be well auerred before they puniſh. For this cauſe the *Baſha's* and other great men of the Port, who are intereſſed in theſe Reuelations, are not well pleaſed when they ſee their Prince goe forth in publique; fearing that the newes of their vnjuſt actions ſhould come vnto his eares. In theſe iſſues the people bleſſe him with their acclamations, and he ſalutes them by nodding of his head, and many times to binde their affections more vnto him, hee drawes forth handfuls of gold and ſiluer and caſts it amongſt them. Two of thoſe men which are of either ſide of him, carry in two purſes of Veluet, two little flaggons of gold enricht with precious ſtones, which are full of boiled water, Cordiall and delightfull to drinke: The *Sultan* makes vſe of it, when he is dry. The reſt of his traine come after: The Dwarffes and Ieſters make a part, as the Apes of the Court, which neuer goes without them, to proue that humane pompes haue alwayes ſomething ridiculous. And all theſe men make the number of about three hundred.

The Sultans entry in pompe.

Theſe are his iſſues when he goes from his *Serrail* into *Conſtantinople*: But when he goes out of the Citie into the fields to make a glorious returne in ſtate, he is better followed, and adorned in another ſort. This is when he will make ſhew vnto ſome forreigne Embaſſadour, and moſt commonly to him of *Perſia* the magnificence of his greatneſſe; to the end he might report to his Maſter the greatneſſe of his Enemy, as hee that hath alwayes looked vpon him with the eyes of Enuy. Hee takes occaſion to goe to his Country Pallace, called the Pallace of *Daut*, or *Dauid Baſſa*, who cauſed it to bee ſtately built two leagues from *Conſtantinople*: The night before he doth aduertiſe his chiefe Officers that he meanes to returne to the Citie, and to enter in Pompe. The chiefe Surueigher giues order for the way and ſtreets, cauſeth them to be pouered with Sand from his Country Pallace vnto *Conſtantinople*: His train, his great men of the Port, and all his Officers ſhew themſelues as is fitting at so Royall an entrie. *Achmat* the First in the yeare 1612. giues vs a president.

   A troupe of about two thousand men at armes march first, they were armed and mounted as was fitting for that day. A stately Regiment of Turkish foot, exceeding braue followed them: After these came the *Cadis* or Iudges of *Constantinople*, with all the Body of Iustice, which were many in number: The *Talismans* and other Doctors and Priests of the *Alcoran* in the order of their puft-up grauity, marched after these Iudges, which is the only way of the Iustice which they hold in their life: The *Grand Vizir*, accompanied with all the other *Vizirs*, and the *Bashaes* and *Beglierbyes* of the Empire, made so stately a Body, as in seeing them, a man might say they were so many Kings, who had by an extraordinary miracle drawne themselues together, much lesse to haue taken them for the slaues of the *Othoman* Monarch: When these were past, there followed the men of the *Serrail*, or the Officers of the Imperiall House, with the tokens of their greatnesse: The first were ten men on foot, who led ten goodly Horses, some of *Barbary*, and others Turkes, with royall Caparisons, whereof the last had the Bitt and Stirrops of massiue Gold, couered with precious stones: the Saddle was white with Pearle and glistering with Diamonds: The *Sultans Roudach* was tied vnto it, with strings of gold, at the end whereof did hang vnto the ground two great tassels of rich Orientall Pearles: Vpon the Saddle they had cast a long Horse-cloth, of rich Cloth of Gold, imbroidered so thicke with Pearles, as they could hardly discerne the stuffe. The rest of the Imperiall Family followed in like order; fiftie *Ianizaries* on foot, either of them leading a lease of Greyhounds, the goodliest whereof had beene presented by the French Embassadour to the *Sultan*, shewed the negligent care of this stately entrie, as if the Prince came only from hunting. The Lackeys or Footmen of his *Othoman* Maiestie, called *Peiks*, *Persians* by Nation, well attired and hauing their heads couered with Caps of siluer gilt like vnto pots, made a small troupe. After these came threescore Archers on foote with their

their Bowes and Arrowes, in the midst of which was the *Sultan Achmat*, attired in a rich Robe of cloth of gold, imbroidered with Pearles and Diamonds; his Turbant was exceeding great, and adorned with fiue plumes of Herons Feathers with an Ensigne of great value, and a band of Diamonds vpon the lower part of his Turbant: He carried in his hand a wand whereon was set a Diamond of inestimable greatnesse and price, which gaue such a light, as they which beheld it were halfe dazled. Hee was stately mounted vpon a goodly Horse, with rich furniturne after an Imperiall manner; the Saddle was imbroidered with Gold, Pearles, and Diamonds; the Bitt and Stirrops were of Gold enricht with a great number of Diamonds, from the horse necke did hang a great tassell of round Pearles beautifull and precious.

This Monarch was followed by three men on horse backe, carrying in their hands the markes of their places being Officers of the Crowne. For, the first who was the *Seohlatar Aga* carried the Royall Sword: The *Tubonter Aga* carried the Turbant: The third called *Chiodar Aga*, carried his Cloke: They were richly apparelled and well mounted: A number of Squires and Officers, which are as Gentlemen attendants followed on horsebacke: A joyfull troupe of Musicians after the Turkish manner came after, being about threescore men on horsebacke, singing, playing on Fife, Claitons, and Trumpets: The rest of the royall Chase came after: There were a hundred of the *Sultans* Pages, whereof fifty carried euery one a Faulcon on his fist, whereof the hoods were enricht with Diamonds: Among them there were many Eunuches, and thirty of the Guard of the Port following them: Fifty Faulconers richly attired, and mounted vpon swift horses, carried their Hawkes vpon their fists. Foure of their troupe had before them on their Saddle-pomell a Leopard couered with Cloth of Gold. A great number of younger Pages, too beautifull to be chaste in a Turkish *Serrail*, chosen among the Children of the Tribute, and vowed to the filthy and vnnaturall loues of the Prince, attired in goodly Robes of cloth of Gold curled, made the pleasing end of this

good-

goodly entry, with a band of young men simply attired, entertained for their Seruice, with all the other Pages of the Serrail. The Embassadour of *Persia*, the chiefe subiect of this magnificence, caused to be cast before his Lodging when the Sultan past, a hundred peeces of Silke: the Archers of his Guard tooke them vp and kept them for themselues.

This Pompe is made when as the Turke is in good termes with the *Persian*: But when as they differ, and that matters are disposed to warre, the estate of things change: The Turke makes shew in his entrie before the Embassadour of *Persia*, of such Souldiers which he hath in *Constantinople* and thereabouts: and entring into the City, from his Countrey Pallace of *Dant Basha*, hee marcheth about the streets with aboue a hundred and fifty thousand fighting men well armed; as *Amurath* the Third did a little before he sent his Army into *Persia*, where hee defeated his Enemies, and got in a short time twelue rich Prouinces from the *Persian*. When as this Prince had made shew of so many warlike troups to the Embassadour of *Persia*, who was come with a deniall of some tribute which had beene promised, hee sent him word by one of his *Bashaes* that all those horse and foote which hee had seene in *Constantinople*, were but the Hens which hee kept in Cages, and that he should consider of the great number which he had in field; the which being led into his Masters Countrey, they would soone deuoure it in passing: Commanding him in the *Sultans* name to leaue the Territory of *Constantinople* within three dayes, and to goe into *Persia*, there to attend his slaues which would visit him. These are the Turkish Emperours issues by land, both particular and generall, who otherwise liue retired in their *Serrail*, where they busie themselues in hugging their *Sultana's* in the midst of the delights and pleasures of that stately place.

P 3   CHAP.

new disaster in the change of their fortunes: Doubtlesse the fauours of the Court are very fraile and inconstant, seeing that a puffe of wind, a word may ouerthrow them: And as wind disperseth smoake, so the great Gardiners discourse doth cause the greatnesse of the *Bassa's* of the Port to wither and fade. The which should teach the Fauourites of Princes, seeing their fortunes are transitory and fading, to imploy their credit in vertuous actions, which may serue them for a solide support, honour their liues, eternize their memory with posterity, and preserue them from ruine. But to speake these things to most part of those of that condition, were to sing vnto the deafe, and to shew colours to the blind: for the great prosperities of the Court blind the mind, and dull the judgements.

When as the *Sultan* hath glutted his desires, with the delights of this Marine walke, and filled his eares with the *Bostangibassi's* tales, he returnes to the *Serrail*, where being landed, the *Azamoglans* draw the *Caiques* out of the water, and lodge them in Vaults made for the purpose, which are within the walls of this Pallace: The which they doe, and put them to Sea againe commodiously and with great facilitie.

Chap. XIX.

Of the Grand SEIGNEVRS Physicians, Chyrurgians and Apothecaries.

GReat Princes in the midst of their Humane felicities are not freed from the crosses and discommodities of life, and much lesse from the infirmities that afflict them, to the end their pride might be humbled, and they should acknowledge themselues to be men. The *Sultan* Emperour of the Turkes seekes ease for his griefes aswell as other Monarches: He entertaines vsually for the seruice of his person, ten Physicians of the most skilfull of the East: Most part are Iewes, for the men of that Nation study carefully in Physicke, and prosper well:

Court of the Grand SEIGNEVR. 113

well: And seeing that the Turkes neglecting Learning doe not attaine to those Sciences which are necessary to make a good Physician. Amidst this number there is one superiour to the rest, called in their Language *Lecchin Bassi*, or the first Physician: Their entertainments are great, and the Presents they receiue make them rich: The first of them is reuerenced in the *Serrail*, they serue him with the same bread they giue vnto the *Sultan*, which is a dainty kind of bread made of the Graine which is gathered at *Bursia* in *Natolia*, reserued for the Princes mouth: He hath what fauour hee can desire in Court, and his Master honours him extraordinarily: Necessitie is a powerfull *Dæmon*, and his vertue makes him also to be honoured. But the merit of Physick hath made it so commendable in the World, and in Court, that many Kings haue crowned it with their owne Diadems: *Sabis* and *Gyges* haue practised it in their estates of *Media*, *Sabid* married it to his Scepter of *Arabia*: *Mithridatus* to that of *Pontus*: and *Hermes* held it as great a glory to bee a Physician in Egypt as to be a Soueraigne King.

When the *Sultan* is sick, his Physicians are cald to visit him; if they hold his infirmity to be of continuance, they are presently lodged in the secret *Serrail* which is the Princes quarter, in Chambers neare vnto him: They giue them two seruants to attend them; and they may not go out of the Pallace, what necessity soeuer doth presse them, vntill the *Sultan* bee recouered or dead. But when hee is in heakh, they are only bound to goe three of them euery morning, into the Apothecaries shop in the *Serrail*, and there to attend vntill noone, if there be any need of their helpe.

The *Sultans* Chyrurgions and Barbers haue lesse libertie: They may not goe out of the *Serrail* where they lodge, but on the day of *Bairam*, which is the Turkes Easter, vnlesse it be by the Princes permission: The youngest of this profession serue him as Pages, some others are Eunuches, which attend the seruice of his Chamber: These shaue him when hee desires, and wash him in his Bathes, when hee goes to tem-

Q   per

See what Marcilius Ficinus a learned Florentine doth write in the first Booke in the Epistle to Thomas Valerius a Physician.

114 | *The History of the* Serrail, *and of the*

por the heate, which troubles him, or to satisfie the commandement of his Law.

The Apothecaries are also lodged in the *Serrail*, their number exceeds both the others: So their Seruice is more ordinary. There are eighteene Masters which worke, and three hundred Boyes which serue them; most of which goe once a yeare to search for Simples on the Mountaines and Valleyes for the composing of their Physicke: Foure Masters most expert in their Art are Superiour to all those: They call them the Priors. The shop of these Apothecaries deserues so many men as serues this great Prince, it is aboue fifty fathome long, and halfe in breadth: The great Vessels which doe beautifie it, furnish it abundantly with all sorts of Oiles, Sirrops, Ointments, Waters, and other liquors proper for Physicke: On the side of it are foure goodly Chambers full of diuers sorts of Drugs. Besides these, there are two others situate towards the Gardens, where during the Spring which doth enamile the Earth with flowres, and the Summer which doth crowne it with Fruits, they draw the essences, and distill the Waters which are fit for Physicke. But in all these Vessels, amidst these Drugs and diuers Quintessences, they find not any remedy which can mortifie the amorous Passions of the Prince, wherewith hee is continually afflicted. They denoure his leisure, interrupt the exercises which are more worthy of his person; and deiect him vnder that which hee is, and make him a slaue to his slaues: for louing them desperately, he liues more in them then in himselfe.

Nullis amor est medicabilis herbis, Ouid, Metamor. l. 1. fab. 9.

The end of the first Booke.

THE

THE GENERALL HISTORY OF THE *Serrail*, and of the *Grand* SEIGNEVRS *Court.*

The second BOOKE.

CHAP. I.

Of the publique Diuan *in the* Serrail, *where they dispatch and iudge all Affaires.*

IN the second Court of the *Serrail*, where is a goodly Fountain, couered with the shadow of many pleasing Cypresse trees, which enuiron it, powres forth a cleere streame, as if it were liquid Christall, is built vpon the left hand, at the end of a long Gallery, a great Hall, whereas the *Sultan* causeth the *Diuan* to be kept foure dayes in the Weeke; that is to say, on Satturday, Sunday, Munday and Tuesday. This word *Diuan* signifies a Colledge, whither

Q 2 many

Let this be spoken without violating the respect, which I owe vnto such persons which relieue the publique by their care in suits, of whom I haue no intent to speake in this place.

many men repaire: whereas they distribute Iustice equally to any that demandit, for what cause soeuer: And the greatest benefit they find, is that the parties are admitted to deliuer their owne causes, hauing no necessitie to consume their goods and their time, (whereof the losse is irreparable) among wrangling Pettifoggers, who enrich themselues by other mens follies. The Turkes policie giues this ease vnto the people, that they will not allow of any: Whosoeuer hath an action against any other, hee brings him to the *Diuan* by the fist, and the other dares not refuse: there by the Iustification of their Acts, if they leaue any, or by a summary and verball deposition of two Witnesses, the cause is iudged with great facilitie, and the execution is not difficult: Or if the judgement be referred after the audience, and committed to some one of the Iudges, the importune delayes, and the horrour of wrangling which is practised in *France*, being not admitted among the Turkes, hinder not a speedy dispatch.

The Officers which assist at this *Diuan* are the *Basha* or *Grand Vizir*, Lieutenant Generall of the whole Empire, who precides: The other *Vizirs* or *Basha's* accompany him, the two *Beglierbeys*, the one of *Natolia*, and the other of *Romania*, two of the prime Dignities of the Crowne, after the *Grand Vizir*: The two *Cadilisquers* or great Iudges of Armies Superiour to all the *Cadis* or Iudges of the Empire: The three *Testardars*, or generall Treasurers for the ordinary and extraordinary treasure, who keepe the *Sultans* Cofers, and receiue that great Reuenew which is leuied in his Estates: The *Nissanzi Bassa* or high Chancellor: The *Netangi*, who is as the Secretary of Estate with vs, which situes monethly, who signes the Commandements, and dispatches with the Royall Signature: The *Bassa's* Secretary with a great number of *Iasitschi*, or Notaries, which are as Registers: The *Chaoux Bassi*, who is chiefe of all the *Chaoux* of the Empire, which carries the *Sultans* Commandements both within and without the Estate, they goe in Embassies, although they be but vild and base Messengers, and execute the Decrees of the *Basha's*; is at the doore of this *Diuan* with a great number

ber of his company, to execute that which the *Grand Vizir* shall command: Hee carries a Staffe of siluer in his hand for the marke of his authoritie. And all these men aswell *Bassa's* as others of inferiour qualitie, come into this Hall of the *Diuan* by foure of the clocke in the morning, with a commendable diligence, to discharge their duties in the administration of iustice, vntill twelue.

The places and rankes are obserued according to the eminencie of their Offices: The *Grand Vizir* sits first in the midst of two long formes fastned to the wals, which looke towards the doore, like vnto the Seats of Audience for iustice in *France*: On his right hand (which is the lesse honourable in Turkey) the *Bassa's* seate themselues. The two *Cadilesquers* are on the left; He of *Romania* or *Greece*, as the most noble Prouince, precedes him of *Natolia*: At the entry of the *Diuan* on the left hand, are set vpon a forme by themselues the three *Testardars*: They haue at their backes all the Notaries or Registers, sitting on the ground with paper and pens in hand, to write what shall be commanded: On the otherside of the Hall opposite to the *Testardars*, is another forme set apart, where the *Netangi* hath also a pen in his hand, being enuironed with his Clerkes and Deputies. The parties which demand iustice, being many in number, are placed in the midst of the *Diuan*, with so great a respect and silence as they dare not spit. This publique Councell is like vnto that of the parties in the *Louure*, with this difference, that in the *Diuan* euery man is admitted for any cause whatsoeuer. All these Officers being thus placed, the parties plead their owne Causes, & they direct their speech to the *Grand Vizir*, who presides in this Councell: The other *Bassa's* neuer speake.: If he doth iudge that the businesse propounded ought to be presently dispatcht, he then decides the controuersies betwixt the parties: If it requires longer inquisition, hee referres the judgement to one of the *Cadilesquers*, if the matter belong to the Ciuill Law: If it concerne the Treasure or Accompts, a *Testardar* is committed; and when there is Question of any falshood, or the verification of a hand or writing, he deputes a *Netangi*. The

affaires

affaires of greater importance, or differences of consequence, which concerne strangers, hee reserues them to his owne judgement.

These imployments detaine them from the breake of day vntill noone: When that comes, one of the Stewards of the *Serrail* appointed for the *Diuan*, presents himselfe in the midst of it, to whom the *Grand Vizir* makes a signe to bring Dinner: Then the parties retire, and the *Diuan* is free for the *Bassa's*; the seruice is made with that frugality that is fitting for Iudges: For a Table, they bring before the *Grand Vizir* a plaine stoole of wood, whereon they set a siluer Bason, and sometimes of Copper blancht, round in forme, and as big as the bottome of a pipe, vpon the brims thereof they set many loaues, in the midst the meate, which they serue one dish after another; One or two of the *Bassa's* are called to eate with the chiefe of the Councell; they bring to euery one a Napkin, wherewith they couer their knees: Their meats are Mutton, wild Fowle, Pigeons, & sometimes Pullets; the drink is of *Sorbee* after their manner, made of water, the iuice of Citrons, and of Sugar, for the *Grand Vizir* alone; the rest quench their thirst with faire water: Their fruit is a Tart or some Cake, wherewith they end their Dinner, which doth not continue aboue halfe an houre: The like is ordained for the *Cadilesquers*, *Testardars*, and all the rest of the *Diuan*: Their slaues dine at the same time. The *Bassa* Captaine of the Sea, is also of the number of those which assist in the *Diuan*, he takes his place in the last ranke of all the other *Bassa's* if hee be not a *Bassa Vizir*; in that case hee mounts higher towards the *Grand Vizir* in the order of his reception.

Dinner being thus ended without pompe, without excesse, and without dissolution, the *Grand Vizir* disposeth of the most notable resolutions which haue beene taken in the *Diuan*, and prepares himselfe to goe and make report thereof to the *Grand Seigneur*; On Sunday and Tuesday, which are the dayes of *Diuan* for publique affaires, and the Councell of Estate. This Prince descends to that effect into a Chamber which is neere vnto it: being artiued, he cals his Officers vn-

to

to him one after another. The *Capigilar Agassi* carries this command. He holds in his hand a long staffe of siluer, like vnto a Beadles Mace: First of all they call the *Cadilesques*, they rise vp, make a low reuerence to the *Grand Vizir*, and follow this Mace-bearer and the *Chaoux Bassi*, who is ioyned vnto him with his other staffe of siluer: Vnder their conduct they goe before the *Grand Seigneur* into his Chamber, they reuerence him and in a manner adore him: For there is not any Soueraigne Prince vpon the earth, whose subiects stand in more feare, nor yeeld him so much reuerence. After this they yeeld him an account of their places, then they retire backwards like men that had consulted with some great Diuinity, and so goe to their houses. The Mace-bearers goe to fetch the *Testardars*, these yeeld the like salutation to the *Grand Vizir* that the others had done; they goe before the *Grand Seigneur*, they speake vnto him of his treasure and of the affaires of their charge; and hauing satisfied him, they retire like the rest, with their heeles first. This custome alwayes to turne their face in retiring is not only practised with the Prince, but also obserued with the *Bassa's*, who according to the Lawes of Turkish Ciuility, would hold it a contempt, if in parting from them they should turne the backe. After the *Testardars*, the Captain of the Sea if he had been in the *Diuan*, goes to relate vnto the *Grand Seigneur*, the estate of his Vessels of Warre, with that of Armes and Munition which are in his Arsenall. The *Aga* or Colonell Generall of the *Ianizaries*, which are the Turkish foot, enters now into the *Diuan*, hee remaines in the second gate of the *Serrail*, being set vnder a Gallery assisted by the Souldiers: He goes first of all to audience to his Master, and returnes to his seate, vntill all the rest be retired; for hee goes last out of the *Serrail*. The *Vizirs* goe one after one vnto the *Sultan*, and being come into his presence they frame themselues to an incomparable respect: They ioyne their hands, and bend downe their heads and eyes to the ground, and stand silent: For amongst them only the *Grand Vizir* may speake vnto the Prince; He comes last with a graue pace, as the party that beares the burthen of all the affaires which

haue

haue beene treated in the *Diuan*; hee yeelds an accompt vnto his Master, who confirmes the judgements, or disanuls them, as he thinkes good. Moreouer, he leaues him instructions in writing, in a Purse of Crimson rais'd Veluet, the which hee layes before him with vnspeakable reuerence and humilitie; then he retires like the rest, vnlesse the Emperour stayes him longer to informe himselfe of the estate of his most important affaires.

Thus the Turkes doe justice to men, whereof the quicke expedition might repaire the defects which they meete with, and yet in that place particularly they are reasonably exact to yeeld vnto euery man that which is due vnto him: The feare of their owne ruine if they had no vertue, were sufficient to make the ballance euen and straight. For the Turkish Princes are accustomed to goe by one of their Chambers vnto a Window, only shut vp with a Lattice, the which lookes into the *Diuan* directly ouer the head of the *Grand Vizir*: From thence he heares what is spoken, and treated; with the complaints of parties, and the Decrees of Iudges; if iniquitie doe sway the minds and mouths of those, to deny vnto the weakest the reliefe which justice doth owe them, against the violent oppressions of the Mighty, the punishment which hee takes is very exemplary. Doubtlesse, as the foundations vphold a house, so justice is a strong support vnto an Empire, without the which it cannot long subsist. Kings, whose principall office is to yeeld it vnto men, ought to cherish it aboue all things; It doth aduance them aboue other men, and makes them to raigne happily; and without it violence drawes all disorders in their Estates, troubles them, and ruines them in the end: They themselues without justice, are like vnto those bodies which are troubled with the falling sicknesse, whom weaknesse and paine afflicts: This diuine vertue should not only be the soule of their Decree, but the soule of their soules: In justice they shall possesse all the other vertues, for it containes them all.

CHAP.

Chap. II.

Of the Azamoglans, *or Children of the Tribute of base condition which serue in the* Serrail, *and elsewhere.*

THe Christians labour so profitably to inlarge the Turkes Empire, as they not only furnish them with occasions, by their wretched diuision, but they also breed them vp men, which in time are the most generous of their troupes, the greatest in their Court, and the most triumphant in Townes & Christian Prouinces. But in this last, force and the constraint which these *Barbarians* vse towards them, makes them more excusable, than when they abandon the reason and the interests of Christianity, to the blind passions of a fatall discord: For they see come into their houses, thoroughout all *Greece* or *Morea*, and in the Countrey of *Albania*, a troupe of the *Grand Seigneurs Capigis*, deputed to make the exaction of the richest, and the most exquisite Tribute, that can be leuied in a Country, the which is of men, the best proportioned, and enricht with the gifts of Nature. There they choose the soundest, the goodliest, and the most actiue of all their Children, out of euery three one, the which they doe euery third yeere; and hauing drawne together aboue two thousand, they lead them to *Constantinople*. At their arriuall, they attire them all, in Robes of Cloth of diuers colours; they giue vnto euery one a yellow Cap of Felt, like vnto a Sugar-loafe. In this Equipage they are led before the *Grand Vizir*, who being accompanied with al the other *Bassa's* and Ministers of the *Serrail*, he makes choice of those that are most actiue for the war: These young men are set apart, and conducted into the *Serrail* by the *Bostangibassi*, or chiefe of the Gardiners, and a part of them distributed where they wanted. Then they circumcise them: being children of Christians they become yong Turks, and for an inconstant fortune of the World and of the Court, they lose the eternall happinesse of Heauen, in the way where-

R *of*

of their first beliefe had directed them. They cause them to learne the Turkish Tongue, and if their spirits be capable of more, to read and write. But all indifferently are instructed to wrestle, runne, leape, shoot, dart an *Azegaye*, and in all other Exercises, which are fit for them which will make profession of Armes.

The rest of this goodly choice of the young Children of the Tribute is in the power of the *Grand Vizir*; Hee doth lodge them, and distribute them diuersly; some are sent into the *Sultans* Gardens and Houses of Pleasure; others are put into the Gallions and Vessels at Sea, which make Voyages for the *Sultana's*; The Patrons charge themselues, and are bound to restore them when they are demanded. They place a good number in Artificers shops to learne diuers trades, whereof they may serue for a Squadron when they shall be *Ianizaries*, and especially in the time of Warre. The *Basha's* and all the great Men of the Court haue their part; They are deliuered vnto them by their Names, Countries, Markes of their face or elsewhere, and by the colour of their haire; they binde themselues in writing, which is contained in a Booke for that purpose, to the end that, if the necessitie of the Warre should force the Captaines to fill vp their companies, in the place of those that are dead, they may take these to that effect. But most commonly they giue the rudest and grossest to these *Basha's*; and they imploy them in their Stables, Kitchins, and other base Offices of their Houses. They which remaine of these *Azamoglans*, are sent into diuers Seminaries, vnder the conduct of diuers Eunuches which haue the charge, and take the care to breed them vp, to bee one day capable to beare Armes, and to serue in the Warre in qualitie of Ianizaries. These Children thus placed the *Grand Vizir* represents them in a Booke to the *Grand Seigneur*. This Prince assignes them an entertainment according to his pleasure, and augments the pay which the great custome doth allow them, which is of foure or fiue *Aspres* by the day besides their nourishment and apparell: Hee assignes the assignation with his owne hand, and sends it by the *Vizir* to the *Testardar*, to the end he may

be

be carefull to pay it according to the order: Hee sees them euery three Moneths, and visits them one after another, calling them by their names, to know the number of those which are dead, and to see how they be fed and gouerned.

But the *Azamoglans* appointed for the seruice of the *Sarrail*, are imployed about base and vile things as the meanest of all those which are of the Royall Family: They serue for Labourers in their buildings, they imploy them in their Stables, Kitchins, Gardens, to cut wood, and to carry it, to lead Dogges to the field as their Seruants, and to doo whatsoeuer their Superiours command them, whereof some haue charge of tens, others of hundreds, and these are also vnder the authoritie of the *Chicaia*, or Steward of the *Bostangibassi*; the toyle they vndergoe, the paines they take, and the miseries which they indure make them the most patient men in the World, and their Masters instruct them to mortification by most rigorous courses: the least fault is rewarded with fiftie blowes with a Cudgell, the which are soundly set on. But their basenesse is not without honour nor recompence: There are charges and eminent Offices among them to the which they succeed by the order of their antiquity, and their patience may make them hope and aspire to the place of a steward, yea of *Bostangibassi*, to shew that there is nothing so base but long labour and inuincible sufferance, may aduance in time. For to come vnto the dignity of *Bostangibassi*, is to be familiar with the Prince, to be great in Court, to speake vnto him when hee walkes, to conduct him at Sea, and to gouerne his Brigandine, and to haue an honourable priuiledge to weare a Turbant in the *Serrail*, which is no lesse than among the great Men of *Spaine* to speake vnto the King with their heads couered.

The Gates of the *Serrail* are the limits of their courses, they neuer goe forth vpon any occasion vnlesse the *Bostangibassi* leads them with him when hee goes out of the Pallace to execute the Princes commandements, and to ruine the fortune of some great Man of the Court, as hee did in the yeare 1614. That of *Bassa Nassuf*, whom hee caused to be strangled in his Bed,

Bed; for these secret Commissions are most commonly put into his hands: When hee takes what number of *Azamoglans* shall be needfull, hee slips in amongst these, the children of naturall Turkes at the entreaty of his friends, yet with the consent of the *Sultan*, and placeth them where they may be aduanced, their Lodgings & abode are about the wals of the *Serrail* towards the Sea, where they dwell in Chambers, they haue their Bathes, their Stoues, and their Kitchins, and liue at their owne will; for they haue their allowance apart: when they haue leisure, they imploy it in fishing, they sell what they take, and reserue the gaines to themselues: They neuer see the *Sultan* but when he comes to walke in his Gardens, or goes a hunting, then they follow him, and Quest in the fields like Spaniels. They doe not supply the companies of foote, when there is any want of Ianizaries, out of this number: If they goe out of the *Serrail*, it is to be better bred in other Seminaries, whilest they are yong: or when they are of riper age, the *Grand Seigneur* giues some of them to his Fauourites, whom he sends out of the *Serrail*, as *Baſſa's* of *Caire*, *Damas*, or some other Gouernments of his Empire; they make vse of these *Azamoglans* for their Stewards, Quirries, Treasurers; and such like Offices in their Family: Moreouer, when the Prince goes a Voyage, or to the Wars, hee leads a great number with him to pitch his Tents, vnlade his stuffe, and to doe other manuall workes.

Chap. III.

Of the Azamoglans, of better breeding and condition, who in time attaine vnto the Dignities of the Turkish Empire.

Vertue hath this proper to her naturall beauty, to make her selfe to be generally esteemed, and acknowledged euen by most barbarous Nations: she doth not only make those admirable which doe poffeffe it, but doth alfo giue the Title of their Nobility to their Pofterity, and makes them commendable. The children that are well borne taken for Tribute from the Chriftians, make triall thereof in Turkey, whereas the Turkes honour their Birth, and feparate them from the reft, to bee better bred and inftructed in Exercifes which make them worthy of the greateft Officers of the Empire: They teach them the Texts of *Mahomets* Law, the ornament of the Turkifh Learning, they inftruct them in armes, and in all things which may adde perfection to men, which are to attend continually neere vnto a great Monarch. They are all Chriftian flaues; but we fhall fee in the courfe of their fortune, that their flauery is a way, by which patience doth lead them to the liberty to command Prouinces, or whole Realmes: and their condition doth teach vs, that it is a happy infelicitie, and an vnfortunate happineffe.

The *Capiaga* or great Chamberlaine of the *Serrail*, brings fome into their number, borne of naturall Turkes, commendable for their good difpofitions, yet feldome and with the Princes leaue. For the cuftome of the Empire in its moft ancient Conftitutions requires that fuch Children fhould be Chriftians Renegadoes, the nobleft and moft ciuill that can be found. So when the aduantages of the Warre, giue vnto the Turkifh Armies victories againft Chriftians, or the taking of their Townes, and they find therein young children to the age of twelue or thirteene yeares, the *Baffa's* referue them for the feruice of the *Grand Seigneur*. For the Turkes hold an opinion, that the Nobility of bloud makes fpirits generous and inclinable to vertue; efpecially when the care of a good education doth polifh and make perfect the gifts of Birth, as they doe in the *Serrail* with thefe young men. The Difcipline, which they caufe to obferue is, fo rigorous, as whofoeuer performes it in all points, becomes the moft modeft, the moft patient, and the moft mortified man liuing. The Mafters which haue charge of their perfons, are white Eunuches, feuere, froward, fantaftique, and fufpicious, as moft of your gelded men be: They neuer fpeake vnto them but in choller, and fpare not

their

their Baſtinadoes, whereof they are very charitable; they make them watch and indure all paines; ſo as many of theſe young men, when they come to the age of twenty yeeres, they ſeeke all meanes to flie this ſeuerity: And although they know that they are in the courſe of a great fortune; yet they had rather get out of the *Serrail*, with the ſimple qualitie of *Spahi* or *Mutaſeraga*, which is like vnto our Men at Armes or light horſe, than to ſuffer any longer the rigours of this Diſcipline. Their number is not certaine, the *Serrail* receiues as many as they ſend; but vſually they are about three hundred. The order and method wherewith they breed them vp, doth teſtifie that the Turkes haue retained nothing of barbarous but the name, and haue ſent vs the effect.

1. Oda.

They call the formes where they inſtruct them *Oda*; this word ſignifies a Chamber: They ordaine foure, by the which theſe young men muſt paſſe, before they attaine to Offices, whereunto the capacity which they learne doth aduance them. In the firſt are placed all thoſe of this condition, which enter into the *Serrail* at a childiſh age: There they circumciſe them if they were not before; being made Turkes, they teach for their firſt Leſſon Silence, and the Countenance they muſt carry for a marke of their Seruitude, and withall a ſingular Reuerence towards the *Sultan*, which is when they are neere him to hold downe their Head and Eyes, and to haue their Hands joyned, or their Armes croſt. For moſt of thoſe which ſerue the perſon of the *Othoman* Prince, neuer ſpeake vnto him, nor looke him in the face. At their comming into the *Serrail* the Prince ſees them, cauſeth them to be enrolled in a Regiſter, by their names and Countries, and commands the *Teſtardar* to be exact in the preſent payment of the Money which is appointed for their entertainment. A white Eunuch ouer-ſeer of all the other Eunuches which teach them, as it were the Principall of a Colledge, takes alſo care to ſee them well inſtructed. After the firſt Precepts they teach them to read and write, and aboue all to pray after the Turkiſh manner, and the worſhip of their Religion, with an incredible care, for the ſpace of ſix or ſeuen yeeres, which is the time they remaine in this *Oda*.

After

After this long terme they passe vnto the second *Oda*, where 2. *Oda.*
more vnderstanding Masters than the first, teach them the
Persian, *Arabian*, and *Tartar* Languages, and practise them
in reading all sorts of written Bookes (for the Turkes vse no
other.) Moreouer to speake Turkish elegantly, the which they
may doe by the knowledge of those three Tongues, whereof
the Turkish Language seemes to be composed. For to heare
them speake they do easily discerne the difference there is betwixt them and those which are not bred vp in like manner.
They adde to these exercises of the mind, those of the Body:
In this *Oda* they teach them to handle the Sword or Semiter,
to shoot, to cast a Battle-axe, to dart a Iauelin or Azagaye,
and to runne lightly; all this is done in places separated from
the *Oda*, at certaine houres appointed with great attention,
where the Eunuches spare not their Cudgels, but beat them
soundly for the least fault. They continue six yeares in these
Exercises, after which they are Men and fit for all paine and
labour.

Then they come vnto the third *Oda*, where they doe not 3. *Oda.*
forget what they had learned before, but practise it still; and
moreouer they learne to be good Horsemen, and to vault with
disposition, to be the more fit and actiue for the Warre: Euery
one according to his inclination doth likewise learne an occupation, to serue the Princes person; one to make Turbants,
another to shaue Haire, to cut his Nailes, to wash him in the
Bath, to make cleane and fold his Clothes handsomely; some
to lead Dogs to the Wood, others to be skilfull in Hawks and
Hawking, to serue for Stewards or Queries, to be imployed
in the Chamber, and to other Offices necessary for the seruice
of great Princes, wherein they grow to that perfection in the
space of fiue yeeres as they are able to instruct others:
Whilest they are in this third *Oda*, they may not see any one
abroad but with great difficulty, and in the presence of an
Eunuch; all conuersation with others is prohibited, but with
those of their *Oda*: But they must doe it with all modesty
and honesty: For if the Eunuch who is their Superiour, shall
enter into the least suspition of the contrary, they shall be af-
sured

sured to be soundly beaten, either vpon the soles of their feet or vpon the backe after the Turkish manner, so as many times they leaue them for dead. They sleepe in long Roomes which may containe fifty little Beds made only of Matteresse: They lie in their clothes, in the night time they haue many lights burning, their Eunnches sleepe among them, betwixt euery ten Beds lies an Eunuch, to keepe them in awe: Day and night their Masters examine them, to see if they be firme and constant in the beliefe of the Alcoran: For being ready to passe to the fourth *Oda*, and from thence to the greatest Offices of the Empire; if they had in their soules any loue of their first beliefe, they might procure some great prejudice to the Turkes estate. Hauing imployed all care, and finding them truly *Mahometans*, they conduct them to the fourth *Oda*.

4. *Oda*.

At their entry into it, they enter their names and Countries again into another Booke, for all passe not into this last place of their continuall trauels: But those only which haue finished their time in the other forme, and by their diligence haue made themselues capable to serue the Prince and State profitably: As labour and rest touch one another, so, the end of one is the sweet beginning of the other. These men finde it in this *Oda*, their Pension is augmented; insteed of cloth wherewith they were formerly attired, the *Sultan* giues them Robes of Silke and Cloth of Gold: They haue liberty to conuerse, with the greatest men of the *Serrail* and with the *Bassa's*, who seeing them entring into great places, adore the Sun rising of their Fortunes, make them great Presents, and seeke to winne their friendship by rich gifts. Besides these pleasing signes of a new happinesse, whereas they were before all shauen, they suffer their haire to grow vpon their Temples, to couer their Eares, an assured signe, that they shall be speedily of the Royall Chamber; they follow the *Grand Seigneur* in all his walkes (where hee is without women) and out of their number he takes the most familiar Officers of his person, and of his Fauourites.

As the *Sechletar Aga*, who carries his Sword.

The *Chioda Aga*, which is he that carries the Roiall Robe, called *Ciamberluc*.

The

Court of the Grand SEIGNEVR.

The *Rechioptar*, or *Rakduntar*, hee which goes at his Stirrop, when he is on horsebacke, or his chiefe Footman.

The *Materagi Aga*, hee which carries a Vessell of Gold full of water when the *Sultan* marches.

The *Tubenter Aga*, hee which doth garnish and carry his Turbant.

The *Chiamaci Aga*, hee that doth wash his Linnen, or his chiefe Laundrer.

The *Camedir Bassi*, or great Master.

The *Chilargi Bassi*, or chiefe Butler.

The *Dogangi Bassi*, or Master Faulconer.

The *Sarrigi Bassi*, or chiefe Cutler.

The *Nanashangi Bassi*, or chiefe Comptroller of the Treasure.

The *Turmachi Bassi*, or *Pirnaagi Aga*, he that pares his Nailes.

The *Berber Bassi*, or chiefe Barber.

The *Amangi Bassi*, he that washes him in the Bath.

The *Teskelagi Bassi*, the great Secretary, or first Secretary of State.

All which are the most ancient of the fourth *Oda*, and stand before the Prince when hee comes out of his Chamber, with that respect and reuerence which they learned in their youth in the first *Oda*; which is to bee silent, to hold their heads downe, and with their eyes fixed vpon the ground, for they neuer speake, nor looke their Master in the face; If hee commands them any thing, it is by signes after the manner of dumbe men, and they doe execute it speedily; they carry his meat, which they receiue at the Court gate from the Stelcards hands who is without, and they deliuer it from one to another, vntill it comes to the Grand Master, who sets it before the *Grand Seigneur*. This Prince is much pleased with the mute conuersation of such men, who dare not entertaine him but by signes; hee causeth them to ride, and to practize running and leaping, he causeth them many times to cast a barre of Iron, and to make such like proofes of their force and actiuity. Hee fauours them with many Presents, as Robes of

S   Cloth

Cloth of Gold, Swords enricht with precious stones, Purses full of Sultanins, and many other things of value. Moreouer to the end that his *Agalaris* may gather the more money, to supply the expences of their Equipage, when they shall goe out of the *Serrail* with the Titles of Gouernours of Prouinces, hee giues them dispatches for Embassies: These men sell them to the *Chaoux*, or bargaine with them for a Moietie or more, of the present which they shal receiue from the Prince, to whom they are sent, the which is of no small importance: For the Princes which hold and depend of the *Othoman*, when he confirmes them in their Dignities, and sends them the markes thereof, by a gilt Staffe, a Throne, or a Crowne, they are bound to giue to him that is sent a Present of that value which is set downe in the great custome of the Empire, the which doth taxe euery one to a certaine summe: And of this number is the *Vallachian*, the *Moldauian*, the *Transiluanian*, the *Tartar*, and many other Vassalls, and Tributaries of the *Othoman* Crowne. This Present is diuided betwixt the *Chaoux*, who receiues it, and the *Agalari* who gaue him, or rather sold him the Commission: Thus they enrich themselues, and make a stocke to furnish themselues vpon the first occasion, the which presenting it selfe by the death of some *Bassa*, they are made either Captaine of the Sea, or *Bassa* of *Caire* or *Damas*, or elsewhere. Besides these great and glorious Dignities, the *Grand Seigneur* doth honour them sometimes with the quality of *Musaip*, that is to say, hee that may speake vnto the Prince, and goe to him in priuate: The which the Turkes esteeme aboue any thing in the Empire, the which the *Othoman* Monarches doo for a double intent, both to gratifie those whom they loue, and to haue men among the greatest of the Court, to enforme him of the *Bassa's* actions, and to discouer their Enterprizes against the good of the Estate and the Princes person. But all the *Agalaris* are not so bountifully aduanced. Those whom the *Sultan* will send out of his *Serrail*, with meaner dignities, he makes them *Aga* of the Ianizaries, *Spahilar Agassi* who is Captaine of the *Spahis*, or at the least *Capigi Bassi* who is chiefe of the Porters.

When

When they goe out of the Royall Pallace, by any great or meane dignity, they carry with them all the wealth they haue gathered together. Many young men whom a desire of libertie, and a curiositie to see the World, rather than any care to aduance themselues, hath made them abandon the exercises of the *Oda*, and their importunities haue forced the Prince to dismisse them, goe forth with the rest without any qualitie of office, and with little entertainment by the day: But when as he that is aduanced to the quality of a *Bassa*, and Gouernour of some remote Prouince, is ready to goe out of the *Serrail*, the *Grand Vizir* sends to receiue him at the Gate, by his *Chicaia*, who is a Steward or Ouer-seer of his house, with a troup of Horse to doe him honour, and causeth him to be conducted to his Pallace, receiues him with all curtesie, giues him many Presents, and doth accommodate him with lodgings for three or foure dayes, vntill his owne be prouided in the Citie: After that he hath giuen order, he settles his Family, and giues the chiefe places, to such as came out of the *Serrail* with him, he stayes sometime in *Constantinople*, vntill his haire be growne, for he was shauen at his comming forth, and likewise to receiue the Presents which the *Sultana's* send him, as goodly Linnen and rich Workes: And those which the *Bassa's* present him; as Tapestries, Horses, Robes of Cloth of Gold, and all sorts of moueables necessary for a man of his condition: He may be at that time about forty yeares old, hauing consumed the best of his dayes, in the expectance of this fortune. They of the other *Oda's* succeed him by the order of their reception, the which is exactly obserued in the *Serrail*, and fauour cannot depriue any man, if he hath not committed some notable fault in the royall Pallace: so as they of the third *Oda* do partly know by the succession what shall become of them, and wish daily, that it would please the *Sultan*, to send some of his *Agalaris* to Offices abroad, to the end they may make place for them.

This new Gouernour parts not from the Court to goe vnto his charge, before hee hath giuen thankes to the *Capiaga* for the care which hee hath contributed to his aduancement, terming himselfe obliged vnto him, and that he would depend of him for a perpetuall acknowledgement of his fauours, intreating him to hold him in his protection, neere vnto the Princes person, vpon all accidents that might happen. He makes this Complement in the *Serrail*, without the Gate of the *Sultans* Quarter; for being once forth hee enters no more, vnlesse the Prince calls for him, to treate with him, concerning the affaires of his charge. Such is their fortune, which haue suffered their actions to be gouerned by patience, and haue laboured to make themselues capable to serue. But such is the choice which the *Othoman* Monarch makes of men, bred and seuerely instructed in their profession about their persons, to be in time the greatest Officers of their Empire, where they neuer aduance to such Dignities, vncapable men, who in the whole course of their liues, haue not learned any thing but to play at Tennice, to cast the Dice, to speake brutishly, and to practize all sorts of vices. Wherefore we must not wonder if the Turkes Estate prospers, seeing that amidst a great number of young men, they can make choice of the best Wits, to be bred vp with care vnder good Discipline, which makes them honest men, and addes to the gifts of a happy birth the perfections of Arte. Nature must of necessitie serue for the ground-worke, to make great Men; Hee that is borne a Foole will be euer so. I haue seene them make choice of the best Wits, to supply their Religious Houses: So they haue alwayes amongst them most Learned and most rare Men; and as long as they shall follow this course, they shall make themselues necessarie, commendable, and admirable: Without a naturall disposition, they may well sowe, but they shall neuer reape, and no man euer made a good Sparrow-hawke of a Buzzard.

CHAP.

CHAP. IV.

Of the foure White Eunuches, the chiefe Men of the Serrail, and of some other Eunuches.

WE haue said elsewhere that the womens *Serrail* hath no other Guard but blacke Eunuches, which are sent young to the Court by the *Bassa's* of *Caire*, to be bred vp to that place. The *Sultans Serrail* receiues none but white, the which are chosen in their infancie, out of that pleasing troupe of children well borne, which are taken for Tribute from the Christians, whose fortune the precedent Chapter doth describe. They are cut or mutilated with their owne consent, and not by force, the which would indanger their liues: The promises of the greatest Offices in Court, and the hope one day to enjoy Dignities whereunto they see such men aduanced, ouer-swayes their will, to suffer themselues to bee cut, the promises are true, for in time they attaine to the greatnesse of Turkey. But the principall of these Eunuches, and the most ancient among them, which are about the Princes person, the first and most powerfull Heads of the *Serrail*, are the foure which follow.

The first is the *Capiaga*, great Chamberlaine of the Empire, in most authority in the *Serrail*; as he who may speake vnto the *Grand Seigneur*, when he thinkes good; he doth alwayes assist neere vnto his person, wheresoeuer he goes, whether he goe out of his Royall Pallace, or enters into that of his women, he followes him vnto the doore, where he leaues men to aduertise him in his Chamber when the *Sultan* retires. Embassies, Packets of Importance, Instructions of Estate, and all great Affaires passe thorough his hands, to come vnto the Prince which make him necessary to all others, and gets him as many rich Presents, and as much money as he can well desire. This without comparison is more beneficiall vnto him, than the entertainment he hath in the *Serrail*, the which is regulated

gulated at ten Sultanins by the day, which make foure pounds of our sterling Money, many Robes of Silke and Cloth of Gold, with such moueables as he desires. Moreouer, his Table is furnished at his Masters charge, and at the same time that his is. Hee carries a Turbant in the *Serrail*, and goes on horsebacke where he pleaseth.

The second is the *Chasnadar Bassi*, or the Treasurer of the Princes secret treasure; hee hath one key and the *Grand Seigneur* another, who doth also set his Seale vnto it. He hath care to lay vp the gold and siluer which comes from Egypt, keepes an accompt of it, and enters alone into this Treasure with the *Sultan*, hee aduiseth him for the gathering together of money, and entertaines him with a subject which was neuer displeasing to Prince: The importance and necessity of his charge, make him to be much esteemed: For gold being the delights of men, whosoeuer hath the ouer-sight, makes himselfe both powerfull and necessary among them: Moreouer, he hath the keeping of all the Iewels of the Crowne, and likewise of those which they present daily vnto the *Sultan*; hee gluts his eyes with the lustre of the goodliest Pearles, and the richest Diamonds that the East doth produce: Those which his Master giues, and wherewith hee doth adorne himselfe on a day of pompe, passe thorough his hands. Hee liues in the midst of the Treasures of the *Serrail*, with hope to succeed to the place of *Capiaga*, if death forceth the other to abandon it.

The third hath the charge of *Chilergi Bassi*, that is to say, great Dispencer. He is, as with vs, the Master of the Kings Wardrobe; by his place he hath a care of the *Sultans* Apparrell, and of other things which belong vnto his person. Moreouer, the pieces of Cloth of Gold, which they send for Presents, the exquisite Furres, the rich Swords, the Plumes of Feathers, and such like which they giue vnto the Prince, and those which hee himselfe giues, are vnder his custody. Hee keepes a particular accompt, to the end they may see the price of that, which enters into this stately Wardrobe for Presents, and the value of that which goes forth in the same qualitie: This exercise keepes him alwayes in breath; for the custome

of

of Turkey, (well practised in the *Serrail*) being to giue and to receiue, doth furnish him with imployment enough to passe the houres of the day farre from idlenesse. He hath vnder him to assist him in this painfull labour a great number of Eunuches. The diligence which he must shew herein, bindes him to remayne in a manner continually within the *Serrail*, his entertainments are his Table, many Robes of Cloth of Gold, a thousand Aspres by the day, or eight Sultanins, with many rich Presents. But the fauour wherewith his Master doth honour him, makes the greatest article of his Reuenew: he hopes by the meanes hereof to enter into the place of *Chasnadar Bassi*, when it shall be void. He carries (for a marke of the honour which he enjoyes) a Turbant in the *Serrail*, and rides within it, aswell as the two former, and he that followes; for these foure Eunuches haue this prerogatiue aboue the other Officers of the *Othoman* Monarch, residing in the *Serrail*.

The fourth is also an old pale withered Eunuch, aswell by the course of his yeares, as the want of that which they haue cut away, who enjoyes the Office of *Sarai Agassi*, which in Turkey is like vnto the Captaine of the Castle of the *Louver* in *France*, but with more lustre and authority, and so he hath more labour and care: For being to look vnto the whole *Serrail*, the ordinary Mansion of the *Othoman* Monarches, hee must performe his charge so exactly, as such Princes will be serued; he doth often visit all the Quarters and Chambers of this stately Pallace, to see in what estate they are, and hath a care to see the meanest Officers doe their duties, (which is more then with vs, to adde vnto the charge of the Royall Pallace the Office of a Master of the Houshold) that the *Serrail* be furnished with all things that are vsually needfull, hee remaines within it in the *Sultans* absence, to maintaine order, and to see that this royall Lodging be alwayes in good estate. He hath the same entertainment with the *Chilergi Bassi*, and hopes if his yeares deceiue him not, to succeed in his place: For the order of the *Serrail*, doth not suffer suffer them to flie vnto great Offices, but it will haue them mount by degrees.

You

You shall not see men there, grow vp in one night like vnto Mushrums or Toad-stooles; long attendance, and long seruices aduance them to the places which they deserue. Thus the *Shasnadar Bassi* aspires to that of *Capiaga*, the *Chilergi Bassi* to that of *Shasnadar Bassi*, and this last to his. These foure Eunuches attend vsually in the Princes presence, only the *Capiaga* may speake vnto him, and not the rest, vnlesse the Prince doth question them about their Offices. Besides these Honours and Offices of the *Serrail*, the Prince doth sometimes honour them with the quality of *Bassa*, and Gouernour of a Realme, as of *Egypt*, *Damas*, or else-where: They also attaine vnto the place of *Grand Vizir*, which is the first of the Empire, and by the authority thereof lead Armies into Prouinces, where they goe to make warre. The which gaue occasion to a generous Gouernour of a place belonging to the Christian, in *Hungarie*, to answere an Eunuch, Generall of an Army, who had summond him to yeeld, that the practice of women was to sewe and spinne, and not to take Townes. The *Grand Seigneur* aduanceth them in this manner to great places without the *Serrail* to a double end; the one to acknowledge their long seruices, the other to haue their places, wherwith to aduance other Eunuches, who during their long seruices haue attended, that they should either die or be sent *Basha's* into some remote Prouinces. For the *Serrail* doth nourish many Eunuches vnder the sweetnesse of these hopes; They may be about two hundred of all Ages.

Such as cannot be aduanced by order of antiquity to these eminent places in the Royall Pallace, are notwithstanding imployed in things of lesse quality; some keepe in distinct places, as Closets or Cabinets, those exquisite things that are giuen as Presents to the Prince, as great pieces of Ambergreece, which the *Bassa* of *Morea* recouers in his Gouernment, and sends to the *Serrail*, many Cods of Musque, great Vessels full of excellent Treacle of *Venice*, soueraigne Methridate, Balme of *Caire*, *Terra Sigilata*, Bolearmoniacke, Bezar-stones, Vessels of *Agath*, Turquoises, Iasper, Chrystall, and other things of price, which they preserue carefully.

and

and neatly for the Princes person, others haue a care of rare Furres, the vse whereof serues for his health, with a thousand other Rarities which they bring from the *Indies*. Besides all this there is employment in the *Serrail* for many other Eunuches, which keepe one place, whither they carry all the rich moueables confiscated, of the great men of the Court, who haue beene executed for the enormity of their crimes, or by the sinister inuentions of Enuie; and likewise of other persons which die rich, for being all slaues their goods belong vnto the Prince. Those Eunuches receiue these goodly moueables, and giue aduice vnto the *Sultan* who goes to see them; and makes choice of what doth like him: the rest is set to sale in the *Serrail*, only to the Officers thereof, and if there remaine any thing vnbought, it is sent to the publique Market of the City, and sold to them that will: The Money that is raised is deliuered into the hands of the *Chasnadar Bassi*, who puts it into the secret Treasure. Some other Eunuches haue for their imployment the charge of other *Serrails* and Seminaries; where the Prince doth cause the youth to be instructed at his Charge, as in royall Colledges, both at *Constantinople*, *Andrinopolis*, *Bursia* and elsewhere. Thus by the wise Policy of the *Serrail* they which serue are aduanced, for an example to the younger sort to flie idlenesse, and assurance that their continuall labour, shall be one day crowned with an honourable and profitable recompence.

CHAP. V.

[*Of many other Officers seruing in the* Serrail, *and the Sultans Person, and of the number of Men which serue in this Palace.*]

BEsides these Eunuches aduanced to great Offices, and those which are vnder them, there is a certaine number of other men, which do vsually serue the *Sultans* person: Some are Groomes of his Chamber, others in a more eminent Dignitie:

nitie : all ordred by thirties, as thirty for his Shirt, thirty for his Waſtcoat, thirty for his little Caſſocke, which the Turkes weare vnder their Robes, thirty for his Furres, thirty for his Turbant, thirty for his Girdle, thirty for his Breeches, thirty for his Stockings, thirty for his Shooes, thirty to make his Bed, thirty to dreſſe vp his Chamber, and thirty to order and diſpoſe of the Moueables, thirty for his Armes, as his Bow, Arrowes, and Semiter; thirty for his Scepter, thirty for his Imperiall Crowne, thirty for his rich Hangings, and as many for his Cuſhions; not that they ſerue all at one inſtant, but by order from time to time.

They which ſerue for his Mouth, are many in number, gouerned by foure principall Officers ſubordinate one vnto another: The firſt is the *Argibaſsi*, who hath a care that euery man doe his dutie. The ſecond is the *Mimmute Pagi*, who doth furniſh the money daily, that is neceſſary for the expences. His place doth giue him a priuiledge to ſpeake often vnto the Prince, to learne from him what he deſires to eat. He hath like vnto the former foure Sultanins by the day, his Table and two Robes yearely, the one of Silke, the other of Cloth of Gold. The third is the *Checaya*, an Office like vnto the Comptroller Generall of the Kings Houſe in *France*, he is in a manner equall in authority to the Maſter of the Houſhold, he reconciles the Quarrels, which Enuy or Pride do breed among the Officers. He hath foure Sultanins a day, and yearely two Robes of Silke and Cloth of Gold. The fourth is the *Mutpariazigi*, which is as a Clarke of the Office; All theſe men imploy their cares, and the authoritie of their places in the Princes Kitchin. Without there ſerue many *Sahangylers*, as Stewards, or rather Gentlemen ſeruants, which carrie the meate; They are neere fifteene hundred men, which ſerue at diuers times in diuers troupes.

The number of other inferiour Officers in the *Serrail* ſhewes that this ſtately Pallace is of great expences, and that the Prince which liues there is powerfull and magnificent. The *Baltagis* which fetch wood for the Bake-houſe and for other firing, are aboue two hundred; The *Boſtangie* or Gardiners,

are

Court of the Grand SEIGNEVR.

are eight or nine hundred, so vast and of great entertainment, are the Gardens where this great Monarch doth walke. The Purueyours only for wilde Fowle or Poulterie, are fiue hundred, the Groomes of the Stable eight hundred, and the other men of the like condition increase the number of the inferiour Officers of the Turkish Emperours house: So as they doe number within the *Serrail*, thirteene or fourteene thousand Mouthes, which are daily fed at the *Sultans* charge, comprehending the Quarter of the Women.

CHAP. VI.

Of the ordinary Victualls of the Serrail, *and of the Prouisions thereof for the nourishment of the Prince, and of those which serue there.*

AN order being so judiciously established in the *Serrail*, and so exactly obserued, it hath not forgotten the necessarie prouision of victuals: They are brought and preserued with admirable husbandrie, contrarie to the ordinarie confusion of Princes Houses. First, the Corne is gathered for the *Sultans* mouth, for the *Sultana's*, the great *Bassa's* and the *Mufti*, (for all of them haue their part) in the Territory of *Bursa*, a Towne in *Bithynia*, where growes the purest and best of all the Easterne parts: They retaine for the *Serrail* eight or nine thousand *Quilots*, euery *Quilot* is two Bushels of *Paris* measure: The Mils erected to that end in *Constantinople* grind it, the great Ouens of the *Serrail* bake it into bread, and this goodly order distributes it by rule, as to the *Sultana's* twentie Loaues a day, to the *Bassa's* ten, to the *Mufti* eight, and to other inferiour persons much lesse, and to some but one. This distribution is contained in a Book, which the chiefe Baker keepes, to cause it to be obserued. The Corne which is appointed for the great number of men, which serue in the *Serrail*, is gathered in *Græcia*, and brought to *Constantinople*, to the quantitie of fortie thousand *Quilots*, and

T 2 distri-

distributed with the like order to those for whom it is ordained. For there they feed men with necessarie sobrietie, to make them labour seriously in any businesse whatsoever.

The Victuals, be it for the Annuall prouisions, or for the ordinarie of the day, are brought and distributed with the like order: About the end of Autumne, the *Grand Vizir* appoints certaine dayes to see the *Pastromanis* made, for the Kitchins of the *Sultan*, and of the *Sultana's*; They are made with the flesh of Cowes that are with Calfe, that they may be the more tender, they salt them as they doe Stags or Hogs in Christendome; about that time they kill to the number of foure thousand. The *Serrail* esteemes this kind of meat, among the delicacies of their Feasts, and the Turkish Families if they haue any conuenient meanes make likewise their prouision; this great store of flesh is for the whole yeere. But the Purueyours doe furnish the *Serrail* daily with two hundred Sheepe, a hundred Lambes, or a hundred Kids, in their season, fortie Calues, fortie Geese, or Goslings; a hundred couple of Wild-fowle, a hundred couple of Hennes, a hundred paire of Pigeons, with some other small Birds which the Poulterers bring. There comes no fish into the *Serrail*, but to please the appetite of some of the *Agalaris* who desire to eate it; then they cause it to bee taken on that side of the Pallace which lookes towards the Sea, the which doth abundantly furnish all sorts of fish.

The excellent Oiles which the *Sultans* Kitchin doth vse, comes most commonly from *Coron* and *Modon*, in *Grecia*, a plentifull soile for Oliue-trees. *Candie* only doth furnish that which is imployed for the Princes seruice: for besides the delicate bountie of this liquour, it is without any ill sent, the which growing old in others makes them vnpleasing. They haue great prouision of Butter in the *Serrail*; the which is brought from *Moldauia*, and other places thereabouts; It comes downe by the blacke Sea in great quantitie but salted, the Turkes doe not seeke after fresh Butter; either for that they know not the quality, or neglect it: Milke is little in vse among them; that which is brought to *Constantinople*, is only ly bought by the Christians or Iewes; If the Turkes make vse of it, it is after it is sowre, for then they say it doth quench their thirst.

Other prouisions of Victuals are drawne from those Prouinces where they most abound, and are best. The Gallions make two Voyages yearely to *Alexandria*, to fraught themselues with Pulses, Sugars, and Spices, as much as shall bee needfull for the *Serrail*, and the chiefe *Bassa's* of the Port; yet the Turkes vse not much Spices, lest it should prouoke them to drinke wine, so expresly defended by their Law. *Egypt* doth furnish Dates, and the best Prunes that come into the *Serrail*. Apples which are the chiefe delights in their Turkish Feasts, and whereof they make a plentifull prouision, are gathered in *Vallachia*, *Transiluania*, and *Moldauia*, and brought vnto the *Serrail* in great abundance: Those which they serue vnto the *Sultan*, are for their delicate sweetnesse bought in *Candy*. *Italy* doth also contribute to the Prouisions of this great *Serrail*; the Bailiffe of *Venice*, residing at the Port, causeth a great quantity of Parmasant Cheese to bee brought for the *Grand Seigneur*, his *Sultana's* and *Bassa's*: they are pleased in the taste, and the Feast would not be acceptable if this meate were wanting.

All these things concerne the food, for their drinke they make a liquour in the *Serrail*, called *Sorbet*, composed of the juice of Citrons, Sugar, and Water; and sometimes they adde Ambergreece, most excellent to drinke; so it is only reserued for the *Sultan* and his women: The greatest men of this Imperiall Pallace make for themselues, as the foure principall Eunuches, of whom wee haue spoken, and some few others: The Ice refreshing it in Summer makes it more delightfull; They make their prouision of Ice from the Mountaines about *Constantinople*, they bring such great store, as the charges (before it be put into those places where they keepe it) comes to twenty thousand Sultanins, or eight thousand pounds sterling. The rest of the Royall Family quench their thirst at those goodly Fountaines, which powre forth delicate water abundantly for the whole *Serrail*: Wine enters not into it without

vio-

violating the Law of the Alcoran, which hath so seuerely forbidden it; and whereof the wisest of the Turkes detest the vse; they call it the Spurre of Sensualitie, and the Tombe of Reason.

The Wood which serues for their Kitchin, is supplied with the like abundance; they measure the quantity by the weight, for so they sell it in *Constantinople*, aswell as in some Prouinces of *France*, and particularly in *Landguedoc*: They cut it in the *Grand Seigneurs* Forrests, and this prouision costs him least of all those that enter into his Pallace. Thirty great Caramonsailes, chosen among an infinite number of his Ships take it in, and sayling by the channell of the blacke Sea, deliuer it into the *Serrail*; his slaues haue cut it downe, sparing good summes of money to the *Chasna* or Treasure without, whereunto the charges would amount, both for the cutting and carriage.

But if the victuals of the *Serrail* be furnished in abundance and excellencie, the Kitchins which imploy them are supplyed with the goodliest Implements, which can be seene in a Soueraigne Princes house. Most part of the greater Vessels are of Brasse, kept so neat and cleane, as the very sight of them will giue content and amazement; the other Implements which are of Copper blauncht, are so great in number as they cannot well be numbred. The losse which happens many times is not small; the foure dayes of *Diuan*, many strangers eate in the *Serrail*, and they which haue learned to furnish themselues at anothers cost, take occasion to practize their Trade, and to take it where they can find it, and steale so great a quantity of Vessels, as the great *Testarder* hath sometimes beene of opinion (to auoid this great losse) to make them of Siluer, and to commit the custodie thereof to some Officer who might answere for them; but the consideration of the great charge, and the feare of an irreparable losse which might befall them, hath alwayes diuerted him.

Such are the victuals and other prouisions, which doe furnish the Pallace of the *Grand Seigneur* of Turkey: If the Reader finds the relation of the Kitchin tedious, which serues for the

the subject of these lines, let him consider that without this Chapter, the others which compose this History could not be. For this wanting victuals to supply the *Othoman* Court, the glory and lustre of his great *Serrail* could not be without them, nor be able to furnish matter for this worke. The members of mans Body (saith the Fable) did one day mutine against the Belly, who they thought slept in perpetuall idlenesse: The tongue speaking for all the rest shewed, that whilst the eyes saw, the eares heard, the hands laboured, and the feet walked, only the belly was idle and at rest, that it was fitting, that in his turne hee should discharge some one of their Offices: They so resolued, they employed it, but nourishment failing them, for the want of the naturall exercise of the belly, they grew cold, pale, and without motion. The truth of this tale teacheth vs, that by labour we must liue, food maintaines life in its naturall functions, and this Chapter furnishing this stately Court wherewith to subsist, giues this History the subject of its imployment.

Chap. VII.

Of the sicke Men, and of such as die in the Serrail.

THe infirmities of the bodie, doe most commonly follow the dispositions of the mind, and dissolution doth sooner cause them than any other thing; Courtiers feele the inconueniences of their Riots. When they of the *Serrail* fall sicke, they put them into a close Waggon, in the which they are drawne by men, and conducted to the Hospitall, whereas the order of this Imperiall house, and the Turkish Charitie, doe what they can to relieue them; the one giues care to the ordinary Physicians, and the other (which as we haue said is very great) forgets nothing to assist them: They are so exactly guarded, as no stranger may speak vnto them, vntill they haue recouered their health, after which they are restored to their first

144   *The History of the* Serrail, *and of the*

first Lodgings, and the exercise of their places. But if they die, the Law of the Court enjoynes, that they of the Chamber or *Oda*, whereof the dead man was, shall be his heires, and share the goods which he hath left, except it be some one of the foure chiefe Eunuches, before mentioned, or the *Chislar Aga* of the *Sultana's*, who is blacke; for then the Prince is sole heire of his precious moueables, and of the abundance of money which this wretched man had so greedily gathered together, by the sinister meanes, which followes the ambitions of the Court; hauing liued poore in his seruitude, to die rich in the same, and to restore to the *Sultans* Cofers, that which his auarice had drawne away. Such Eunuches doe vsually leaue great wealth in Moueables (for the Turkes haue no Lands) and particularly when their long seruices haue aduanced them to the Dignities of Gouernours of Prouinces, then they haue liberty to dispose of a third part of their estates, to make a Will, in the which the *Sultan* is alwayes Executor, hee giues shares to the Legataries; and many times takes all for himselfe, by the right of his Prerogatiue, and that of Master, not only of the goods, but also of the persons of his Empire: for all men being his slaues, hee is their first and lawfull heire.

Chap. VIII.

Of the Grand SEIGNEVRS *hunting.*

MOst of the Turkish Emperours, in the effeminacie of their Idlenesse, where they wallow wretchedly in the bosomes of their Concubines, haue taken hunting for a pleasing diuersion: But some finding it more pleasing than others, haue loued it with more passion. *Baiazet* the first of that name, (who raigned in Turkey when as the weaknesse of *Charles* the sixth, suffered the disorders in *France*, which had like to haue ruined it) was so transported with this exercise, as he therein spent the best of his dayes: his Court was fuller of

Hunts-

Huntsmen than any other; whosoeuer went to aduance his fortune, must goe with a Hawke on his fist or a lease of Greyhounds in his hand; for the best course to rise in Court, is to follow the inclinations of the Prince, how brutish soeuer they be: Then a Faulconer grew great, and a Rider got an Office, but a vertuous man was rejected and grew poore. What priuate men did, to merit this Monarches fauour, forreine Princes did imitate to winne his loue. *Iohn* Earle of *Neuers* sonne to *Philip* the Hardy, Duke of *Burgundie*, accompanied by the Lords of *Tremouile*, *La Marche*, *Couey*, *Philip* of *Artois*, Earle of *Eu*, Constable of *France*, *Vienna*, Admirall of *France*, *Boucicault*, Marshall of *France*, the Lords of *Breze*, *Montrell*, *Montquell*, *Helly*, and many others, led to succour *Sigismond* King of *Hungary*, a generous army of *French*, against the Turkes which were in *Nicopolis*: Bad intelligence and rashnesse ruined them, their troupes were defeated by the succours of *Baiazet*, the men were put to the sword, the Earle of *Neuers* taken Prisoner, with the chiefe of the *French* Nobility: The Turkes Prison is rough, and a Prince how great soeuer must suffer. *Philip* the Hardy to mollifie the sauage humour of the Turke, and to bind him to better vsage of his Sonne, sent him Presents, and particularly many white Ger-faulcons, whereof he made great accompt: and to testifie the pleasure which hee receiued, he inlarged the Prison of this young Prince, and led him often a hunting. There in the *French* obserued the brutish passion of *Baiazet*: His Faulconers had cast off a Ger-faulcon after a fowle vnseasonably, he grew into a fury, and would presently haue put two thousand of those men which followed him to death with their Hawkes vpon their fists, if the earnest intreaty of the Earle of *Neuers* had not diuerted him: Then hee vented out his choller in words, and told the *Burgonian*, that hee did more esteeme a good Hawke or a good Dogge than any of his men; and (adding this brutish speech) he said he could haue as many men as hee pleased, but for good Hawkes, or good Dogges he could hardly find them.

In his hunting whosoeuer did hurt a Dogge vnaduisedly, he

V was

was guilty of Treason, and was punished in like manner: But Hee, who with his powerfull Hand controules the pride of Princes, measured him in the like manner. *Tamberlaine* King of the *Tartars* defeated him soone after in battaile, tooke him with his Wife, and made lesse account of his person than of a Dogge or a Hawke: When hee dined hee caused him to be set vnder his Table in a Cage of Iron, and cast him bones to gnaw: Ministring matter to History, to write this example to Posteritie, to the end that Princes that loue hunting, may not suffer their reason to be surmounted with the fury and brutish impatiencies of this exercise. The hunting traine of this Prince was so great, as for hawking only hee had seuen thousand Faulconers, which were entertained vntill the raigne of *Mahomet* the Second, who comming to the Empire, looked vpon this fearfull troupe of Faulconers with amazement; and as he had no inclination to hunting he casheer'd them all, and answered the intreaties of great Men, who spake to haue them restored, with these words: *God forbid, that I should giue my bread to such vnprofitable persons, ordained for so vaine a pleasure.* Hunting is an honest recreation, easeth the minde, exerciseth the body, and he that loues it, shewes the quicknesse of his spirit, and the agilitie and disposition of his person: But the time which hee imployes must be measured, free, and not stolne by violence from more serious imployments, the which ought alwayes to be preferred before this commendable pleasure. Hunting must be generous, and they must take that by force which they pursue, and not by cunning and policie, as to set Nets and Toiles for beasts, then it is base, idle, and forbidden by the wise, who haue laboured to settle flourishing Common-weales vnder the gouernment of good Lawes.

Plato amongst others In his booke, de legib. dial. 7.

Solyman the Second, he which tooke *Rhodes*, and erected the Turkish Crescent in the best Townes of *Hungarie*, did often spend his time in hunting; during his Raigne, hee imployed a whole yeare, which was in the yeare 1531, when as *Italy* apprehended that the great preparation of a fearefull Nauall Army, had beene made for their ruine, and the *Venetians*

tians prest with jelousie, that it should cause some dangerous tempest in their Gulfe, vnder pretext of seeking the Pyrats of *Malta*, which did annoy the Turkish Merchants. they sent vnto the Kings of *Hungarie* and *Polonia*, to the end they would intreate *Solyman* not to trouble himselfe to send his Army into their Seas, and that they would promise and vndertake, to keepe the *Leuant* Seas free from all Pyrats: It succeeded according to their desire, *Solyman* being retired to *Andrinopolis*, spent the whole yeare (as we haue said) in the pleasure of hunting.

The Turkish Emperours which haue succeeded him loued this exercise. *Osman* the last dead, entertained a great number of Huntsmen and Faulconers. These Princes hold it a glory to make a shew of them in their stately entries into *Constantinople*, as wee haue formerly obserued, where among the troupes of Huntsmen, wee see Faulconers with their Hawkes on their fist, haue a Leopard at their Saddle pomell couered with Cloth of Gold; they hunt the Hare or the Stag many times with some content; they pursue the Boare, although the vse of it be forbidden by their Law: If they take any, they giue the flesh to Christians, or cast it away, and reserue the skinne to couer Bookes for the which it is very good, and preserues their Volumes long: Those which haue come into my hands bound at *Constantinople*, are excellently well couered with Boares skins, although they be not artificially done as with vs at *Paris*.

But Superstition the Soueraigne Mistris of Turkish Spirits, hath a share in this pleasing exercise, when they hunt vpon the day of their Coronation, or when as they conceiue the designes of an important warre, they hold it for a good presage if they take the first beast that is put vp; but this pleasure of hunting doth not so possesse them, as it makes them forget the care of serious affaires. The Turkish Emperours haue been accustomed in these sports to take the aduice of their *Bassa's*, of the occurrents which concern the estate; they cal them vnto them in the field, they speake vnto them, and command them to deliuer their opinions: In Court they call this manner of con-

consulting, *The Councell on horsebacke*: whereby wee may learne that this Nation is not so barbarous as men conceiue, and that if they raigne so powerfully ouer so many Prouinces and Realmes, it is not accidentally and by chance; their care and judicious Councell giue vnto their Empire a wise Gouernment.

Chap. IX.

Of the traine which followes the Grand Seigneurs Court.

THe number of men lodged and fed in the *Serrail*, which amounts to fourteen thousand mouths, would make those imagine, which know not the power of the Turkish Emperours, that many Soueraigne Monarchs, lodged together, had drawne all the Officers of their houses into one Pallace. And truly he whom they serue hauing vanquished and ruined many Kings hath made an vnion of their Crownes: His *Serrail*, when he lodgeth there, containes in him alone the Emperour of *Constantinople*, him of *Trebisonde*, the Kings of *Ierusalem, Babylon, Damas, Egypt, Cypresse, Thunis, Algier, Fez*, and *Morocco*, with an infinite number of other smaller Soueraignes, whose Empires, Realmes and Principalities hee doth possesse: So as so many Officers as are in his Pallace, seruing his greatnesse, serue many Crownes. But when he goes out of his *Serrail*, to vndertake a Voyage into some remote Prouince, the traine and followers which increase his Court is wonderfull. Thirty sixe thousand *Ianizaries*, make the number of his ordinary Guard on foot, fortie foure thousand *Spahi*, which are as light Horsemen, make the Cauallery; two thousand *Capigis* or Archers of the Port follow him: These beside their ordinary Guard, execute the Office of the Ministers of Iustice, with men of meaner condition that are vnder them: Two thousand *Solachis*, which are Guards on foot about the *Sultans* person, are of his traine: Foure thousand

sand *Chaoux*, Men imployed in Embassies, and in the executions of Iustice march after him. There are also fifteen hundred *Sahangylers*, or Gentlemen Seruants, which carry his meate vnto the chamber doore, where the Pages receiue it and deliuer it to the *Capiaga*, who sets it vpon his Table. The number of men for baser vses is not lesse, if we consider wherein they are imployed, there are three thousand Groomes of the Stable, and a thousand Riders for hunting; the *Balthagis* which cut the wood, and bring it to the Kitchin are eight thousand: There are a thousand *Thanegys*, which are Purueyours, or Victualers: two thousand fiue hundred *Therezi*, or Tailors to the Court, sixe hundred Bakers. And if the Voyage be made for the warre, the Officers of the *Arsenall*, which are Commissaries of the Artillery and others, make fortie six thousand men: The *Gebegys* which make Armes, and repaire and keepe cleane those which are already made, are fourteene thousand: seuen thousand *Tufechgys* or Gun-makers, follow with their Tooles and ambulatory shops: eight thousand *Topeys*, which are the Cannoneers, increase the traine of this monstrous Court. I omit a number of pettie Officers, for that I haue not their names.

The beasts of burthen are vsually twentie thousand, that is to say, ten thousand Camels, and ten thousand Moiles, which is the ordinary for the *Sultans* house, not reckoning the traine of the *Bassa's* which follow, the which is not so small but in seeing them march apart, you would take it for the traine of a Soueraigne Prince; for the Turkes carrie in their Voyages all sorts of Commodities, to the end they may be accommodated aswell in Field, as in the Townes of their abode. The supputation of the number of men that follow this Court, amounts to a hundred fiue thousand, sixe hundred, when the *Sultan* trauels in a time of peace; but if hee goe to the warre, his Court is composed of a hundred and foure score thousand men, beside the Souldiers. So as who is hee, that seeing this fearefull Court to march, would not beleeue that it is a whole Nation, who hauing abandoned their owne houses, goe to conquer new habitations. Certainly, that which History relates

lates of the Descent of the Northerne Nations, as *Cimbrians*, *Sicambrians*, *Gothes*, *Vandals*, *Burgonians*, *Normans* and others, is plainly seene there by the number of men; but with this difference, that those did but passe, and these remaine still, and adde to the continuance of their tedious Raigne, the Rule and power ouer many other Nations, neere and afarre off, from the principall seat of their Empire.

Chap. X.

Of the greatnesse of the Turkish Bassa's.

THe brightnesse of the Sun doth not only shew it selfe in the body of its Spheare, but it doth also shine in the greatest Starres. And Kings who are in their Estates what the Sun is in Heauen, do not only shew in themselues the lustre of their magnificence, but it doth also shine in the wealth of the great Men of their Court. This is seene more visibly in Turkey than in any other place of the World, where the Turkish *Bassa's* display in the pompe of their great riches, the proud power of the Emperour, from whom they haue receiued it. *Machmut Bassa*, *Beglierbey* of *Europe* enjoyed so great treasures during the Raigne of *Mahomet* the Second, as the annuall Reuenewes thereof, would haue defraied a powerfull Turkish Army. This example would put them to silence, which bragge so much of the treasure of old *Crassus*, the yearely rent whereof, they say was able, to entertaine a Roman Army. The least of the Turkes Armies would containe many of theirs. As this *Bassa* had beene the most powerfull, and the most sumptuous, that euer the *Othoman* Court had aduanced to the height of an extraordinary fortune, it shall not be vnfitting to deliuer briefly by what meanes hee came vnto that greatnesse. He was by Nation a *Græcian*, and in his infancy his Mother who was a *Bulgarian*, led him one day with her, from the Towne of *Nebopride*, to that of *Senderovia*; she met casually with the Turkish horse, some of them

seeing

seeing this young childe wonderfull beautifull, tooke him away by force, and carried him as a Present to the *Sultan* their Master: The Prince loued him, and in a short time made the greatest of his Court know, that beauty is many times a powerfull motiue to a great fortune, hee was placed among the best respected Pages of his Chamber, where hee spent his younger yeeres in the midst of the delights of the *Serrail*, after which he had the charge of *Aga*, or Colonell Generall of the *Ianizaries*; afterwards he was honoured with the qualitie of *Bassa*, then he became *Vizir*, & mounting daily higher, *Romelia* or *Europe* had him for their *Beglerbey*: The magnificences which he shewed, during the possession of so much wealth, would be tedious to relate. One only example shall suffice for all. *Mahomet* the Second, caused the eldest of his children to be Circumcised; the custome of the Court will haue great Men to giue him Presents, as wee haue formerly spoken: all performed it; but that of *Machmut*, mounted neere to a hundred thousand *Sequins*, which would make fortie thousand pounds sterling. The Ocean must bee vast and great, which doth breed such great Whales, liuing and walking Mountaines: And the *Othoman* Court must be stately, seeing the *Bassa's* encounter with such fortunes.

But it may be that of *Machmut* will seeme stale, for that it happened an age before ours: to satisfie those which loue new things, and to augment the proofes of this verity, that the Turkish *Bassa's* are great, we will adde an example which many haue seene of late yeeres. It appeared in the *Leuant* in the yeere 1614, and in the person of *Nassuf Bassa* Grand Vizir of the Empire, whose treasures were so great, as they found in his Cofers at the time of his death a Million of Gold in *Sequins*, and in siluer Coine eight hundred thousand Crownes, three bushels of precious Stones not wrought, a bushell of Diamonds not set in gold, and two bushels of great round Pearles of inestimable value: His other furniture was equall to his treasure; he had a thousand goodly Horses in his stable, whereof the least was valued at a thousand Crownes: Moreouer, he had foure hundred Mares of *Arabian, Egypt,*

the

the goodliest that could be found in those Countries, with many thousand of Camels and Moyles. His Armory was full of the richest Swords that could be found in the *Leuant*, and elsewhere: The least had the hilts of siluer: One was so enricht with Diamonds vpon the hilt, as it was valued at fiue thousand pounds sterling. The rest of his moueables were no lesse precious, his *Persian* Carpets wrought of Gold and Silke. The great quantity of Cloth of Gold & of Silk of most excellent workes; the rich beds, and all, that excesse of a monstrous fortune can draw into the Pallace of a Fauourite, exceeds the imagination of men, and giues occasion to say, that with the spoile of such men, they might not only enrich many houses, but many Cities.

 Such rich and sumptuous Courtiers go with no smal trains: when they march in field, and vndertake a Voyage, be it for their owne particulars, or to receiue the possession of the Gouernment of Prouinces, wherewith the *Sultan* doth honour them, the baggage which goes before, and the great number of men which follow them, doth equall, yea, exceed the attendants of the Soueraigne Princes of *Europe*: Such a traine may busie the eyes of those that see them passe, for a whole day, for so much time is necessary for the least entry into a Towne, and yet many times they supply the want of day by Torch-light: It is the care of such *Baffa's* to shew themselues great to the eyes of the World: which makes them prodigall in their expences, to be attended by many thousands of houshould seruants, (if they bee not ill serued being a difficult thing, but such a number and troupe should be importune and troublesome) to whom they giue many *Eunuches* to command them. They take a delight to bee well mounted, and withall to haue as many horses, as would serue for diuers Regiments: They will haue their Baggage, to seeme the more stately, to be carried by twelue or fifteene hundred Moiles, and as many Camells. The number of the Concubins which they entertaine in imitation of the Prince their Maister, imployes the care and watchfull diligence of many black *Eunuches*, which they appoint to keepe them, and consume their great wealth.

Their

Their Lodgings are stately *Serrails*, which they haue built with incredible expences; as wee may see in the *Hippodrome* of *Constantinople*, by the *Serrail* of *Hibraime Bassa*, whereof the Turkish Emperours haue beene heires, the which is capable to lodge a great King. Their Moueables and Ornaments of their Hals, are equall to their greatnesse, wherein they spare no cost, as the only acquisitions which the Law of their seruitude doth allow them: for being all slaues, they can purchase no lands nor possessions, the which doth generally belong to the *Sultan* their Soueraigne. But if of Caitiue slaues they be so great and so proud in their wealth, what must the Master be who hath made them such?

CHAP. XI.

Of the affronts which the Turkish Bassa's are forced to pocket up in Court, and the disgracefull Chastisements which they suffer.

THe honours and greatnesse of the World haue their counterpoise; shame and contempt followes them at the heeles: All that clime vp may descend, yea fall. Thus the diuine Prouidence hath wisely ordained, to teach man not to build his assurances thereon; and to binde him to seeke them in that which is constant & eternall. The Court is the Theater, wherein the Tragicall Scene of change, shewes it selfe; griefe goes hand in hand with pleasure, and is an inseperable Companion; he cannot be long a Courtier that hath not tried it. That of the Turkes doth many times make it sensible to the greatest *Bassa*'s; in the midst of the glorious dignities of the Empire, they feele the displeasure, to see themselues shamefully intreated by the commandement of their Soueraigne. For when he hath an intent to blemish their Names with eternall infamy, hee causeth the crouper of their Horses to be cut, whilest they are vpon them; an affront held in Turkey, the greatest that a man of their condition can receiue. So was

Mu-

Mustapha Bassa intreated in the time of *Selym* the first, Father to great *Solyman*. This Prince hauing vanquished the *Sophy of Persia*, & triumphed in *Tauris*, the chiefe Citie of that Realme, was forced to leaue it, when as he saw his souldiers inclined to mutinie, saying plainly that they had rather lose all, then to spend the Winter in *Persia*. This Deniall was very sensible, & he thought to be reuenged on those whom hee should find to be the Motiues: they perswade him that *Mustapha Bassa*, who had credit among the Footmen, had induced them to Mutinie; hee dischargeth his choler vpon him, and seeing him on horsebacke, he sent to cut his crouper by a Iester which followed him: The *Bassa* perceiued it, and the disgrace which he receiued, made him to end his dayes in the midst of the cares and griefe, which a man of his qualitie doth feele, when he thinkes he hath lost the reputation, which made him to liue gloriously in the World and Court.

The infamy of this affront comes not alone; it hath for a companion, the disaster of a shamefull punishment, which the great men of the Port or *Sultans* Court receiue, when hee holds him guilty of some small crime: When he hath caused the Crouper of some of their horses to be cut, he doth likewise cause others to be whipt by his Slaues: as it happened in the time of *Amurath* the Second, to the *Aga* or Colonell of the *Ianizaries* or Turkish foot, who being conuicted to haue brought in some Hirelings at the Muster, the Emperour caused him to be taken and whipt. But this punishment is not so insupportable vnto them, as the affront of cutting the Crouper, as if the Leather of the Harnesse of their Horse, were more sensible vnto them than their skins? So much a false opinion doth deceiue them, as they hold that a disgrace which is not, and are not troubled for that which should be most sensible vnto them. An example, which teacheth, that most things which disquiet the mind of man, are vaine, and forged in a depraued imagination. For it is more easie to suffer a hundred Croupers to be cut, than to endure fifty lashes with a whip vpon the body. But such are the affronts & punishments which follow the greatnes of the Turkish Court, in the person of their *Bassa's*.

Nimio otio ingenia, naturâ infirma, & muliebria, inopia vera iniuria lasciuientia, bis mouentur, quorum pars maior constat vitio interpretantis. Senec. lib. In sapientem videde.

CHAP.

Chap. XII.

In what stile the Grand SEIGNEVR *writes unto his Bassa's.*

THe greatest dignities of the World, are not the most happy, (said an Ancient) and the condition of great Monarches hath seemed miserable to some, for that they had little to desire, and much to feare; for being advanced to the height of humane greatnesse, they cannot desire more, but continuing in the languishing of their spirit, they sometimes conceive jealousies and imaginary terrours, and many times such as are true; the which troubles their rest, disquiets their lives, and fils them with tedious conceits. So saith the Master of Princes in the holy Writ, in these few words, delivered by a Prince, *The heart of Kings is inscrutable.* Certainly truth doth teach vs, that if Crownes and Scepters be weighty, as charges of care and trouble, the Office of Kings is painfull; for there is nothing so difficult to man, as to command well, whereon depends the knowledge of raigning well. The Prince which commands must obserue three things, that what he desires may be just, for the publique good, and concerne his owne glory. The which is done by well aduising. The Ottoman Monarches, as Princes retired within their Serrail, and not much communicable, commanding matters daily by writing, and the stile which they vse in writing that which they command, is particular vnto them. We shal hardly find in Histories any one example of a Monarchie or Common-wealth, in the which the Superiours haue commanded so imperiously, and hath beene obeyed so speedily, as with the Turkes; their letters breathe nothing but threats, and they speake no other language but that of cruelties. Behold some examples of those, which the *Sultans* haue written to their Bassa's. In the yeare 1602. *Mahomet* the third hearing of the losse of *Alba Regalis* in *Hungarie,* which the Christians had recouered, and holding this place to be of very great im-

Cor Regum inscrutabile, Prou. 25.3.

Experiendo didicisse quam arduum quam subiectum fortunæ, regendi cuncta onus, Tacitus lib. 1. Annal.

importance, hee sent an Army vnder the command of his *Grand Vizir*, and wrote to *Serdar Bassa*, his Viceroy in *Hungarie*, a letter in these termes. *Alba Regalis as I heare is taken by the Christians, recouer it speedily, or resolue with thy selfe to die shamefully.* *Serdar* had no sooner receiued this Letter, but he leuies men in all parts, to increase the *Vizirs* Army; and goes with him to the siege of this place, batters it, and forces it to yeeld by composition, yea, they enter by the breach; the Christian Souldiers hauing abandoned it after the signing of the Articles, to saue the goods which they had in their Lodgings. This example shall be fortified by another, which will teach vs that this rude stile of the *Othoman* Monarches, makes their *Bassa's* to doe impossible things. *Solyman* the Second hearing that the Christians preuailed much in *Hungarie*, and that his men decayed, he resolued to goe thither in person with a powerfull Army, which was the last Voyage he made; he aduanceth and passeth the Riuers of *Tisse* and *Danow*, his Scouts bring him word, that the Riuer of *Draue* was so ouerflowne, that it could hardly be past without a Bridge: he presently dispatched *Assambeg* to make one, and gaue him fiue and twenty thousand men to labour with diligence. *Assambeg* arriues, and finds this Riuer so fearefully ouerflowne, as it was rather like vnto an Ocean, which surrounds a whole Country, then a Riuer which hath its bed and current: This accident stayes him suddainly, to labour in it he thought he should but drowne men in sport: He giues aduice vnto his Master, and writes vnto him that it was not more difficult to make a bridge vpon a Sea tost with stormes & tempests, than vpon the Riuer of *Draue*, whose waters had made a generall Deluge ouer the whole Countrey. *Solyman* sends backe the same Post, with a Cloth like vnto a long Napkin, and there-withall this answere: *The Emperour* Solyman *commands thee by the same Post, which thou hast sent vnto him, that thou cause a Bridge to be made vpon the* Draue, *what soeuer thou findst; and if thou hast not finished it before his comming, hee will cause thee to be strangled with this Cloth.* *Assambeg* receiues this Letter, reads it, and seeing that hee must

must make this Bridge or die, hee labours, hazards all, and loseth many thousand men; yet notwithstanding this overflowing of the water, hee finished a Bridge in sixteene dayes ouer the Riuer of *Draue*, being fiue thousand fiue hundred fathome long, and fourteene broad, supported by Boats tyed one to another with chaines of Iron. *Solyman* past his Army ouer it, and went to lay his siege to *Seghet*, where he died. *Assambeg* had good & strong excuses, not to attempt the making of this Bridge, any other Prince but a Turke would haue allowed of them: But hee who was (as the Turkes be) a bad husband of mens liues, would haue it done at what rate soeuer. The threat of those Letters which wee haue related are with some condition. But the Turkish Princes many times write absolutely; as it happened in the yeare 1614, in the person of *Nassuf Bassa, Grand Vizir* of the Turkish Empire. The Emperour *Achmat* the first would haue his life and his treasure: He sends vnto him being in *Constantinople*, the *Bostangibassi*, with two Letters written by his own hand, whereof this was the tenour of the first: *Faile not presently vpon the receipt hereof, to send mee by the* Bostangibassi *the Seales of my Empire*. *Nassuf* obeyed, and deliuered them into the great Gardiners hands; hauing receiued them, he drew another of the Sultans Letters out of his pocket to *Nassuf*, whereof these were the words: *After that thou hast sent mee my Seales, send mee thy Head by him that shall giue thee this Note*. This command was rough, and the stile of his Letter troublesome, yet hee must obey; not of force; for *Nassuf* was in his house with a Family of abouet wo thousand men, and the Gardiner had neither sticke nor staffe, and was only assisted by ten or twelue Rascals vnarmed, which were *Capigis*, or Porters of the *Serrail*. *Nassuf* suffered himselfe to be strangled, and the *Bostangibassi* carried away his head in the view of all his great Family, whereof the least Scullions might haue broacht him with their Spits, with his goodly traine: Yet no man moued, seeing the people of the *Serrail*, and knowing that it was the Princes pleasure, their Armes were their teares and sorrowes. Thus this rough manner of writing proues very beneficiall

to

to the Turkish Princes, and they reape many commodities thereby. First, they are not forced to giue money to the Gouernour of a strong place, who is not faithfull or profitable, to draw him out of it, and to buy with great summes of money (as they doe in other places) the Townes and Forts of their Estates; the least of their Letters drawes forth a Gouernour, where they place whom they please; they compasse great enterprizes, causing that to be done by feare which loue cannot doe; they are lesse betrayed in affaires of importance, and are generally exactly obeyed.

Chap. XIII.

Of the malicious inuentions and poysonings which the Turkes vse one against another, and especially great Men.

Ambition hath brought other Vices into the Court, where shee imployes them in her designes. Slander and Treason are the Counsellours of her detestable inuentions, and poysoning puts them in execution. But this last finds more imployment in the Court of *Mahometan* Princes than in any other part of the World: They vse this abhominable meane to revenge injuries, and to content their passions: And after their example the great Men and *Bassa's* imploy it: Former ages, and the disorder of that wherein we liue, furnish examples. In the yeare 1379, *Mahomet* the old King of *Granado*, a *Mahometan* Prince, meaning to be reuenged on the Court of *Castile*, and to ruine *Don Henry* King thereof, couers it with the goodly shew of a rich Present, experience hauing taught him, that of all humane things, gifts haue the most easie accesse into Courts. Hee therefore resolues to cause a paire of royall Buskins to be made imbroidered with Gold, with the rarest inuentions that could be deuised, and to make them more glorious, hee did enrich them with an infinite number of precious stones, and sent them into *Castile*; Don Henry receiues them, admires them, and well

plea-

pleased with so rare a Present, hee doth publiquely commend the magnificence of the Turkish Prince. But hee doth soone learne to his cost, that poyson is rather among gold and precious stones that among pouerty. Hee puts them on the next day, but presently the poyson wherewith they were infected, layes him in the bed of death, and depriues him of life. Spaine hath beene alwayes subject to such accidents whilest the Mahometans commanded there; and the Kings thereof had cause to feare a double poyson: For whilest the Turkish Princes did attempt their persons by poyson, the Alphaquis, and Priests of the Alcoran, poysoned the soules of their subjects by the contagious impurities of a false and brutish Doctrine. A little before the death of the King of Castile, he of Leon called Don Sancho, was poysoned by the inuention of a Turke, who taught Gonzalo, his Lieutenant at Leon, the detestable meanes to kill his Master in giuing him an Apple, the which this wretched Lieutenant performed: This was at the same time when as a Deluge of fire came out of the Ocean, the which carried his flame farre into Spaine, but in a great Country, and of many Burroughs and Villages, made heaps of ashes as farre as Zamora. The Spaniards write it, and Moyerne Turquet in the seuenth Booke of the historie of Spaine.

These examples shew the malice of the Turkes against the Christians; but they doe no lesse among themselues. A Turkish King of Fez, not able to endure the prosperities of him of Grenado, called Ioseph, a Mahometan like himselfe, he resolued to take away his life: Hee sends to visit him oftner than he had accustomed, he makes a greater shew of friendship, and after he hath receiued many effects of his, hee sent him for a Present a Cassocke of Cloth of Gold of great value, King Ioseph receiues it, and puts it on, but hee had not worne it a day, but the poyson wherewith the Prince of Fez had infected it, seased vpon him, and gaue him such cruell conuulsions and torments, as his flesh fell away in pieces, and his Physitians knew not the true cause of his disease, nor could apply any remedie: Thus hee of Grenado died by the damnable inuentions of a Moorish King. The like villanies which were practised among the ancient Turkes, are vsed at this day in the *Leuant*, at the Court of *Constantinople*, and in other places, whither they send great Men to eminent charges. In our dayes a Turkish Courtier affected by all meanes possible the dignitie of *Bassa* of *Aleppo*; the beauty of the place, the lustre of this dignitie, but rather the great gaine which the Vice-royes make, inflamed his desire to the possession of this Gouernment; to attain vnto it he purchased by great gifts the affections of the *Agalaris*, or Fauourites of the *Serrail*, which are the Eunuches attending the Princes person: These men content his ambition, and obtained the gouernment which he desired from the *Sultan*; hee receiues the Letters, takes his leaue to goe vnto his charge, hee arriues and is receiued with the applause of the people; but he had scarce begun to enjoy the first honours of this new dignity, but another doth dispossesse him by the same meanes which he had vsed; hee gets the friendship of the Eunuches, and gluts their auarice with greater gifts obtaining Letters for this place. He was aduertized hereof; the displeasure which he conceiued to see himselfe deceiued by the Courtiers of the *Serrail*, to whom hee had giuen much more money than hee had gotten in so short a time, that he had beene *Bassa* of *Aleppo*, made him to draw his dearest friends about him, to resolue with them how hee should gouerne himselfe in this important businesse. Many were of opinion that he should refuse the entry into the Towne to this new *Bassa* who was vpon the way, vntill he informed the *Sultan*, the *Mufti*, and the *Grand Vizir* of the couetous disloyaltie of the *Agalaris*; and this Counsell was conformable to his apprehension. But one of the company drawing him aside, told him, That hee which came to displace him, brought a Commandement from the Prince, wherein it was dangerous to vse any opposition; that, obedience was the safest way in such affaires; but he would teach him a meanes to make the continuance of this new Gouernour shorter then his had beene, that he must strictly imbrace the *Bassa* which came, and testifie vnto him a ready obedience to the *Sultan*, and all loue and friendship to him; and after this to take him out of the World by the meanes of a poysoned Present: They

re-

resolued it, and laboured in their designe. In the meane time the new *Bassa* arriues, the other receiues him, and yeelds him the place. It is the custome of the great men in Turkey, to giue Presents to the new Gouernor when they enter in charge, some to testifie that they are welcome, and others to gain their affections. This discontented *Bassa*, who left his charge before the ordinary time, would not be the last to present this new commer. He giues him a poysoned Handkercher, imbroydered with Gold and great round Pearles, the price thereof could not be easily valued: The new Gouernour receiues it with vnspeakable joy; for great men hold nothing so sweet in their places, as to take whencesoeuer it comes; but God doth many times suffer that such greedy Takers, are taken in taking, as it happened to this *Bassa* of *Aleppo*: The Handkercher of price, which was the price of his life, contents him: Hee admires the worke, lookes vpon the great Pearles, and his hands doe not abandon it, vntill the poyson forced him; the which exhaling and infecting the *Bassa*, they grew weake and make him to leaue it; whereupon hee died and left the gouernment which he had not enjoyed: The other *Bassa* flies speedily to *Constantinople*, redemands the gouernment, whereof he had beene dispossest, and grounds his reason vpon his speedie obedience, and forceth the iniquity of the Fauourites to consent that hee should enjoy it. Thus couetousnesse had depriued him of a Dignity where it had first placed him, and poysoning restores him: Whereby wee may Iudge what these Gouernours can be that are setled by such meanes. It is certaine that the like offences are committed daily in the Turkes Court by the *Bassa's* thereof, who imploy their greatest care, to find out the most subtillest poysons, and how to employ them cunningly one against another. The most ordinary which they vse is drawne from Toads: They cause a Toade to sucke the Milke of a woman that hath an extraordinary red haire: When it is full they beate it gently with a little wand, they put it into choler, its poyson mingles with this Milke, and it bursts in its rage; this poyson is so violent and strong, that in rubbing only the stirrop of his horse

Y whom

Mustapha Bassa intreated in the time of Selym the first, Father to great Solyman. This Prince hauing vanquished the Soppy of Persia, & triumphed in Tauris, the chiefe Citie of that Realme, was forced to leaue it, when as he saw his souldiers inclined to mutinie, saying plainly that they had rather lose all, then to spend the Winter in Persia. This Deniall was very sensible, & he thought to be reuenged on those whom hee should find to be the Motiues: they perswade him that Mustapha Bassa, who had credit among the Footmen, had induced them to Mutinie; hee discharged his choler vpon him, and seeing him on horsebacke, he sent to cut his crouper by a Iester which followed him: The Bassa perceiued it, and the disgrace which he receiued, made him to end his dayes in the midst of the cares and griefe, which a man of his qualitie doth feele, when he thinkes he hath lost the reputation, which made him to liue gloriously in the World and Court.

The infamy of this affront comes not alone; it hath for a companion, the disaster of a shamefull punishment, which the great men of the Port or Sultans Court receiue, when hee holds him guilty of some small crime: When he hath caused the Crouper of some of their horses to be cut, he doth likewise cause others to be whipt by his slaues: as it happened in the time of Amurath the Second, to the Aga or Colonell of the Ianizaries or Turkish foot, who being conuicted to haue brought in some Hirelings at the Muster, the Emperour caused him to be taken and whipt. But this punishment is not so insupportable vnto them, as the affront of cutting the Crouper, as if the Leather of the Harnesse of their Horse, were more sensible vnto them than their skins: So much a false opinion doth deceiue them, as they hold that a disgrace which is not, and are not troubled for that which should be most sensible vnto them. An example, which teacheth, that most things which disquiet the mind of man, are vaine, and forged in a depraued imagination. For it is more easie to suffer a hundred Croupers to be cut, than to endure fifty lashes with a whip vpon the body. But such are the affronts & punishments which follow the greatnes of the Turkish Court, in the person of their Bassa's.

CHAP.

Nimio otio ingenia, natura infirma, & muliebria, inopia vera iniuria lasciuientia, bis mouentur, quorum pars maior constat vitio interpretantis, Senec. lib. *In sapientem virum non cadere iniuriam.*

tuses, destinated to so damnable an vse is not small: the Eunuches which haue them in guard are alwayes neere them, to beautifie them outwardly, they plaite their haire with Gold, and sometimes with Pearles, they perfume them, they attire them in Robes of Cloth of Gold, and adde to their naturall beauty whatsoeuer Arte can inuent: what vertue, what wisdome, what pietie can be found in a Court composed of such men? He that is the Head and commands them, doth furnish this pernicious example; for the *Sultans Serrail* is full of such Boyes, chosen out of the most beautifull of the East, and vowed to his vnnaturall pleasures: This doth countenance this disorder and corruption in the *Othoman* Court: Such as the Prince is, such are most commonly the Courtiers which follow him: the principall Maxime which they giue for a precept to their fortune, is to follow the humours and manners of the Prince, whatsoeuer they be, yea, many times they incite the Prince to these disorders. The miseries and diasters which happen daily in Turkey, are too many to be couch't in this Historie. The great Men kill or poyson one another for such subjects, Families are in combustion, Wiues make away their Husbands, and Husbands their Wiues. *Mahomet* the second Emperour of the Turkes, was stabde in the thigh, and if any misfortune seeme monstrous among them, this vice which is so monstrous doth produce it: Men well bred abhorre it, Heauen detests it: When it was borne vpon the Earth, Idolatry was her sister Twinne. So being the auersion of Nature and the contempt of the Author thereof, Heauen doth punish it, and casts forth the fire of his wrath vpon those which are polluted therewith; whole Townes haue been consumed, men eternally lost, and the memory of the one and the other in execration vpon the Earth. The Turkes doe not punish it; they alleage, as wee haue obserued in the History of their Religion, that God hath reserued the chastisement to himselfe; and they bring an example of a miserable wretch who had abused a young Boy which stab'd him. This Sodomite being thus slaine, *Mahomet* their Prophet sent his Kinsmen to open his Tombe, and see how many wounds he had;

Sodomia & idolatria simul inceperunt simul creuerunt, D. Tho. 4. sent. dist. 1. q. 2. a. t. 1

they

they came and saw no body, but found in the place a blacke and smoakie stocke. Hence they say, that seeing the diuine Iustice doth punish those that are culpable of this offence, they must leaue the execution to him, and in the meane time suffer this vnnaturall excesse to any. The Turkish Ladies detesting these damnable affections of their husbands, haue also abandoned themselues by their example or for reuenge, to another disorder: the following Chapter will shew it. For the husbands are many times the cause of the losse of their wiues; and the contagious example of their vices, giues them occasion to ill, and to faile in their faith to him, who had first broken it.

Chap. XV.

Of the Loues of the great Ladies of the Turkes *Court, and of their violent affections among themselues.*

THe prouocations of a hot Climate, the seruitude of women restrained, and the bad example of loose and luxurious husbands, are the principall Motiues of the loues, whereunto the Turkish Ladies abandon themselues. Some to haue free exercise, take occasion to see their Louers, when as they are allowed to goe to the Bath, to receiue the Purifications which their Law doth enjoyne them: others better qualified, from whom the commoditie of Waters and Stoues which are in their houses, hath taken away this pretext, make vse of other men. Sometimes they borrow the habit of their slaues, and thus disguised goe to find them they loue: When this course is difficult, by the encounter of some great obstacle, they imploy men and women (whom they reward) to find them subjects which may please their eyes, and content their passions; but this last meanes is more apparent and better knowne in *Constantinople*: for such Messengers of loue discouering themselues to some that refuse them, they diuulge

their

their secret. They addresse themselues vsually to Christian strangers of the West, and if they can finde Frenchmen, the seruice they doe vnto their Mistresses is the more pleasing: The disposition of their humours, the grace of their bodies (say they) and the ordinary courtesie of their Nation, makes them more desired: But it is dangerous to serue the passions of such Louers, where the recompence and the reward of a painfull loue, is a Dagger or a Glasse of poyson: For these cruell women, when they haue kept some young stranger three or foure dayes hidden in their Chambers, and haue made vse of him vntill he be so tired and weary with their lasciuiousnesse, as hee is no longer profitable, they stab him or poyson him, and cast his bodie into some Priuie: Whether it be that they feare their affections should be discouered, or that their light and inconstant humours, doth alwayes demand new subjects, or that it is the nature of their lasciuious loue, to change into Rage and Fury tragically cruell. They which are aduertised at *Constantinople*, auoid this danger, and reward their pains which speake vnto them with a flat deniall, but not without danger: For such Messengers aswell as the great ones that imploy them are Witches, and reuenge a deniall vpon the person of him that made it, as it happened of late yeares to a French Gentleman, which was at *Constantinople*, when as the Baron *Sancy* did serue the King there as his Embassadour: This Gentleman going to the *Diuan*, which is the publique Audience of the *Serrail*, was encountred by a woman, whose age, habit and discourse did shew plainly that shee did pleasures for the Turkish Ladies: Shee came vnto him and vsed these words: Hast thou the courage to see a faire Lady, which is in loue with thee? He who knew well with what Merrils such Ladies are accustomed to crowne their Louers which haue serued them, excuseth himselfe for that time, pretending some important businesse which drew him to the *Serrail*: But he promiseth at his returne to content her desires, intreating her to attend at the passage. In the meane time he goes to the *Serrail*, followes his businesse, and hauing dispatched it, returnes to his Lodging another way, and leauing the woman in in the impatiencie of a deceitfull attendance, she saw her selfe in the end deceiued by this Frenchman: who to reuenge this affront, had recourse to her Witchcrafts, and imployes them against him: They worke their effect, and this Frenchman found himselfe suddainly seized with a kind of Palsey: The sicke man tooke his bed, and was continually afflicted with sensible paines and convulsions. The Physicians were called to his help, but all their lerning could not find out the cause of his infirmitie, nor prescribe a remedie: Some dayes past in these extremities, after which an old Turkish woman offers to cure him; she visits him, and hauing looked vpon him, she told him in her gibbridge: I will soon cure you: But tell the truth, haue you not refused some Lady that sought your loue? By her Charmes she expelled those which tormented him, and restored him to health: After which, this man going in *Constantinople*, hee encountred a woman which told him in his eare; Remember another time not to abuse the courtesie of Women which affect you, and deceiue them no more by your vaine promises.

All the women of Turkey, and especially those of *Constantinople*, doe not tie their affections to men only, they grow passionately in loue one with another, and giue themselues to false and vnlawfull loue, especially the wiues of men of quality, who liue coopt vp in *Serrails*, vnder the guard of Eunuches. This vitious appetite doth domineere ouer them so tyrannously, as it smothers in them the desires of a naturall and lawfull loue, and many times causeth them to loathe their husbands. This disorder may grow for that their affection wanting a lawfull prize, they tie it to a strange object: Moreouer, the reuenge of the vnnaturall loue to their husbands, carries them vnto it; for most men of those Easterne parts, and the greatest are giuen to that beastly and brutish lasciuiousnesse. These Ladies loue one another most ardently, and come to the effects of their foolish loues, they imbrace one another, and doe other actions which loue seekes, and modestie forbids to write. They whom this strange loue makes slaues to others, goe to finde them in the Bath to see them naked,

ked, and entertayning them vpon the subject whereof they languish, make such like discourses in their Language: *They had reason to say that the Sun did plunge it selfe in the waues, seeing that you are in this water, the which by Nature should quench the fire, but it kindles my flames when you are in it. Is it possible that you should receiue to the enioying of so rare a beauty, other persons than those of your owne sexe, which are like your selfe? Fly the imbracings of Men, which contemne vs; and haue no loue but for their like, and enioy with vs the Contentments which they deserue not.* When as a foolish womanish Louer, hath made such like discourses, shee goes into the Bath, and burnes with a flame which it is not able to quench, she imbraces her Louer, kisseth her, and attempts to doe that (although in vaine) which I must heere conceale: And these loues of woman to woman are so frequent in the *Leuant*, as when any Turks are resolued to marrie, the chiefe thing which they inquire of, is whether the party whom they affect be not subject to some woman whom they loue, or is beloued. Thus these people liue farre from the light of true Faith, in the darknesse of *Mahometan* ignorance, which haue carried them to the excesse of all sorts of vices.

Chap. XVI.

Of the foure principall Bassa's *of the Port.*

THe foure chiefe *Bassa's* of the Port, and the foure prime Wheeles, which mooue this vast and powerfull Turkish Empire are the *Vizir Azem* or the *Grand Vizir*, the Captaine of the Sea, the *Aga* of the *Ianizaries*, and the Captaine of *Constantinople*, called the Captaine *Bassa*: Their places are the chiefe of the Empire, and the glory thereof giues them respect with the Prince, to be honoured by great Men, and feared by the people. The *Vizir Azem*, or *Grand Vizir* holds the first place next vnto his Master, he is Lieutenant Generall of the Empire, and Armies, high Chancellor and chiefe of

the

the *Diuan*, which is the Councell where Iustice is administred; the Captaine of the Sea is high Admirall, and Generall of Nauall Armies. The *Aga* of the *Ianizaries* commands all the Turkish foot, as sole Colonell thereof. And the Captaine of *Constantinople* gouernes the Citie, and takes knowledge of the chiefe affaires which passe. These foure *Bassa's* differing in Offices and Honours are notwithstanding powerfull in authoritie, the which is of such weight, as they giue and take the Crown from their Soueraigne Prince when they thinke good. We haue seene the experience of late yeares, in the persons of *Sultan Mustapha*, and *Osman*: *Achmat* ended his life and Raigne in the yeare 1617, hee left two young sonnes; *Osman* and *Amurath*: He knew by experience that the weight of such a Crowne could not be borne by a Childe, and that the absolute gouernment of the Turkish Monarchie required a man: He called to the succession of his Scepter, his brother *Mustapha* who had beene fourteene yeares a Prisoner in his *Serrail*, and made him to taste this sweet change, to come from a Dungeon to a Throne, and from the fetters of a tedious captiuitie, to that power to command the greatest Estate vpon the Earth. But the great rigour of his command, and the extrauagances of his inconstant humour, made him odious to the Captaine *Bassa*; he gained the other three, who drew the Souldiers and some great men vnto their party, they vnthroned him, put him into his Prison, and set vp *Osman* sonne to his brother *Achmat*. This example was in our dayes: but that which followeth is so fresh, as the newes hereof came when I was labouring about this worke. *Osman* not well satisfied with the affection of the *Ianizaries*, (who are the sinewes of his Estate) and disliking some of the foure *Bassa's*, had an intent to change the Seat of his Empire to *Caire*, and to abandon *Constantinople*; he prepares himselfe, gathers together as much Treasure as hee could, and couers his designe, with the pretext of a Pilgrimage to *Maque*, where he said his intent was to accomplish a vow, and to make as great a gift as euer Prince made vnto a Temple of what Religion soeuer. When as he had mannaged his enterprize vnto the day of his

de-

departure, when as his Galleyes were readie, and the *Bassa* of *Caire* come with an Armie to receiue him; the *Ianizaries* were aduertised, they runne to the *Serrail* with the consent of the *Aga*, the people are moued, the Captaine *Bassa* stirres them vp, they take the *Sultan* in his Chamber, kill some great Men in his presence, dragge him into a prison, and there make him to suffer a shamefull death by the hands of an Executioner, hauing drawne *Mustapha* his Vncle out of Prison again, and crowned him the second time Soueraigne *Sultan* of the Turkish Empire. That which is here set downe for true proofs of the authoritie and power of these foure great *Bassa's*. They are not alone in greatnesse, although that no man doth equall them in all the *Othoman* Court; There are two *Beglierbeys* (that is to say Lord of Lords) the one of *Romania* or *Greece*, the other of *Natolia* or *Asia* the lesse. The *Nissanzi Bassa* or ordinary Chancellour, who signes all the Dispatches of the Court; three *Testardars* which are the high Treasurers, thorough whose hands the Reuenewes of the Empire doth passe. The *Rais Kintap*, whose charge is to keepe the Books, Papers and Records of the Empire. Besides these there are many others of lesse consideration. Doubtlesse, as Whales are in the vast and deepe Seas; so great and eminent Dignities are in great Empires, and those of Turkey make those which enjoy them to seeme like so many pettie Kings about the person of a great Monarch.

Chap. XVII.

Of the Tymar, Tymarriots and Pensioners of the Port.

THe Turkes giue two sorts of pay to their Souldiers; the one is called in their Language *Vlefe*, which is payed daily by the Treasurers of the warre; and is the entertainment of ordinary Souldiers: The other is called *Tymar*, or pension assigned vpon Houses, Lands, or whole Burroughes; this is

Z   not

not giuen but to men, who by their valour haue done some notable seruice to the Prince, and deserued well of the publique: These Pensions are honourable, the recompence of their vertue, and the marke of their merit. It seemes that the Turkes haue borrowed the name of this recompence from the *Gracians*, who called it *Tymarion*, and *Tipi*, which signifies Honour. Such Pensioners are called *Tymariots*, they are most commonly *Spahis* and Horsemen, who enjoy the honour and profit of such Pensions taken out of the Lands in Turkey which belonging all vnto the Prince, by the rights of Soueraigne Master of the persons of all his Subjects, who are his slaues, he giues them to such as haue made themselues worthy by their good Seruice; as they doe with vs the Commanders of Military Order, or the Fees or Lands which the Princes haue instituted in our Countries to honour Gentlemen of merit, and to binde them to serue them vpon all occasions. It is true that the continuance of such fees, doth farre exceed that of the *Tymar*, for they passe vnto their Successors, and this is temporall, and no man is suffered to enioy it any longer than it shall please the giuer. If the *Spahi* be not in his Equipage fit for a Souldier, if hee doth not serue with that care and diligence as hee ought, the Iudges which the *Sultan* appoints to visit the *Tymar*, depriue him, and recompence another that may serue better, so the *Tymarriots*, or Pensioners of the Turks Court, are not vnprofitable mouthes, as in other places; there the credit of an insolent Fauourite, cannot take them from vertue, to giue them to the idlenesse of some one of those which follow him, and idolatrize the greatnesse of his fortune.

Chap. XVIII.

Of the Grand Seignevrs *Fauourites aduanced to the greatnesse of the Empire, and of their fall.*

FEw Kings haue beene without Fauourites; and what reason were it to debarre the most eminent among men from
that

Court of the Grand SEIGNEVR.

that which is allowed to the most abject, that is to loue one man aboue all others, and to honour him with the effects of their friendship, by honours and greatnesse, whereof they are the Masters and absolute Disposers? Doubtlesse the Soueraigne of Kings, who came into the World to teach both Men and Kings perfection, hath not denied them this libertie, when as he himselfe gaue them an example, louing and fauouring aboue the small number of men which were in his Ordinary Court, him whom hee thought most worthy of his fauours. But few Fauourites haue beene without insolencie, whether it be that most Princes are not much carefull to make choice of men, whose vertues haue made them worthy of their friendship; or that the nature of fauour and honour which follow them, be such, as it blinds their vnderstanding, and puffes vp their spirits with pride. This History hauing taken for its principall Subject, the Court of the *Othoman* Monarches, it shall seeke no farther for examples of this truth.

Iesus Christ had Saint Iohn the Euangelist for his Fauourite.

Hibraim Bassa Fauourite to *Solyman* the Second, had attained to the height of greatnesse which hee enjoyed by such degrees. He was a Christian, borne of a very base extraction: at the age of seuen or eight yeeres, they which exact the tribute of Christians Children, tooke him from his Fathers house, and conducted him with a troupe of other young slaues to *Constantinople*: At his arriuall he was giuen vnto a *Bassa*, who caused him to be bred vp carefully, and soone after presented him to *Solyman*; This Prince to whom *Hibraim* was equall in age, tooke him into his affection, his seruice was alwayes more pleasing vnto him, than that of the other slaues: He honoured him with the charge of *Capiaga*, who is Captaine of the Gate of the inner *Serrail*: From this place hee came to that of *Aga* or Colonell of the *Ianizaries*: Then the example of some great Men of the *Othoman* Court, ruined by the inconstancie of Fortune, gaue vnto his spirit the first apprehensions which the great Dignities of the Court giues vnto Fauourites which enjoy them, and serued as a bridle to restraine his passion: hee besought *Solyman* not to aduance his fortune so high as he might fall with the greater ruine: Hee

Hibraim fauourite to Solyman

Z 3   shewed

shewed him that a meane prosperitie, was more safe than all the greatnesse, wherewith he would honour him: That his seruices should be sufficiently rewarded, if hee gaue him wherewith to spend his dayes in rest, farre from the necessities of life. *Solyman* commended his modestie, and meaning to aduance him to the chiefe Dignities of his Empire, he sware vnto him neuer to put him to death whilst he liued, what change soeuer should happen in his Court. But the condition of Kings which is humane, and subject to change, and that of Fauourites which is proud, and vnthankfull, shall cause *Solyman* to faile of his promise, and *Hibraim* of his faith and loyaltie, as wee shall see. In the meane time this Fauourite becomes a *Bassa*, and soone after *Grand Vizir*, and Lieutenant Generall of his Masters Empire; his credit, his traine, his wealth, and the pompe of his greatnesse, teach euery man that hee is the Arbitrator of Turkey. But his fortune is too great to be without Enuie; and it seemes vnreasonable, that the highest trees which are on the tops of the highest Mountaines, should be free from the violence of the windes: The Princesse Mother to *Solyman*, and *Roxillana* his wife, the best beloued of his *Sultana's*, enuie the credit of *Hibraim*, and his vnlimited authoritie is insupportable vnto them: They practize his ruine, and imploy all their power both within and without the *Serrail*, to dispossesse him: he finds it, and judging that the affections of a Mother and a Sonne are so naturall, and the loue of a Wife and a Husband so strong, as there is not any fortune nor fauour in Court, which should not feare the encounter, he resolues to draw his Master out of *Constantinople*, and to remooue him from the imbracings of the one and the conuersation of the other, and from the perswasions of them both. To effect it with the more pretext, he propounds the designe of the Warre of *Persia*, and being in Counsell with three or foure *Bassa's*, he perswades *Solyman* in this manner. Sir, Great Kings must haue great designes: Their principall office is not only to preserue the estate which their Ancestors haue left them, but also to inlarge it and to extend the limits; the Sword wherewith the *Mufti* did gird

Velut arbitrum regni agebat, ferebaturq, digredient eo, magna prosequentium multitudine, saith *Tacitus* in the 13. Booke of Annals, speaking of *Pollus* a freed Man to *Claudius* and his Fauourite.

your

your Greatnesse, on the day of your Coronation, is not so much a signe of your Soueraigne power, as that you are bound to maintain and defend the truth of our Alcoran, and to publish its beliefe farre: The *Porsian* hath alwayes beene an Enemy to your Estate and Religion, and their Kings haue not had any stronger passion, then to see the ruines of the one and the other: The Historie of the Warres which our Predecessors haue had against them doth furnish many examples; now you may be reuenged of their insolencie, and lay at your feet these ancient Enemies of Turkey. *Tachmas* who is their King, is a man without valour and experience, his people are yet in necessitie, being the remainders of the warres past: Your Empire is flourishing, you are borne to great matters, and to you alone the destinies haue reserued the glory of an absolute triumph ouer the *Persians:* Heauen doth promise it, Honour binds you, the weaknesse of your Enemy inuites you, your Treasures and a great number of fighting men, which attend your Commandements in Armes, furnish you with meanes. Goe, goe, then great Prince, adde vnto your Crownes that of the Realme of *Persia*, and to the Bayes which your valour hath gathered in *Hungarie* and at *Rhodes*, the Palme to haue subdued *Persia*, and to haue tamed the most troublesome of all your Enemies. To these perswasions hee added a tricke of his Trade. In *Damas* the chiefe Citie of the East, there liued an excellent Magician, called *Mule Aral*, he drawes him to *Constantinople*, and makes vse of his Predictions to further his designes; he speakes with him, and hauing taught him what to say, hee brings him to *Solyman*. This Sorcerer foretold the *Sultan*, that hee should take the principall Places of *Persia*, and should be crowned King of that Realme: All this makes him resolue to goe to horsebacke, and the warre was concluded: The teares of the Mother, nor the sweet kisses of the Wife, could not frustrate this designe: These poore *Sultana's* see the order of the Estate ouerthrowne by a Fauourite, and their persons contemned by *Hibraim*, who carried him from them, and drew him farre from their just jealousies; but the mine, into the which insolencie dragges it selfe, is ineuitable.

Hi-

Hibraim by this retiring, deferrs his losse, but doth not auoid it; hee shall returne from the warre of *Persia* to dye in *Constantinople* strangled with a Halter: The sequell of the historie will tell vs. In the meane time *Solyman* departs, with aboue six hundred thousand men, most Souldiers: *Hibraim* goes before to make the way with a powerfull Armie, he passeth at *Aleppo*, and fortifies it: From thence he goes to *Carahemide* a Towne vpon the Frontiers of *Mesopotamia* or *Dierbetch*, built vpon a strong situation: *Vlama* a great Noble-man of *Persia* commanded therein: his qualitie and valour had bound *Solyman* to make him gouernour; hee had formerly married the Sister of *Scach Tachmas*, sonne to *Ismaell Sophi*, and then King of *Persia*, who discontented for some disgrace in Court left *Persia*, and came to serue the Turke. *Hibraim* gaue him thirtie thousand men, and sent him before to discouer the Enemies countrie. *Vlama* who knew the language and the countrie, approached neere vnto *Tauris*, whereas *Sultan Musa* a neere kinsman to the King commanded: Being aduertised of the approach of the Turkish Troupes, and finding himselfe too weake to attend them, abandons the Citie: *Vlama* enters and takes it: *Hibraim* who followed him neere came speedily, fortifies it, and in a new citadell which he caused to be made, hee placed three hundred and fiftie peeces of Ordinance, and sent to aduertise *Solyman* of this good successe. Neuer fauorite held himselfe so happie, nor so powerfull ouer the enuie of his Enemies: But he shall finde his misreckoning. *Solyman* aduanceth, comes to *Tauris*, and stayes three weekes, to see if *Tachmas* had any will to come and encounter him. But hee had neither power nor will. Hee was retired into the Mountaines, expecting greater forces than his owne, that is to say, that hunger and the necessitie of all things, with the rigour of winter, might force his Enemie to retire: They followed soone after: the Northern winds, the Snow, Frost, and want of victualls forced *Solyman* to take his way to *Curdistan*, which is *Assyria*, hauing left thirtie two thousand men in Garrison within *Tauris*, vnder the command of *Ulama*, of *Iadigiarberg* and *Siruan Ogly*. *Tachmas* who

was

was watchfull seeing the Turkish Army farre from *Tauris*, approcheth with ten thousand men: The Garrison go forth to encounter him and charge him; but *Iadigiarberg* a notable Coward, growing amazed fled, and put all the rest in disorder, and gaue the aduantage to *Tachmas*, who recouered *Tauris*, and brought a notable change, causing the three hundred and fifty Cannons which were in the Citadell to be moulten, whereof he made *Manguris*, which is a Coine of *Persia*, and so that which was the terrour of his people, became the delights of their affections: *Solyman* in the meane time conquered *Curdistan*, and *Baggadet*; he tooke *Babylon*, where he was crowned King of *Assyria* by the *Caliphe*, but not of *Persia*, as the Magitian had promised him. Winter was now spent, and the Spring approached: *Ulama* and *Hibraim* perswaded *Solyman* to returne to *Tauris*, to punish the rashnesse of *Tachmas*: He returnes with his Army, and being within few dayes march, *Tachmas* abandons the City and retires, burning and razing whatsoeuer he found in the way, to stay his Enemy from following: The Turkes re-enter *Tauris* and their rage puts all they find to fire and sword, not sparing senceleffe things; the stately Pallaces became the subject of their furie, and the Citie was the pittifull remainder of a sacke and a cruell spoyle. *Solyman* retires, giuing order that his chiefe forces should be in the Reare, lest the enemy should follow and charge them behinde. *Tachmas* was wonderfully discontented, to see this fearefull spoile in his Country, and in the Capitall Citie of his Realme, and could haue no reuenge; when as one of his *Satrapes*, or Gouernours, a *Caramanian* by Nation and the most resolute man in his Court, sirnamed *Deliment*, for his courage, (that is to say Foole) offered himselfe, and promiseth (so as hee would giue him troupes) to follow the Enemie and to ouertake him, and when hee should thinke least of it, to make him pay for the spoile which he had made in *Persia*. *Tachmas* grants what he demands; *Deliment* goes his way, he runs or rather flies towards the place where the Enemie was: His Spies bring him word, that the Turkes were camped neere vnto *Bethlis*, tyred

with long marches, and with the toile of a troublesome way; that they slept without Guards, without watch, and without any Sentinels, so as it would be easie for him to surprize them, if he would make his troupes to double their pace: *Deliment* makes more speed than they requi ed, hee drawes neere vnto the Turkes at the shutting vp of the day, and in the night goes to surprize them, inuirons them, chargeth them, beats them, kils the greatest part, and takes the rest prisoners, few escaping by flight. *Solyman* vnderstood the next day of the losse of his men, and seeing the small troupes he had remayning, findes foure hundred thousand men wanting, of those which followed him from *Constantinople*, the which were dead in *Persia*, either slaine by the Sword, or famished with hunger, or frozen with colde, the which made him returne towardes his *Serrail*. He comes to *Aleppo*, and soone after to *Constantinople*, and detests in his soule, the Counsellour of this Voyage and the Warre of *Persia*: The *Sultana's* finde at his returne, an ample subject to ruine *Hibraims* fortune; and to be reuenged of the presumption hee had vsed against them. They obserue the murmuring of the people against this Fauourite, and what the great men spake of him, and make it knowne to *Solyman*. Moreouer, as they were busie to ruine his greatnesse, they discouer that this *Bassa* fauoured the House of *Austria*, and that he had secret intelligence with the Emperor *Charles* the Fift, an Enemy to his Master: This treachery being auerred, it did wholy ouerthrow that which the *Sultana's* had already shaken. *Solyman* to whom they had made knowne the truth of all this, concludes his death; but the promise and oath which he had made vnto him not to put him to death whilest hee were aliue, suspends the execution vntill hee might find a Dispensation by the aduice and authoritie of the chiefe Preists of his Law; hee takes counsell of the most Learned; one of the number giues him a pleasant *Expedit*, to free himselfe of the *Bassa*, and yet to keepe his word. You haue sworne, Sir, saith he, not to put him to death, whilest you are liuing; cause him to be strangled when you are asleepe: Life consists in a vigilant action, and he that sleepes doth not truly liue: so you
may

may punish his disloyaltie, and not violate your oath. Doubtlesse if *Solyman* were dead when hee slept, according to the saying of this *Talisman*, hee hath reuiued many times whilest he liued. This Prince seekes noe more, he contents himselfe, to haue found a Clergie man which absolues him for this deed: He sends for *Hibraim Bassa* to the *Serrail*, hee causeth him to supp with him, and supper being ended hee letts him see his crymes by his owne letters written to *Charles* the fift, and *Ferdinand* his brother; hee reproaches his ingratitude, and commands his dumbe men to strangle him whilest he slept, and thereupon went to Bed. Thus ended the life and greatnes of *Hibraim Bassa* fauorite to *Solyman*: For an example, that if the fortunes of the Court shine like gold, they breake like glasse. His Maister had aduanced him more then hee desired, fearing a fall in the beginning of his fortune, into the which he did precipitate himselfe by his disloyaltie: he supported the continuance of his greatnesse vpon his Princes Oath: But they were humane, and their nature is to haue no other stay, but the declining where they slide. A Courtiers fauour is neuer durable, if it hath not Iustice and Pietie for Companions, which makes them zealous towards God, and well deseruing of men : If these parts be found in a Fauourite, they make enuie to yeeld ; and impose silence to the bitterest slander. *Hibraim Bassa* had not these good qualities: his former seruices had deserued some share in his Masters affections ; but his pride against the *Sultana's*, and his treachery against *Solyman* made him vnworthy of that which he enjoyed. So the Lion of *Lybia* wipes out with her long taile the steps of her feet: the insolencie which followed, defaced all the good which went before. To enjoy the fauour of the Court, they must haue so strong and generous a spirit, as they must neuer suffer themselues to be transported with pride, nor dejected with amazement, but remayning in a commendable equality, continue couragiously in doing well.

Cuncta mortalium incerta; quanto plus adeptus foret tanto se magis in lubrico distitantis Tacit. li. 1. Annal. speaking of *Tiberius* who discoursed in in this manner to the Senate.

    The example of the fortune and disaster of *Hibraim Bassa* shall be followed in this History with that of the great credit, prosperities and disgraces of *Bassa Derneir*, a Fauourite to

Dernier Fauourite to Achmat

Ach-

Achmat the first, Brother to *Sultan Mustapha*, who raigned of late yeares. This man of a base condition laboured in the Gardens of the *Serrail*, when as hee began to enter into fauour: *Achmat* in his Garden-walkes, seeing his jouiall humour, tooke many times delight in his tales, stayed to see him worke, and in the end so affected him, as without knowledge of any other merit, he made him *Bostangibassi*, or great Gardiner; This charge (as we haue said) is one of the goodliest of the Turkish Empire, being then void by his death who had enioyed it: Therein *Dernier* serued with so great care, and made himselfe so pleasing to his Master, as he bound him to make him greater. The Generall of the Sea dies, and *Achmat* giues him the place: he doth it with that lustre and pompe which followes this dignitie; he causeth the Galleyes to be armed, goes to Sea, takes all he meets with, and sailes so happily as the inconstant windes seemed to fauour him, and the most inconstant Elements seeme to joy in the happinesse of this new Fauourite; his courses are fortunate, and his returne glorious: But the Sea of the Court more stormie than the Sea it selfe will one day teach him that it doth amaze the best Pilots, and will make him feele to his disgrace, a more troublesome shipwracke, than he could haue found vpon the waues of the *Leuant* Seas: The reception which hee found at his returne, and the triumph wherewith hee is honoured after the taking of many Christian Vessels, are felicities which flatter, and deceiuing him, make him imagine that happinesse it selfe did him homage. *Achmat* cherished him more than himselfe, and had no rest, vntill hee had aduanced him to the height of the prosperities of the Court: That is to say, to the Dignitie of *Grand Vizir*, Lieutenant Generall of his Empire: Soone after it fell void, and hee bestowed it on him, with these words of affection: There is not any thing in my Estate, how great soeuer it be, which thy vertues, and the affection thou bearest to my seruice, hath not well deserued. Thus *Dernier* became the first man of the Turks Court, and his Master was sorry, that hee could not make him the prime Man of the World. In this charge hee restored many
good

Nihil esse tam excelsum, quod non virtutes istæ, tuusq́; in me animus mereantur, Tacit. lib. 1. Annal. *Tiberius* spake so to *Seianus* his Fauourite, who demanded *Liuia* in Marriage.

good Lawes, which disorder had ouerthrowne; hee reduced euery man to his duty, strooke terrour into the Magistrates: and let the Souldiers know that they were vnworthy to make their Musters, and to receiue the pay, if they be not in case to serue. These things doubtlesse had crowned his name with new glory, if violence and crueltie had not blemisht him: He caused more men to be executed in one day, than his Predecessours had done in a whole yeare: The least suspition of a Crime was culpable of punishment, and this Fauourite made lesse acoount of the life of men, than of the Coleworts which hee had sometimes planted in the Gardens of the *Serrail*. But violence is neuer durable, and that Fauourite which followes it suffers himselfe to bee led to his owne ruine. *Hee that kils, shall be killed* (saith God) *hee that loues bloud shall perish in bloud*. Doubtlesse, it is a miserable thing in Princes Courts, and prejudiciall to a whole Estate, that a base fellow, and a man of nothing, without vertue or merit should be aduanced to the qualitie of a Fauourite; master the affections of his Soueraigne; and enjoy the prime Dignities of an Empire: For such persons are most commonly cruell; contemne the Nobilitie, and make no account of vertue, as being ignorant of the one and the other. *Dernier* in all these Offices had gathered together great treasures, the which with his extraordinary seueritie, furnish matter of Enuy to the other *Bassa's*, who all joyntly vndertake his ruine, and labour so carefully therein, as they find meanes to entertaine *Sultan Achmat*, with the insolencies of his carriage: he heares them, beleues part of that which they tell him, and growes so violently jealous of the credit and authoritie of *Dernier*, that he resolues to free himselfe of him; he concludes his death, and commands the execution to a troupe of the *Capigis* of his *Serrail*, who receiued commandement to strangle him, as soone as he should come: But hee will trouble them to performe it, they shall not finde in him a delicate fauorite, bred vp from his youth in the softnesse of the Court, he will defend his life couragiously, and let them see that a man, which hath long time handled a Spade and a Mattocke, is not soe easily mastered. *Achmat* sends for

A a 2 *Dernier*

Dernier to the *Serrail*; he comes and is scarce entred when he suspects the partie which was made against him; he goes into the *Grand Signeurs* quarter, being there, this troupe of *Capigis* fall vpon him to seaze on him, and to put the Halter about his necke; he frees himselfe from them, and stands vpon his defence although he had nothing in his hands, and with his fists scatters them brauely; hee beates one of their Noses flat, puts out the eye of another, and strikes out his teeth that held the Halter, and puts him out of breath which had taken hold of his Arme, and remaines free in the midst of al them which did inuiron him, and durst not take him: The feare of punishment which doth attend those which doe not speedily execute the will of the *Sultan* in such affaires, and the shame that one man alone disarmed should slay them all, aduised one of the troupe to fetch a Leauer, wherewith approaching to *Dernier*, he gaue him so great a blow as hee brake his thigh, and ouerthrew him; then they put the cord about his necke and strangled him. Thus hee ended his life, which gouerned the whole Turkish Empire, and strooke a terrour into the greatest: The iouiall humours and the humble discourses of the Gardiner, had raised him to the greatest fortune that a Courtier could find in all the world; and the insolencie and pride of the *Grand Vizir* had humbled him, and deliuered him to the mercie of a dozen Rascals which strangle him: For a new example, that fauour is not durable, if it hath not moderation for its companion, and Iustice and Piety to support it. His bodie is buried without pompe or honour, his treasure came vnto the *Sultan*, and his name was so forgotten, as in three dayes they did not know in Court if there had beene any such man. The which may serue for a lesson to great Men, which possesse their Princes, that the course of a boundlesse and proud fauour in Court is like the flight of a Bird in the Aire, the passage of a Ship at Sea, or the gliding of a Serpent vpon the Ronos, where there remaines no shew.

Nassuf Fauourite to Achmat This thing happened at *Constantinople* in the yeare 1606. But of a later date in the yeare 1614. *Nassuf Bassa*, of whom we haue formerly made mention, *Grand Vizir* of the Turkish Empire

Empire and fauorite to the same *Sultan Achmat*, gaue (by the fall of his fortune) as much amazement to the East, as his prosperities had giuen admiration: his riches were greater and his credite more absolute then the two former fauourites; but his extraction and Birth as base as theirs, and his pride equall. Hee was Sonne to a Greeke Priest, borne in a little Hamblet neere to *Salonica*. The Collectors of the tribute tooke him from his Fathers house in his infancie, and led him to *Constantinople*, where hee was sold for three Sultanins, (which is foure and twentie shillings of our sterling money) to an Eunuch of the *Serrail*, who bred him vp vnto the age of twentie yeeres. Then hee sold him to a steward of the *Sultana* Mother to *Achmat*, to serue him in his charge. This Man soone found in his slaue the eminent gifts of a free spirit, which is inlightned with dexteritie: and holding him fit for greater affaires then those of the houshold, wherein hee imployed him, hee gaue him the ouer-sight of the building of a rich and stately *Mosquee*, which the *Sultana* Mother caused to bee built at her charge, to bee an immortall marke of her pietie and magnificence. Hee prospered so well in this charge, and gaue so good proofes of his Iudgement, as hee gaue good content vnto the *Sultana*, and had such part in her liking and affection, as shee made him Superintendant of her house. In this Dignitie hee let the whole *Serrail* See, what an able and sufficient Man may doe when hee is imployed in affaires; his merite came vnto the knowledge of *Sultan Achmat*, who would haue him to his seruice. Thus hee changed Master, and mounted to a new Dignitie. *Achmat* gaue him the place of *Capigi-bassi*, soone after he made him *Bassa* of *Aleppo*, where hauing finished the time, which they giue to such Gouernors, they honoured him with the Dignitie of Gouernor Generall of *Mesopotamia*: hee passed from *Constantinople*, hauing the traine, attendance and pompe, of a Turkish Vice-roy. The commoditie of this Prouince, Frontier to *Persia*, filled his Cofers with treasure, and his Spirit with ambition. Hee knew that hee was very necessarie for his Master, he saw that the Neighbour-hood of the *Persian*, might by secret intel-

ligences

ligences with him bring him great wealth. This imagination flatters him, and his auarice followes him: hee abandons his fidelitie to the offers which the *Persian* King made him, and practiseth in secret with his Ministers, and fauoureth what hee can, the Enemy of his Soueraigne Prince. *Achmat* is aduertised, and louing him still with passion, dissembles his cryme and resolues to gaine him to himselfe, to dis-ingage him from the *Persian*, and to content his ambition with any thing hee could desire in his Empire. To this end hee sends for him to *Constantinople*, and at his ariuall gaue him the place of Grand *Vizir*, which *Serdar* had newly left, and with it the best and richest of this *Bassa's* spoyles. Moreouer he promised to giue him the *Sultana* his Daughter in Marriage. All these things are signes of the great bountie of *Achmat*, thus to honour a Traitor, who deserued rather a shamefull death, then the first dignitie of the Turkish Empire; they will in like sort be a testimonie of the ingratitude of the fauourite, who will abuse them. For an example that too indulgent a Prince to a notable Traitor, doth furnish him with meanes to do worse. *Nassuf* being now *Grand Vizir* & with assurance to be Sonne in law to his Master, goes to horse-backe, and in qualitie of Generall of an Armie, leads the forces of Turkey against the *Persian*, enters with them into his Countrie, makes a generall spoyle, and forceth *Ka Abbas*, who is King at this Day, to demaund a peace, and in the meane time grants him a truce for six Monethes. Hee parts from *Persia*, leading with him the Embassadour of *Ka Abbas*, hee comes to *Constantinople*, enters in pompe, hee is receiued not onely as the vanquisher of *Persia*, but as the restorer of the *Othoman* estate. The custome of Turkey binds the *Bassa's* when they returne from their gouernments, and the Generals of Armies from the Warre, to make a present vnto the *Sultan*. *Nassuf* at his comming exceedes the magnificence of all the Presents that euer entred into the *Serrail*, since the Turkes estate was setled; for besides a thousand rarities which hee brought from *Persia*, to the Sultan his Master; he presented him with a Million of Gold coyned, and within few dayes

after

after married his Daughter. This is the ascent and height of his fortune: Behold the descent. Achmat saw that Nassuf exceeded the ordinary of all the other Vizirs which had serued him, that his treasure did equall his, if not exceed it: He conceiued a jealousie (abundance of riches is many times criminall and offensiue to Princes) and growes into distrust of his actions. The Bassa's hauing some vent thereof by some of the Aguilaris, Eunuches of the Chamber, labour to informe him of the carriage of Nassuf: The Bassa of Babylon knew more than any Man, they cause him to come to Constantinople, and obtained secret audience for him: This Man did plainly discouer vnto the Sultan, that the Bassa Nassuf betrayed him, for the which hee drew great Pensions from the Persian, to whom hee wrote the secrets of his most important affaires. Achmat well informed of the disloyalties of his Fauourite, resolues not to leaue them vnpunished, and presently concludes his death: He giues the charge to the Bostangibassi, which is the great Gardiner: Nassuf is aduertized by the Sultana, which was most fauoured, being his Pensioner, that Achmat was much discontented with him: This amazeth him, hee faines himselfe sicke, and keepes his bed; the Bostangibassi comes to his Lodging, and demands to speake with him in the Sultans name, hee excused himselfe vpon the discommoditie of a violent purgation which troubled him: The Bostangibassi presses it, and tels him that hee would not returne vntill hee had spoken with him; that the Sultan had commanded him to see him, in what estate he was, & to learn from himself the newes of his health. Then Nassuf commanded they should suffer him to come: There the Bostangibassi complements with him concerning his indisposition, and assured him that he should be soone cured: he might boldly speake it, seeing hee carried the remedie in his pocket. After such like discourses of courtesie, he drew out of his pocket a commandement from the Sultan written to Nassuf, to send him the Seales of his Empire. Nassuf obeyeth, causeth them to be brought vnto his bed, wraps them in his Handkercher, seales them with his owne Seale, and giuing them to the

Auri vim atque opes principibus infensas esse, said *Sosibius* Gouernour to *Britannicus* in *Tacit. lib. 11. Annal.*

the *Bostangibassi* kisses them, and intreats him to assure his Master, that he had kept them faithfully, and had neuer sealed any thing which was against his seruice: Then hee thought that the discontentment whereof the *Sultana* aduertized him, would haue no other sequell but to depriue him of his charge, which they call in this Court to be made *Mansul*, and that by the helpe of his friends and the force of money, hee might be restored in a short time. His misreckoning was not farre off; the *Bostangibassi*, being now in possession of the Seales of the Empire, drew forth another Commandement to *Nassuf* from the same *Sultan*; to send him his head: Then *Nassuf* cried out, calling Heauen and Earth to witnesse of his innocencie; he desired to speake with the *Sultan*; and intreats the *Bostangibassi* to conduct him; he excuses himselfe, that he had no other charge but to see him strangled by ten or twelue *Capigis* which attended him: Vpon this refusall he contested long; but seeing to deferre his end, was but to prolong his distemperature and griefe, he resolues to die, only hee demands of the great Gardiner to suffer him to goe and wash himselfe in a Chamber neere by, to depart this World in the estate of puritie, according to the Turks beliefe, which hold the washing of the body for the purification of the soule: This grace also was denied him. Then he abandons his life to the *Capigis* who were about his bed: they put a cord about his necke, and not able to strangle him so speedily as they desired by reason of his extraordinary fatnesse, one of them drew a Knife out of his pocket, and cut his throat. *Achmat* would see him dead, to be the better assured; and then appointed his buriall among the common people without any honour. Such was the fortune of *Bassa Nassuf* and such his fall: His good wit had raised him to these great Dignities of his Empire, and his pride cast him downe, hauing long enjoyed the fauour of his Master, and made no good vse of it: His riches equall to his fortune were extraordinary; the Officers of the treasure, which were imployed to take an Inuentory of his goods, found in his Cofers in Sultanins, (which is a Coyne of Gold) fiue hundred thousand pounds sterling, in Siluer coyned three hundred and

Tacitus in the fourth Booke of his Annals, speakes as much of Suilius in these words, Quem vidit sequens ætas præpotentem venalem & Claudij Principis amicitia diu prosperè, nunquam bene

and eight thousand pounds sterling, the quantitie of three bushels of precious Stones not yet wrought, a bushell of Diamonds not set, and two bushels of goodly round Pearles. His Armory was furnished with aboue a thousand rich Swords, whereof the least had the Hilt and Pomell of siluer, and amidst this number there was one all set with Diamonds, valued at twentie thousand pounds sterling money: The Chambers of his Lodging and his Wardrobe, were richly hanged with Tapestry of *Persia* and *Caire*: Many rich stuffes of silke and gold excellently wrought, did augment the quantity of his precious Moueables: In his Stables were found aboue a thousand great Horses of price, foure hundred and fortie Mares of *Arabia* and *Egypt*, as beautiful as any Painter could represent, with all there were many thousand Camels and Moiles for his Baggage when hee trauelled: In his base Courts they numbred a hundred thousand Oxen, Kine, and Sheepe: the number of his slaues exceeded foure thousand. With this great wealth he might haue done great good, if he had had a friend to giue him good counsel (but great prosperities haue not any) who might haue contained him by wise aduice, within the limits of his dutie. Thus the fauours and pomps of the Court passe away. Those of Turkey, culpable of the least crymes, yea those which are innocent are of no longer continuance. For if the Court in what place soeuer, bee a Sea full of waues, that of the *Ottoman* is alwayes beaten with stormes, and tost with Tempests: The winds of the *Sultana's* passions, which are most cherished by the Prince, the couetous desires of the Eunuches which serue him, and are his familiars, banish the calme, and are the cause of such like shipwrackes, if they doe not pacifie the greedinesse of the one, in glutting them with presents, and the auarice of the other by great pensions. And although they take this course most commonly, yet notwithstanding they are oftentimes allarmed, suffer troublesome apprehensions, and liue alwayes in feare and disquietnesse. To teach men, which admire and adore the lustre of such fortunes that their perfectest ioyes are fruitfull in sorrowes: And when they thinke to make their Paradice in this World, then they carry their Hell with them. B b CHAP.

Chap. XIX.

Of the Grand Seigneurs *Armes and Seales.*

THe Turkes who esteeme vertue by its price, haue no Armes, nor Sirnames: The Lawes established and seuerely obserued among them, which haue made them so powerfull vpon earth, would thus banish out of Turkey (although somewhat preposterously) this subject of vanity in Families, and force men rather to support their glory vpon their owne merit, than in the vertue of their Ancestors which is not theirs: For this cause in their Monarchy, the sonne of a great *Bassa*, is lesse esteemed than he of a *Waterman*, if he hath lesse vertue: All the aduantage hee can challenge, to be borne of vertuous Parents, is to tearme himselfe their sonne. As for example, *Mustapha* the sonne of *Siruan*, shall be called *Sirnanogli*, that is to say, the sonne of *Sirnan*: The rest of his glory must be supplyed by himselfe, and not borrowed from his Father. Their Emperours haue no Armes, and the Family of the *Othomans* neuer beare any. They defaced, in the siege of the *Grecian* Empire, those of the most Illustrious Family of the *Paliologus*, who were the Soueraigne Monarches, who carried gloriously the Titles of their triumphant prosperities, by foure Letters separated distinctly, which the *Greekes* call *Vita*, and not *Fusils*, as some haue dream't; those Letters, signified in the same Language, Βασιλευς Βασιλεων Βασιλευων Βασιλευοντων, that is to say, *King of Kings, raigning ouer them that raigne.* It is true the Turkish Princes, haue some kinde of Marke or Ensigne, rather of their Empire than of their Family: for when as they represent it, they paint the Globe of the World, with a Crescent or halfe Moone on the top; and in their Armies, their Ensignes haue no other deuice but the same Crescent: their Towers and Steeples carry it, yea the Pilgrimes which goe to *Mecqua*, carry it on the top of their staues: the which shewes that this Crescent is rather a marke of their Religion, then of the Imperiall Race. Wee

haue

haue obserued in our History of their Religion, the Miracle which *Mahomet* their Prophet brags hee had done, when as he repaired the Moone which was torne, and all in pieces, after he had drawne it from Heauen and put it into his sleeue. The Turkes which count their Moneths by Moones, shew the veritie hereof, when as they prostrate themselues in the beginning thereof, before the Moone, and lifting vp their eyes to his brightnesse, they pray vnto God that hee will grant them the grace to begin happily, to continue in like manner, and to end with good successe the course of this Starre.

The Imperiall Seale of the *Grand Seigneurs* of Turkey, hath no other figure, but certaine *Arabian* Characters, which expresse their name, that of their Father, and note the pride of the felicity whereof they brag. *Achmat* the Emperour, who died in the yeare 1617, had caused these words to be grauen in the Seale, wherewith his Patents were sealed: *Achmet ibni Mehemet Cham Sadet*: that is to say; *Achmet sonne to Mehemet, Emperour alwayes victorious*. The other *Othoman* Monarches, haue in a manner the same deuice, the names onely changed: It is true that the *Arabique* Letters are so interlaced one with another (in a manner like the Cyphers, wherewith they expresse their names in *France*) as few men in his Estate, can expound them: only the *Vizir*, or he which seales hath the perfect knowledge. This manner of grauing their Seales only with Letters, hath beene imitated only from their Prophet: For the Turkish Monarchy, and all that depends thereof, hold it a glory to haue for their principall support, the Religion which he professeth, and to haue no other interest but his: *Mahomet* the Authour of the Alcoran, caused words only to be grauen in his Seale, and wordes without truth; which were these, *Mahomet the Messenger of God*. This Seale was made seuen hundred and fiue or six yeares before that *Othoman* the first Prince of that Family, which raignes at this day in the East, had seated the Turkish Monarchy: and since, we doe not read that any Turkish Emperour hath had any other Armes for their Seales than the Characters and *Arabique* words. Thus these men by words not

Bb 2 cast

cast into the wind, as many other Princes doe, but grauen, haue by the esteeme which they haue made of the vertue of men which haue serued them, subdued the Emperour of *Constantinople*, rauished that of *Trebisonde*, seazed vpon *Egypt*, *Palestina*, *Damas*, *Pamphylia*, *Cilicia*, *Caramania*, and all *Natolia*, vanquished *Rhodes* and *Cyprus*, triumphed ouer *Gracia*, *Albania*, *Illyria*, and the *Triballiens*, and likewise doth by his Armes possesse the best parts of *Moldauia*, *Transiluania*, and *Hungary*, and without doubt, their Conquests had extended farther into the Prouinces of Christendome, if Heauen had not giuen them bounds, and stayed their courses, by the troubles of the *Othoman* House, and the death of its Princes.

Chap. XX.

Of the Death, Mourning, Funerall, and Burying, of the Grand SEIGNEVRS, Emperours of Turkey.

THe Kings which receiue tribute from so many Nations pay it vnto death, and the condition of their perishing life, makes them to suffer this equalitie with other men, to returne vnto dust the common beginning of all men liuing: the which should incite them the more to forget the glory of their Name, and to repaire by their goodly and royall actions, the shortnesse of their dayes, to the end they may passe from the disquietnesse of an vncertaine Raigne, to the eternall rest of a heauenly command, and change their Crownes which are not durable, to the Diademe of an Empire which hath no end. The Turkish *Sultans* spend their dayes farre from these wise thoughts in the shadow of their *Serrail*, in the midst of pleasures, with their *Sultana's*; the effeminacie of their exercises, doth blemish their glory, and dulls their spirits, corrupts the humours of their Bodies, and shortens their liues: For delights Il more men then the sword. When they are sick, the *La-*

ni Bassi, who is the chiefe of the Phisitians, assembles the rest within the *Serrail*, and shuts himselfe vp with them, where they labour for the cure of their Maister, with that care which wee haue formerly mentioned. Remedies are but for helpes, they draw them not from the Bed, whereas their life and pride must haue an end: They die, and leauing their Scepters and Crownes, with all that which the World adores, they carry nothing with them but the good they haue done liuing, yet vnprofitable to their soules health, seeing they haue not Truth for their Guide. The Prince which is to succeed puts on Mourning, and attires himselfe in blacke for a short time; hee couers his head with a little Turbant, and doth testifie by his exterior shew, the griefe hee hath for the losse of his Predecessour, although that in his soule, hee feeles the most sensible joy that euer hee had. Thus *Solyma* the Third shewed himselfe before the Body of *Solyman* the Second his Father, who dyed in *Hungary* at the siege of *Siphet*: All the *Bassa's* weare little Turbants in signe of Mourning. And if then Emperour dies as then *Wursedas Solyman* did, all the Ensignes and the Standard Royall, are turned downward towards the ground, vntill the new *Sultan* takes his Royall Robes, and puts on a great white Turbant, the which is done soone after. Then they cry as wee haue formerly related; That the soule of the Inuincible Emperour *Sultan N.* enjoyes the immortall glory and eternall peace: That the Empire of *Sultan N.* may prosper with all felicitie. But they interre them all in *Constantinople*, since they settled the Seate of their Empire in that place. Before, their Tombes were erected in *Prussia* in *Asia*, the place of their first Domination: their Funerals are made in this manner.

The Emperours Body is carried in a Coffin couered with Linnen very rich, or of Veluet. His Turbane is set before it, with a Plume of Herons Feathers. The *Talismans, Sansons, Alphaquis, Derwis,* and the like rabble of the Alcoran, carry in their hands Tapers lighted, to shew that their Prophet is the Ape of Christianity; goe before singing in their Language such Verses, *Alla rahumani arhamabula Alla,*

illa

190   *The History of the Serrail, and of the*

illa Alla, Alla humana Alla, that is to say, *Mercifull God haue pittie on him, there is no God but God, God is God.* They also say these words : *Iabilac hillala Mehemet resullaha tungari hanhorum burue,* which signifieth, *God is God, and there is no other God, Mahomet is his Counsellour, and his true Prophet.* Before the Corps doth march the *Mouis feragas,* who carries the Emperours Tulbant vpon a Lance, with the tayle of a Horse tied neere vnto it : The *Imicadrens,* the *Solachi,* and the rest of the Imperiall Guard follow the Hearse. After these, the Officers of the Sultans house march in order vnder the conduct of *Capugirbassi,* or Master of the Household ; The *Mehunder,* heralds in mourning, carrie the deceased Grand Seignors Armes ; and the Royall Standard dragging vpon the ground : The *Bassa's* and all the great Men of the Port, yeelding their last duty vnto their Master, assist at their Funerall pleasantly attired in mourning : They haue a piece of Grey cloth hangs before and behind from the head to the foot, like vnto that Frock which the Brethren of the Hospitall of the Charity in the Suburbes of S. Germain at Paris do weare ; some of them, for that they will not seeme too sorrowfull, tie only a long piece of Linnen cloth, to the end of their Turbants, which hangs downe vnto their heeles. At this great Mourning the masters in the Ottoman Court, hold their Ranks in this Funerall Pompe, whereas the Men take but a paire of the Conuoy, Beasts supply the rest, with lesse griefe and more teares : For all the Sultans great Horses are at his Interment, they carry their Saddles turned vpward, and better couered than the Bassa's in their Grey Frockes ; they haue blacke Veluet hanging vnto the ground : They weepe and sigh without heauinesse : They put *Assagoth* or Tobacco into their nostrils, to make them sneeze, and into their eyes to draw forth teares : Such is the vaine pompe of the Turkish Sultans, who being vnable to binde men to wepe for their losse, constraine beasts to shed teares : In this manner they conduct the body, (the head first after the Turkish manner) to the Tombe where they will inclose him, it is vsually ioyning to the Mosquee, which the deceased Sultan hath caused to be

built

built, in a Chappell apart: the Sepulchre is couered with black Veluet. If the Prince died in the Warre, they lay his Semiter vpon it; if not, his Turbant is aduanced, and set against the wall neere vnto the Tombe, with rich Plumes of Herons feathers for an Ornament; two Candlestickes which carry great Tapers gilt, are at the foot of the Sepulchre: Some Turkish Priests which are instituted to that end, repeate continually the *Azoares* of the Alcoran in their turnes, and one after another sayes the Turkes Chapelet; whereof wee haue spoken in the History of their Religion, and pray continually for the soule of the deceased. On Fridayes these Imperiall Tombes, are adorned with new Couerings, and strewed with flowres: They which come on such dayes pray for the dead, or powre forth their teares, and take a Nosegay when they returne. Sometimes they doe also set much meat, to giue Almes vnto the poore, and they call to these Funerall Feasts, not only poore Beggers, but also Beasts, as Dogges, Cats, and Birds, the which are honourably receiued, and feasted with as much liberty and safety as the Men, who seeing the pawes of Cats in pottage with their hands, dare not chase them away: But contrariwise they owe them respect and succour, as those whom misery hath made their equals, and therefore capable to receiue the effects of the Turkish Charity: For the *Mahomets* hold opinion, that to giue Almes vnto Beasts is a worke no lesse meritorious before God, than to giue vnto Men: for that, say they, these poore animals possesse nothing in this World, where they are destitute of all temporall goods, necessary for the maintenance of life. Thus they shut him vp in sixe foot of ground, whom all the World could not containe, and whose vnrestrained ambition aspired to more Empire than the Earth containes: And after that he had bin a terrour to Men, and the cruell scourge of many Nations, he is made the subject of Wormes, and their ordinary food. In this manner passeth, and ends the glory of the World.

FINIS.

THE HISTORY OF THE COVRT OF THE KING of *CHINA*.

Written in *French* by the *Seigneur Michael Baudier* of *Languedoc*.

Translated by E. G.

LONDON,
Printed by *William Stansby*.

The Preface.

THe care of Men flyes to the Indies, and all the East to seeke for Drugges, and Remedies which may purge the body from those diseases which doe afflict it. And this labour drawing out of the Histories of the like Orientall Region, examples, the which exposed to the view of the publique, may in imitating them purge many disorders, and in time cure mens mindes of the passions which trouble them. That which hath drawne Me to the texture of this worke, are the rare and eminent qualities of the spirits of China, who in the particular World wherein they are inclosed, furnish wise Counsels, and true Maximes to reforme the disorders of other Nations. Their History little knowne to vs, being as it were curtailed in this little Worke describes them the means, the truth whereof will be lesse offensiue in our dayes, than that which we might haue made more glorious in a greater Volume, in that which we haue seene, and the affaires which are neere vnto vs. The wise and iudicious Reader may see in the relation of the Court of China, two powers alwayes working, by the which that great and vast Kingdome is happily gouerned: That is the assured recompence for vertue, and the infallible punishment of vice; and without being at the charges of so long a Voyage, nor incurring the dangers which are encountred, he may with-

Like vnto those two Diuinities whereof Themistocles made vse in the gouernment. Πειθὼ καὶ Βία.

The Preface.

out parting from his owne House in reading these leaues, see the Court of China, be present at their Pompes, and stay there as long as his leasure will giue him leaue. Hee shall not see flattery enter the Royall Palace in Pompe, & to shut the Gate against truth; nor dissembling to hold the place of friendship, nor fauour to rob vertue of her honours and rewards. Flatterers are so banished, that neuer any Monarch of China had any cause, like vnto that Prince of the Antiquitie corrupted by delights, to binde them to a Wheele, to wash their foule mouthes in the water, and to expresse in turning them about, the inconstancie of their base practice. These Courtiers do not trust the weight of their prosperities to such weake supports, as the Elephant doth the weight of his body to a tree halfe sawed in sunder and ready to fall: the felicities which they enioy haue for a solide foundation, the basis of their vertues. He shall not see by the course of the inconstancies which rules in other places, this wise Court to change its countenance often, and like vnto Mida's Altar, to be sometimes of pure gold, sometimes of ordinary stone; the order which wisdome hath setled there makes it alwayes equall. It were a very extraordinary thing to find a Courtier there, honoured one day like a God, and chased away the next like a Deuill. The merit of them of China hath dismounted Fortune from her inconstant wheele, and hauing disarmed her of her wings, hath set her vpon a firme Rock. So he that shall read this Tract, of what profession soeuer he be, he shall see Learning in recommendation, Armes in esteeme, Iustice reuerenced, and Arts honoured: So as admiring the good qualities of them of China, and enuying their durable felicities, he shall haue nothing to wish them but the light of true Religion, which they want; and may say in himselfe, that Vertue wanting reward is fled from vs.

Parasitos ad rotam aquariam ligabat, & cum vertigine sub aquas mittebat, ru susque in summum reuoluebat eosque Ixionios, amicos vocauit, Ælius Lampridius in Heliogab.

Hodie tu Iupiter esto, Cras mihi truncus eris ficulneus inutile lignum, Horat. Satyr. 8.

THE HISTORY OF OF THE COVRT
Of the KING of *China*.

HE Realme of the *Sines*, whose manners ancient Writers haue related vnto vs, is called by them of the Countrey *Taybinco*; by their Neighbours *Sancley*, and by the people of *Europe*, *China*: It lies vpon the extremitie of *Asia*, vpon the East and South, it is watered with the waues of the great Ocean; towards the West, the higher *India* confines with it, and on the North, the *Scythians*, and *Massagets*, are their neerest Neighbours. It hath in Circumference or Circuit, nine thousand fiue hundred and sixteene *Dies* (a measure of their Country) or three thousand French Leagues; In Diameter or length, eighteene hundred Leagues. In this vast and immense space, are contained fifteene goodly great Prouinces; fiue hundred fourescore and eleuen Cities, fifteene hundred fourescore and thirteene Townes, and an infinite number of Burroughes: fifteene Cities are the Metropolitan or Principall of the Realme, stately and commodiously built vpon goodly Hauens of the Sea, or vpon the fertill bankes of great Nauigable Riuers. The Prouinces are *Paguie*, *Canton*, *Foquien*, *Olan*, *Quinsay*, *Susuam*,

The names, situation, greatnesse, and qualities of the Realme of China.

To-

Tolanchie, Canfay, Oquian, Aucheo, Honain, Xanton, Quinchen, Chequean, Saxij, or *Sancij*: They are gouerned in particular by the administration of a Vice-roy: except *Pagnie* and *Tolanchie*, which are immediatly ruled by the care of their Soueraigne, and the aduice of his Councell; for he resides in them, as neerest to the *Tartars*, their ancient Enemies, to the end that his Royall presence as the Sunne of the Estate, might disperse the fogges and Cloudes of troubles, which would obscure his glory. The admirable bounty of the Country makes all the Earth to enuy it: The Inhabitants breathe the Aire of the Easterne part of the World: Wine, Graine, and Fruit, are in abundance, for the fertile Land yeelds encrease thrice a yeare. They haue store of Wooll, Cotton, and Silkes: They gather Perfumes; Meitals are found there, Gold and Siluer abounds, Diamonds glister, Pearles are fisht, the Sea obeyes to their Nauigation: Great Riuers water it, and the *Chinois* may disdaine and contemne the helpe and assistance of other Men, and the Commodities of their Prouinces. They are inclos'd and shut vp as it were in another World, Nature hath furnished them with great Mountaines which locke them vp; and Art by the industry and care of King *Tinzon*, hath drawne a Wall fiue hundred Leagues long, very high, and aboue fiue and twenty foot thick, which doth finish the enclosure of that which Nature had left them (as it seemes) of purpose; to the end that knowing their forces, they might make a World apart: Although Histories say, that the inroades and spoyles which the *Tartars* made vpon them on that side, aduanced the project, and made them to hasten the Worke.

<small>The fundamentall Lawes of the Estate.</small>

The principall Lawes vnder the wise conduct whereof they liue, in the midst of an assured peace, ful of all felicities, are first, that the Scepter of the Realme of *China* neuer fals to the Distaffe, and that the Males only and not the women succeed to the Crowne. Secondly, that no man of the Countrey shall presume to goe out of the Ports thereof to any forreigne parts, without expresse leaue of the King himselfe, and not of his Officers: and that no stranger shall be admitted to enter, with-

without the like licenſe: whereby they preſerue inviolably the purity of their good cuſtomes, and with the helpe of this great wall they hinder the entry of Strangers into the Realme, and their cares keepe vices out of the Court, which in other places are familiar to Courtiers. If happily any ſtranger creepes in amongſt them, he is preſently diſcouered of euery man; for to that end they long ſince ſetled a cuſtome amongſt them, to cauſe them to cruſh and make flat the Noſes of their Children when they are borne: So as all the *Chinois* haue flat Noſes: Which makes a ſtranger in their company ſeeme to haue a different countenance. Thirdly, the Charges and Offices of the Eſtate, are not giuen but to very capable men, and indowed with rare and eminent qualities. That no Man ſhall be held Noble, vnleſſe he be vertuous. That the Children of great Men, cannot be admitted to their Fathers Offices, nor haue any part in the glory of their Reputation, if they doe not equall or ſurpaſſe them, tying Nobility by this meanes to the perſon, and not to the bloud. Fourthly, that the Children of Merchants and Artificers how rich ſoeuer they be, cannot mount higher than their Fathers Trades; vnleſſe ſome rich gift of the minde doth ſo recommend ſome one aboue the reſt, as he may profitably ſerue the Eſtate and publique: Then, and by the expreſſe leaue of the King, after long ſtudy and many painfull exerciſes, he is made *Loytias*, that is to ſay Noble, with the luſtre of a pompous ſolemnitie, as we will ſhew in its place. Fiftly, that idleneſſe bee puniſhed as a capitall crime; and to baniſh it out of the Realme, they prohibit vpon great penalties, to giue Almes to thoſe that ſhall demand it; for the poore maymed in their members, or afflicted with diſeaſes, are ſent to their Kinsfolkes, whom the Law enioynes to taxe themſelues, and to furniſh food and other neceſſaries for theſe poore afflicted people: If the Kinsfolkes be poore, the Kings Purſe and the publique Charity feedes them in Hoſpitals, and other Houſes Inſtituted to that end, but the blind and the lame, which may worke eate not the bread of the poore; They force them to get their liuings, turning Mils, and doing other Workes, the gaine whereof ſupplyes their neceſſities.

This

The Province, Towne, & the Kings Pallace.

This great Kingdome vnder the conduct of so good Lawes, is gouerned by one Soueraigne King, who liues commonly in the Prouince of *Paguie*, or *Pagule*, in the City of *Tabin*, otherwise called *Suntien*, which signifies in their language a City of Heauen: *Marcus Paulus Venitus*, calls it *Quinsay*, the which is so great, as it fils the spirit of those that read the extent with admiration, and being but a small patterne of the Realme, shewes plainly what the whole piece is: It hath in length as much as a man can well goe in a day on horseback, from one gate vnto another: The bredth is halfe as much, and the circuit most vast: The Suburbes which are many containe altogether as much as the City: The *Chinois* haue heretofore leuied in this Towne vpon vrgent necessities, of an important Warre, an hundred thousand foot, and an hundred thousand horse. I was present in the yeare 1616, when as a *Flemmish* Iesuit newly come from *China*, related vnto the King, being in the *Louver*, the wonders of this Royall City; he gaue it in length twice as much, as is from *Paris* to *Pontoise*, which is seuen *French* Leagues: The rarities which hee spake of, are conformable to the History; he shewed himselfe in the Kings Cabbinet, attired after the manner of *China*, whereof the habit was pleasing. There are three royall Pallaces built in this great City, the one at the entry towards the East, the other in the midst, and the third at the other end towards the West: The King of *China* hath made choice of the first for his Mansion, of so vast a greatnesse, that to see the particularities, a man cannot imploy lesse than foure whole dayes: It is wholy enuironed with seuen great and spacious Walles, so as within the distance of one from another, there are easily lodged ten thousand Souldiers, which make the ordinary Guard of the Pallace. The number of goodly Chambers, rich Wardrobes, and precious Cabbinets, amount to aboue fiue hundred. There are threescore and nineteene Hals, all richly built with admirable Art; foure of which are most remarkable in this Palace: The first is of metall cast, curiously wrought, with a great number of figures: The second hath the floore and seeling made of siluer of great value; the third

is

of the King of China.

is of massiue Gold, excellently enameled: But the lustre, beautie, and value of the fourth doth farre exceed the other three: It is beautified with many Iewels of price: within it there shines a Royall Throne all couered with Diamonds, and a great number of Carbuncles, the which with other precious stones giues such a light, as the Hall is as light in the darkest Night, as if there were many Torches burning: This fourth is called the Hall of the Kings Treasure, and so it containes it. In these foure Halls the King giues audience to the Embassadours of Forreigne Princes, and measures the honour which he will doe them at their reception in these Halls; For those of meaner Princes his Tributaries, are not receiued but in the first Hall: Those that are more eminent in, he second: & such as come from great Kings which doe not acknowledge him, in the third and fourth. Hee also keepes his Court in these Halls, and giues audience there to the principall Officers of his Crowne.

Mary of Medicis Queene Mother to the King, the honour and admiration of her age, who by the lustre of her rare and incomparable vertues, hath carried the glory of her Name, to the most remote Regions of the Earth, sent him in the yeare 1616, a stately Present of rich Tapestrie, and her great pietie had no other designe in this Present, but the glory and honour of him who had made her the greatest Princesse in the World: for shee did it to the end, this Prince should giue more free accesse to those that went into his Realme, to turne their soules from the false worship of Idols, by the light of the Gospell, and to put them in the way of their saluation. Hee which had charge to present it, which was this *Flemming* of whom we haue spoken, assured mee, that the King of *China* would cause a rich Hall to be built of purpose, proportionable to the Tapestry, wherwith hee would hang it, and would esteeme it the richest Moueable of his Pallace: For *China* which hath before vs found out the goodliest inuentions of Art, hath not yet that of rich Tapestry. This stately Pallace doth furnish the King with the delights of walkes; he hath goodly Gardens enameled with all sorts of Flowres,

A present from the Queene Mother of France, to the King of China.

Dd wa-

watred with goodly Fountaines, whereas the sweet murmur of their boyling springs, summons the birds with their notes to make a naturall consort of pleasing Musique; In their goodly Allies, hee charmes the troubles and cares which follow Royaltie, and grow vnder Crownes. The number of the women which he entertaines, are his most ordinary Company; He takes delight to contemplate, in their faire countenances, more Roses and Flowers than his Gardens doe produce. On the side of these Gardens are many goodly Orchards, which yeelds all sorts of delightfull fruits; and farther off, extend great Woods, some cut, others of high growne trees, whereas somtimes he takes his pleasure in hunting. They are enuironed in some places, with many large Pools, all couered with wild fowle, amidst the which the Swans which couer their hideous blacke skins with white feathers, seeme the most beautifull vnto the Prince, and doth silently teach him a wise lesson, that goodliest shewes in the World and Court, couer many deformities and hide treacheries. The Kings of *China* haue often tried it: The diuisions of their Estate, the troubles thereof which haue continued one and fourtie yeares, the Treasons and Massacres which haue beene committed euen vpon their Kings persons, vnder the vnfortunate Raignes of *Yanthei*, *Laupi*, *Guirgey*, *Quiancy*, and *Soutey*, are true testimonies in their Histories.

This is the reason why at this day, they liue so retired in their great Pallaces, and in steed of Pages and Gentlemen Attendants, they are serued only by women, with whom they vsually conuerse, they commit the care of their breeding vnto them, & relie vpon them for the preseruation of their healths: Not but that their persons are guarded by men: There are as we haue said, ten thousand men, armed in guard without the Royall Pallace, besides those which are at the Gates, and vpon the staires of the same Pallace, and likewise in the Hals. For the Princes of *China* haue not beene free from the malice of women. King *Trouson*, surprized with the rare beautie of his Fathers Widdow, found by his pursuit, in the vaine enioying of his loue, the losse of his life. This goodly Queene called *Canso*, who was one of the miseries of the State, wearie

of

of the troubles of the World, and the vanities of the Court abandoned them after the death of the King her husband, to enjoy quiet and rest farre from them, in the which a soule enjoying it selfe finds happinesse and felicitie: She shut herselfe into a Monastery of Religious women of *China*, in the which the Deuill, vnder the worship of Idols, causeth himselfe to be adored by the goodliest women of the East: There laying at his feet the Crowne she had vpon her head, she put on a Vaile like vnto the rest, and did liue in the simplicitie of this Order: *Tranfon* her sonne in Law, who was a greater worshipper of her allurements than she was of her selfe Gods, is aduertised; and followes her: to serue for an example, that Kings aswell as other men, liue in the thing beloued; he entertaines her at a Grate, Courts her, and perswades her to leaue her vaile, and to resume the Royall Crowne vpon her head the second time: Shee heares him, beleeues him, and going out of the Monastery, makes it knowne that many times the Deuotions of Women are like Vessels of Chrystall, which breake with the first knocke: she marries him. But what good can happen by this inconstant diuersion and change, from the World to a Cloyster, and from a Cloyster to the World: Doubtlesse, a woman willingly vnfrockt, is a dangerous Creature in a State or a Family. *Cause* resumes the Ambition which shee had trodden vnder foot, and to Raigne alone vnder the name of her infant Sonne, she caused King *Tronfon* her husband to be slaine, then being Mistris of her will aswel as of the Realme, she abandons her Reason, her Honour, and the glory of her Majesty to her lasciuious passion: shee became Wife to many Husbands, or Friends: There was no great Man in Court, to whom her Imbracings were not allowed, yea, offered. This filthy life of a Princesse, who should haue beene an example of vertue in the State, offended all the World as a publique scandall: Shee couers it in some sort, and marries againe, but to continue her disorders, she weds a man of no worth, who allowes any thing. Vices follow one another; from this incontinent and lustfull life, shee fals to cruelty: her children more carefull of honour than herselfe, testifie only by their sorrow, the griefe they haue for her bad carriage: she causeth them to be murthered; to aduance vnto the Crowne of *China* a Nephew of hers, who was a support and countenance to her lust, in the which she had raigned fortie yeares, too long a time for so lewd a woman. In the end the *Chinois* grow weary of her disorders: They send for a base sonne of her Husbands, they crowne him, and acknowledge him for their King: His name was *Tantzon*, hee seized vpon this impudent woman, caused her Processe to be made, and put to death by the hand of an Executioner. This was the end of the Princesse *Canse*, who had beene the cause of so many disorders in the State, and was in the end the cause of her shamefull ruine.

But the Kings of *China* haue for these latter ages, liued much retired in their stately Pallaces. There hath beene some which haue neuer gone forth in publique, but on the day that he was crowned King, and tooke the accustomed oath: If the people see him at any time, it is thorough a glasse window: They say they doe it to preserue their Royall Dignity, and the respect which is due vnto them, and moreouer to auoid the Treasons which may be practized against them. This kind of liuing thus close, doth not diminish the loue and reuerence, which the people owe vnto their persons: For the Gouernours and Magistrates know how to maintaine it, and to make them obserue it: and moreouer in the principall Townes of the Prouinces of the Realme, whereas the Vice-royes make their Residence, they haue beene accustomed to hang vp in a publique place a rich Table of pure gold, in the which the portraite of the King is represented to the life, vailed with a curtaine imbroydered with gold: The *Loytias*, which are the Knights, and the Officers of Iustice goe daily before it to make lowe submissiue Reuerences; giuing vnto the publique this example of an exteriour respect towards their Soueraigne, which many times doth excite an inward loue. The dayes of solemne Feasts, which they celebrate at the new Moone of euery Moneth, they vnuaile this Table: The people see it plainly, and euery man runs to salute it.

In the perpetuall abode of these delightfull Pallaces, the
Mo-

Monarches of *China*, haue no other cohuersation, nor ordi- The Kings wo-
nary company but Women: For besides those which serue men and their
him, which are many in number, they haue thirty Concubins, Marriages.
the fairest that can be found in all their Kingdome, and one
only Queene which they marry, and make companion of
their Scepter. They were accustomed in old time, when they
had a will to marry, to inuite all the Knights and Noblemen
of the Court, to a Royall and solemne Feast, commanding
them to bring with them their Sonnes and Daughters: They
did it, with a designe to lodge some one of their Daughters in
the Throne of *China*, and added to their beauties all the ornaments of Art: The Feast being ended, these Virgins were
placed in a great Hall, according to the order of their Race,
and not the ranke of their qualitie. Then the King if he were
not married, or the Princes his sonnes (if he were) came into
this Hall to entertaine the Ladies, and to choose out of their
number those whose graces and perfections of beauty had giuen most power to captiuate their affections by the sweetnes
of their charmes. The *Infanta's*, Daughters to the King did
the like among the young Knights which had beene at the
Feast: They had libertie to choose out of their troupe, him
whom they held most worthy to be their husband. But all
worldly things passe, especially those of the Court; so this custome is extinct. The Kings of *China* doe all marry now to
their Kinswomen, the first degree of proximitie or neernesse,
of bloud only obserued, and sometimes the second. After the
King hath thus taken a Wife, hee makes choice of thirty
Friends, which the Law of his Religion allowes him to keep,
and they are commonly the fairest of his Estate: These not a-
ble to attaine vnto the honour to be these wiues (for he marries but one) hold it a glory to enjoy his Imbracings. They
know well their children shall be legitimate, and that after
his death they shall be honourably prouided for, and married
to the greatest of the Court. For in his life time hee makes his
Will, before he be sicke, leaues them portions, and names for
their husbands thirty of the most eminent Knights in his
Court, which are to marry. Being dead, and the Obsequies
per-

performed, he which succeeds vnto the Crowne, causeth these thirtie women which haue serued his Predecessour, to be richly attired, and adorned with all sorts of precious Iewels; Hee causeth them to be ranked in goodly Chaires in the midst of this fourth Hall, whereof we haue formerly spoken, and causeth their faces to be couered, so as they cannot bee knowne. Then he cals into the same Hall the thirty Knights, whom the deceased King had named by his Testament, the which according to the order of their antiquity, or that of the nomination of the Testament, goe one after another, to take one of these women thus vailed by the hand, and leads her, without discouering her face, presently to his house, where they see what chance hath giuen them, and soone try whether the deceased Prince hath bequeathed them a pleasing or importune Legacie; for from that time they hold them for their wiues.

The Ladies of the Court of China.

The other Ladies of the Court are married, not according to their owne desires, or the blind passions of loue; but according to the will of their Parents, who know how to choose men, whose age and merit may not be vnequall to their youth and condition. It is the custome of *China*, that the husbands giue portions to their wiues in taking them, for they bring not any thing but their beauty & vertues; They deliuer the money promised before they marrie them, and they giue it to their Fathers and Mothers, for a small acknowledgement of the care, which they had in breeding them: So as, it seemes, the iniustice of this Law, doth force men sometimes to buy bad Merchandizes at a deare rate, when as in Marriages, they encounter with indiscreet spirits, and extrauagant humours; But, there is another Law which doth sweeten their displeasure, if they conceiue any: for hauing bought them, they may lawfully sell them againe. This doth seldome happen: The Ladies of *China* are so well bred and so honest, as they giue their husbands more cause to cherish them, than to put them out of their Families: The merit of their vertue hath brought the glory of their Reputation into our Countries, they which are so remote from vs so many thousand Leagues, and dwell in the extremity of the World; for an example to vertuous Ladies

Their Marriages.

dies, that the renowme of their perfections shall be neuer extinct. The vertue of these Ladies of China, being growne with them is become so solid with time: For from their infancies, they breed them vp in the loue of honesty, and the hatred of vice; they shut them vp perpetually, and imploy them without ceasing, to the end that Idlenesse the nursing mother of Vices, mollifying their spirits, should not draw them into some disorder. This care to breed them vp in this manner, is expresly commanded to Parents, by a Law which hath beene inuiolably obserued for many ages, in the Realme of China, established by the first King which swayed the Scepter, called Vitey. This Prince knowing that the idlenesse of women had beene the cause of great disorders, which had ruined Common-weales, ouerthrowne whole Estates, and in his time had troubled many Realmes; Hee ordained vpon great penalties, that the Wiues of Artizans should worke on their husbands Trades; and those of other men should imploy themselues with workes of the Needle, or to spinne Linnen. This Law was so strictly obserued, as he would haue his owne Wife obey it: Thus the women of China labour continually, and the Queen her selfe, who at this day weares the Crowne of that Realme, is continually busie in spinning of Gold and Silke, or to make some rich worke with the Needle, which serues for an Ornament to the Altar of her vaine Idols. This is the reason why you shall seldome see any women in the streets, they are all imployed in their houses: If any Ladies of the Court goe forth in publique (the which happens seldome) it is to visit their neere Kinsfolkes, when they are dangerously sicke: They goe couered in Chaires carried by men, where thorow little grates artificially made of gold or siluer, they see and are not seene. Another inuention of the Kings of China, which haue loued the modestie and chastitie of women, hath beene of no small moment to cut off their courses and vaine walkes. They ordained that the Mothers should bee carefull, to binde vp streight their Daughters feet in the Cradle, to the end they should not grow, perswading their credulous sexe, that the beauty of a woman consisted in hauing a little foot; and they

Their employployments.

Their going forth in publique.

be-

They haue all little feet.
beleeue it so constantly, and presse them so violently in their tender age, as they are incommodated, and in a manner lamed; the which is another reason why they so willingly keep their houses. It were a difficult thing to perswade them the contrary of this opinion, and to diuert their spirits from this foolish crueltie, thus to rack their feet in the estate of innocencie: For if any of them had the face of Angell, and the foot indifferently great, shee will hold herselfe the foulest creature in the World. It is true that this vaine beliefe, to hold them faire which haue very little feet, is not only at this day in *Asia*: some of these Easterne parts, haue followed it with as much passion. *Elianus* reports in the thirteenth Booke of his diuers Histories, and the three and thirtieth Chapter, that the faire *Rhodope* of the Towne of *Naucratia*, bathing herselfe one day, in the Chrystall streame of a pleasing Fountaine, had left her clothes vpon the banke, vpon a heape of Roses which her Gentlewoman had gathered; when as an Eagle which sought her prey seized vpon one of her Pattens or Shooes and carried it away. This Bird whom they haue held to be the Messenger of Warre, and carries the lightning of Heauen, was then, of peace and loue: for being lost in the Cloudes, she fell farre off in the Citie of *Memphis*, which is now the great *Caire*, and let the Patten fall at the Kings feet, who then gouerned *Egypt*. This Prince judging of the forme of the foote by the Shooe, which was wonderfull little, and by the foote the perfection of the Ladie, imagined that shee was faire enough to deserue to be crowned Queene of his Estate, and Companion of his Scepter: hee sent men into all parts to informe themselues what that Ladie was from whom an Eagle had taken a Shooe: They found her, (this fortune was too great to flie from it and hide her selfe) and brought her to their Prince, who tooke her to Wife. Thus the Easterne beauties haue little feet, and from this foolish opinion, the wise Politicians of *China* haue drawne this benefit, thereby to contain the women in their houses. They are neatly and richly attired in Silke and Gold: Pearles, Diamonds, and whatsoeuer the couetousnesse of men doth fish for in the Seas, and

Their apparel.

digge

digge out of the Mines, is as much in vſe there as in *Europe*. Their habits are in some sort like to those of the Spanish Ladies, and their rich attires of their head are not borrowed, they are made of their owne haire, artificially pleated, and wreathed with little treſſes of gold, and rais'd to the top of their heads in forme of a Crowne, bound about with a band couered with precious ſtones: All this Pompe although it depends of the vanity of the World, is notwithſtanding agreeable with their Chaſtities; for they haue alwayes had, as wee haue ſaid, the glory to be very chaſt.

The Kings of *China* neuer die without iſſue Male: the number of the women, whereof we haue formerly ſpoken, furniſh them heires enough for their Crowne. The firſt which is borne of any of thoſe, is the lawfull Succeſſour of the Eſtate: the reſt are bred vp with all the Princes of the Royall bloud, in Cities remote from the Court, which the King hath aſſigned them for their portions, where they liue with all ſorts of pleaſures and delights in ſtately Pallaces. But they are forbidden vpon paine of death to goe out of theſe Pallaces, and to come to Court, vnleſſe the King cals them. The moſt buſie and actiue cannot goe from their Pallages, vnleſſe they will incurre the penaltie: Yet theſe prohibitions doe no way diminiſh the reſpect, which they owe vnto their perſons: The Gouernours of the Prouince and Townes, are bound to goe and viſit them vpon all Feſtiuall dayes, which are the firſt dayes of euery Moone: If they or the Magiſtrates paſſe on horſebacke before their lodging, they ought in reuerence to light, and if they be in their Chaires, to goe out of them, and goe on foot without traine or pompe, vntill they be paſt the Lodgings; the gates whereof, to the end that none ſhould pretend ignorance, are painted with the colour of the Princes Liuery. Thus the eſtate of *China* enjoyeth (farre from the troubles of Ciuill Warre) the ſweetneſſe of peace: and the Princes of the bloud Royall, liue ſat and riot in the riches of the Court, in ſafety of their perſons, in the midſt of all pleaſures and recreations, reſpected and honoured as Demi-gods, without any care of the affaires of the Prouince wherein they liue, what ſhould in any ſort

The King of China's children, and the Princes of the bloud Royall.

trouble the calme and tranquillity which they enjoy.

The Courtiers of China.

The Courtiers of the King of *China* are all *Loytias*, that is to say Knights: They are of two sorts: The one are by the merit of Learning, the others by the valour of Armes: And you shall not see in all this number, that the blind rashnesse of Fortune, or the fauour of the Court hath aduanced any to this Dignity: They mount by the degrees of vertue; the which guides the one in this manner. The generall Visiters whom the King (by the aduice of his Councell) sends euery third yeare, throughout all the Prouinces of his Kingdome, in the execution of their Commissions, they haue nothing so much recommended vnto them, as to see the yong men which are bred vp in Colledges, to make them capable to serue the publique. They examine them, choose the best wits, and hauing found them capable to be imployed therein, they make them *Loytias* in the Kings behalfe, that is to say, Knights, giuing them both the Priuiledges and Ensignes; these are, a Girdle of gold and siluer, and the Hat garnished with two Brooches of gold in fashion of a Palme, hauing two labels hanging behind, like those of a Bishops Mitre: They cause them to take a solemne Oath, which is to serue the King and Publique faithfully and carefully in those charges wherewith they shall be honoured: That in the exercise thereof, they shall not take any Present from any person whatsoeuer, but shall content themselues, with the Pension which the King shall giue them, being sufficient to supply their necessities, and the lustre of their Dignities. The pompe and magnificence which is obserued, when they make these new Knights, testifie a publique Ioy; that Vertue is aduanced to charges of Honour, and the Empire shall be serued and gouerned by able and sufficient men. Then these *Loytias* goe with the new Markes of their new Dignities to Court, they visit the chiefe of the Kings Councell, and the other Ministers of the State; these receiue them and imbrace them; their Names are presently entred into a Booke, which serues to that vse: They are commanded to stay in Court, vntill there be some places void, whereunto they may be preferred: In the meane time they polish themselues, and

Loytias by learning.

adde

of the King of China.

adde vnto their learning the practice of the World, making themselues capable to doe well: when as occasions are offered to aduance them, some are sent Gouernours into a Prouince, others are made Lieutenants in another, and some are Soueraigne Iudges. The other sort of *Loytias* or Knights are made of grace (as the *Chinois* say) and by the will of the King, which are the Treasurers of the Realme, and the old Captaines which haue serued worthily. But I doe not see any extraordinary fauour, in this second Creation of Knights: For although these bee not made by examination, like the others, who are learned, what Grace doe they vnto them, to giue them that which their valour hath well deserued, in the ordinary hazards and dangers of warre: For the Law of the Court of *China*, doth not refuse to any man the recompence of his valour: The meanest Souldier may pretend it, and obtaine it: If they should see in *China* a Souldier lamed in the Trenches, to be reduced to that misery as to craue Almes in the street, they would impute it a crime to him that should suffer it, and the Realme would hold it selfe vnworthy to haue men to serue it at need. These last Knights are neuer aduanced to the gouernment of Prouinces or Townes, the Law of the State giues them to those that are learned, who are within their Realme esteemed aboue all other things. These *Loytias* or Courtiers, are ordinarily attired in Silkes of diuers colours; They haue Robes and Cassocks which couer them: The Gouernours, and such as haue the principall charges in the state, weare their Cassocks embroydered with gold and siluer from the Girdle downwards: They haue all long Bonnets: They weare on the Crowne of their heads a tuft of long haire artificially pleated and wouen with gold. Superstition the Mistris of their spirits, hath aduised them this kind of Periwicks: They beleeue that at their death they shall be pulled vp to Heauen by this handfull of haire: Their Priests more proud than so, weare not any, but are all shauen: For they preach that they haue power enough by the merit of their condition, to mount vp into Heauen of themselues, and not to be drawne vp forcibly by the haire: But they all labour in vaine:

Loytias by Armes.

Their habits.

Ee 2 Heauen

Heauen receiues no Idolaters, whether they haue long haire or none at all. These Courtiers doe also weare the Nailes of their left hand extraordinary long, with the like designe as the haire, as if they must scraule or scramble to goe vp into Heauen. Certainly the Court hath beene alwayes the abode of many fooles, and the Courtiers spirits forge strange and ridiculous imaginations. I haue obserued this difference in their Historie, that these men with long Nailes doe not scrape and get so much, as those of other Countries which haue shorter. Their Language is very much polished, and differs wholy from that of the other men of *China*. Their ordinary entertainment when they are together, is not as else-where of friuolous and idle subjects, nor of the shamefull encounters of the filthy exercises of a Brothell house; but of politique affaires: They propound Questions of Estate, they shew the meanes to preserue a Realme, they deliuer those which serue to increase it; and fortifie their discourses with some examples drawne out of their History. Their carriage is graue, and their countenance serious. When they goe forth in publique, they are carried in rich Chaires of Iuory: They alwayes hold their eyes fixed vpon one thing, with that seuerity which hath bin taught them from their infancie: Their Guards and seruants are about them, and their Friends follow them: They lead many Horses of shew after them, and they carry many Parasols to defend them from the heate and discommodity of the Sunne: If they be aduanced to any charge or gouernment in the Estate, many Officers of Iustice march before them, to make way: Some carry great Reeds hardned in the fire, to punish those which in their way shall be found conuicted of any light insolency; One of the troupe carries at his brest a Table fring'd with gold, in the which is written in great letters, his power which marcheth with this pompe. When these Courtiers meet, they salute one another in this manner: They stretch out their Armes, and bend them like a Bow, then they interlace their fingers one within another, & make a low reuerence, accompanied with some honest complement, as this *If I could as easily find occasions to serue you as I desire*

Their going forth in publique.

Their manner of salutation.

encounter your person, I would testifie vnto you sincerely how much I am yours, and should liue the most contented man of the Court. They also say often: I wish you all sorts of felicities, not so much as your vertuous merit, (the World hath not sufficient, that were to wish an impossible thing) but as much as a man may haue. The complement ended, they stand long in a courteous debate who shall part first to continue his way. The men of meaner condition, as simple Burgesses, vse this manner in their Salutations: They claspe the left haud, and couer it with the right, and carry both vnto their brests, making a low reuerence, and pray him whom they salute, to belieue that their friendship, is not only in the exteriour shew of the Ceremony, but hath also its principall seat in the heart, where they sweare they will preserue it inuiolably: This spoken they passe on, and continue their way. Doubtlesse there is not any Nation, how rude and barbarous soeuer, which hath not receiued the lawes of courtesie, and embraced them; and they which at this day reject them rashly, are barbarous spirits, and haue nothing of a man but the outward shew. When the distance of places where they are, hinders the complement, and entertainment by mouth, they doe it by missiue Letters, with the neatnesse of the Court of China. They gild all the margent of their paper, which is most fine, made of Reeds, they limne it, and write in the midst, what their affections or courtesies doth dictate: They put vp their Letter without sealing in a purse made of the same paper, daintily gilt and painted, and so seale it vp: These Missiues thus gilt are sold by the Book-sellers of the Court, yea ready written, so, as there remaynes nothing to doe but to signe them, and the vse is so ordinary among the Courtiers, as they themselues in their Visitations, giue them one vnto another for the greater assurance of their friendship. For the complements which are but by words, haue no other support but winde, and they which are by writing, remayne for a gage of that they promise. Thus by the rules of courtesie, and the strict obseruance of the Lawes of the Realme, these Courtiers of China liue in quietnesse and peace, and their discretion hath banished from

Their Missiue Letters.

Ee 3. the

the Court, the rashnesse of ill grounded quarrels, and the fury of Duels: Yet insolencie which hath brought other vices into the Court, hath kept her place to induce the most susceptible of her Counsels to offend others by words: The which happens sometimes amongst them, when as they speake injuries which are as ridiculous to vs, as they are sensible to them, for that they ground the offence vpon the Oracles of their Religion; for one of their Prophesies threatens their tranquillitie with troubles in this sense: *That a day will come when they shall be subiect to men which haue long Beards, Aquilin Noses, and great Eyes like vnto Cats eyes.* Thus, these men described in this manner, being odious vnto them in opinion, when they will doe an affront to any one, they call him Cats eyes, which among them is the greatest injury that can be done vnto the honour of an honest man. When as in the commerce of the Court, their ambition pursues any businesse, they desire to know the euent before they come, and to this end they cast their ordinary lot, which they vse in this manner: They haue two little peeces of wood like two Nutshels tied together with a little thread, and when as they haue called vpon the assistance of their Idoll, they cast them in its presence: If these peeces of wood, fall with the hollow parts vpon the ground, they hope for the accomplishment of their wishes in their affaires; but if the hollow parts be vpwards, they vomit out all kinds of Injuries against their Idoll, and begin to cast the lot againe; but if it doth not encounter well, they take the Idoll and beate it, put it in the water, and many times broyle it in the fire, and continue still their lot vntill it be fauourable vnto them; then they take the Idoll, imbrace it, and set it with all honour vpon its Altar, they sing Hymnes vnto it, and offer it Wine and the most exquisite meats they can find. Certainly in the madnesse of these Courtiers of *China*, we see in some sort the portraite of the impietie of some others which liue in a better Religion; who in the disorder of their affaires, challenge innocent Heauen as guilty of their misfortunes. These Courtiers of *China* haue another kind of lot: They cast into a vessell many little stickes, vpon either of which, is written a letter

of the King of China.   215

ter of their Alphabet, and when as they haue well shaken the vessell, they draw out one by the hand of a little childe, and looke with what letter it is marked, then they search in a Booke the leafe which begins with that letter, they reade it, and interpret that which they find written therin, to the good or bad successe of their affaires. Thus men are men, and in all places the Court is a Sea, whereas Ambition sayles and labours with Oares towards the accomplishment of her designes, and spares not any kinde of inuention to attaine vnto it, how sinister soeuer it be. Their deuotion which hath nothing for object but wood and stone, cut and fashioned into Idols, is also a Courtier, that is to say, Cold, done for fashion sake, and with negligence: And their Sacrifices are in some sort the Image of loue fit for Courtiers. They retaine vnto themselues the best part of that which they offer, and giue vnto their gods that which they would refuse themselues: If they kill a Heyfer or Boare, they offer vnto the Altar only the tips of their eares: If they sacrifice Fowle, they offer the clawes and bils, and eate all the rest: They present great vessels of wine, but themselues drinke it, after they haue consecrated, and powred forth some few drops: for in Court all is for themselues, and nothing for Heauen. The History accuseth them to faile of their faith and promise: It sayes they doe not measure the continuance but by their priuate interests, and doe not keepe it but so long as they list. But what good can you expect from men and Courtiers, who alwayes wallow in delights: The fertility of the soyle, the sweet temper of the Aire, the tranquillity of the State, the abundance of riches, and withall the falshood of their Idolatrous Religion, doth plunge them into all sorts of pleasures, capitall Enemies to vertue: They which are least voluptuous of their troupe, are the *Loytias* of learning, whose condition and their ordinary imployment, in more important affaires of State, keepe alwayes in labour and exercise, the which being of it selfe incompatible with vices, the children of Idlenesse, smothers them in their birth. When these Courtiers trauell in the Countrey, they make vse of Caroches which goe with sayles

Their deuotion.

Their faith.

Their delights

Their Caroches with sayles.

vpon

vpon the Land, as well, and in a manner as swiftly as ships vpon the Sea: For an example that the winde driues, guides and gouernes all in Court: And if in *China* the Coaches of great men goe with sayles, in other places the spirits of Courtiers goe with the wind: For if the world be nothing but vanitie, the Court which is the quintessence, sels, giues, followes, and adores the winde.

The King of *China* is serued and followed by such Courtiers; but his Councell, makes the sounder and better part of his Court: For Kings cannot be without it, being (when it is good) the preseruation, yea, the increase of their Estate, and without Councell the most powerfull Monarches loose and ruine themselues, by the weight of their owne greatnesse. The King of *China* makes choice of his Counsellours among the most learned; of greatest experience, and the wisest of his Realme: In the choice and election which he makes, fauour hath no voice, only merit and vertue speake: For this Prince doth practise as well as any Monarch of the earth, the aduice of the wisest of Kings, who counsels his like, *Not to admit into their Counsell, Spirits ill made, ignorant and vnaduised, who carry themselues where their passions driue them.* The Counsellours of the Estate in *China*, must, with the honestie of their liues, and the integritie of their manners, be learned in the Lawes of the Realme, and haue taken the degree of *Loytias*, they must be learned in Naturall and Morall Philosophy, and well seene in Judiciary Astrology. Their Religion expresly requires this last part, for that (saith it) they which are at the Helme of an Estate, should by their knowledge haue an eye to the future, foresee the tempests and stormes, auoid the Rockes, preserue themselues from shipwracke, and guide their ship happily. They are thirteene in number, twelue Counsellours, whom they call Auditours, and a President, which is among them as the Chancellour with vs. They sit in Councell in the Royall Pallace, the place where they assemble, is worthy of the pompe and magnificence of the Monarch of *China*; there are twelue stately chaires set for their sessions, six of massiue siluer, and six of pure gold; In the midst whereof

The Kings Councell.

of vnder a cloth of Estate of cloth of gold, beautified with two Serpents wreathed together of gold, which are the royall Armes, shines a seate of pure gold enricht with precious stones, in the which the President of the Councell sits, or the great Chancellour of *China*. This worthy preparation for these Counsellours of State is proportionable to the subject wherein they deale: For if Councell be a certaine diuine and sacred thing, as flowing from God, wee must not hold it strange, if in *China* they honour it in like sort. These men in these rich seats, giue the best and soundest aduice for the glory of their Prince, the good of his Estate, and the ease of his subjects: Their life without reproach, and the wisedome of their spirits inspire them to serue their King worthily. From such men they learne the wise Maximes and Instructions, how to gouerne well, and not from Counsellours whom Auarice disquiets, and Delights peruert and corrupt, and whom Ambition puffes vp: For who will seeke a liuely Spring in a filthy puddle, or draw troubled water to drinke? saith a wise Counsellour and Chancellour of Antiquity. When as any one of these men of the Estate dyes, hee which followes him in order of reception enjoyeth his place, by the Law so strictly obserued in *China*: *That the seruices of euery one should haue the recompences which their conditions may pretend*. They mount by degrees, and there is not any need to demand permission from the Prince. But to fill vp the last place, the Councell makes choice of him that is held the wisest and of greatest experience in the Kingdome; If he be absent, he sends for him: Being come they present him vnto the King, who confirmes or disauowes his election; but that happens seldome: The Counsellour newly chosen takes an Oath in the Kings hands, after this manner: *That hee shall doe Iustice to euery man according to the Lawes of the Realme, and that in this exercise, or in the nomination of Gouernours or Iudges of the State, passion nor affection shall euer supplant (for his part) vertue and merit: That hee shall receiue no Presents: That hee shall preserue with all care the peace of the Realme, and aduertize the King and his Councell of any thing that he shall know to be*

pre-

preiudiciall to his seruice. After this solemne Oath, hee is put into the possession of his charge in one of the thirteene Seats of the Councell Hall. The Imperiall City doth celebrate the solemnity, the whole Realme solemnize that day, and the people rejoyce, by Playes and publique Feasts: Doubtlesse, the passengers haue reason to rejoyce, when as wise Pilots are called to the Gouernment and conduct of the Vessell: For a King which beleeues Councell, hath need of wise and well aduised men, which may counsell him without passion. The President only of this Councell may speake vnto the King, which hee doth alwayes vpon his knee, with a singular respect: When as hee is sicke, it is the ancient Auditor of the golden Seats. Happy in truth are the men of *China*, which liue in a Realme, whereas vertue receiues her honours and reward: But more happy if the worship of the true God did guide them to eternall felicity, by the meanes of a better Religion, then that which doth diuert them. Although the Realme of *China* be of a very great extent, as we haue already said; yet the Kings Councell is aduertized monethly of all that passeth in the Prouinces, which are most remote from the Court; The Viceroyes or Gouernours are bound to giue continuall aduice by Posts. The President of the Councell hauing receiued it, giues an account vnto the King, and informes him exactly, of all that which passeth within his Realme: And if the disorder of any Prouince binds the Councell to dispatch some one from Court, it is done with incredible diligence, and with that secresie which the affaires of Estate, doe many times require. He which is sent departs secretly, arriues vnknowne, and informes himselfe of that which hath past, and then if it be needfull makes himselfe knowne, and shewes his power. Finally, these Counsellours of Estate, not by dozens as in other places, but twelue in number, hold the first and most eminent Rankes of the Realme; For there being no ... Marquesses, Earles, and such persons of that Illustri... , the Law of the Country remouing from Court ...es of the bloud, they receiue in their places, the duties which they would yeeld vnto them; they
visit

of the King of China. 219

visit them with great respect, they speake to them on their knees, and they shew them an extraordinary veneration.

By the aduice of these wise Councellours of State, the King giues the Offices of his Realme, to those whom vertue, and their rare merits haue made most worthy. These charges, or the most eminent are sixe in number. The first is that of Vice-roy of the Prouince, whom in their language they call *Comon*: He is the Soueraigne Magistrate, and in his gouernement represents the royall person of his Master. The second is the *Infuanto*; Hee is next to the *Comon* Gouernour of the whole Prouince as in our Countries a Lieutenant Generall for the King. In euery Towne of the Prouince remaynes a Gouernour, called *Tutan*, who besides the care hee hath to rule the place which is committed vnto him; he is also bound in the execution of his charge to relate vnto the *Infuanto*, the principall affaires of the place where he commands, who doth aduertise the *Comon*, and the *Comon* giues aduice to the King and his Councell. The third is the *Ponchasi*, or Superintendant of the Treasure, who hath many inferiour Officers vnder him, and a compleate Councell: Hee payes with the money that is brought vnto him, all the Officers of the Prouince, and consignes the remainder into the hands of the *Tutan*. The fourth is the *Toior*, who is Captaine Generall of the men of warre which are in the Prouince, be they horse or foot. The fift is the *Anchasi* or President, and Soueraigne Iudge of the Iustice; as well in Ciuill as Criminall causes: His Iudgement decides defintiuely, the controuersies which are brought before him by appeale from inferiour Iudges. The sixt, is the *Aytao*, or President of the Councell of warre, whose chiefe charge consists in leuying of Souldiers, aswell for the Armies by Land as Sea, and to furnish and prouide that which is necessary, for the Garrisons which are vpon the Frontiers. Moreouer, he hath the care to obserue strangers, which come into the Prouince, and to examine them exactly, to know from whence they are, and to what intent they are entred in the Realme, and to aduertise the Vice-roy diligently of all. These charges haue the greatest lustre & glory of the Realme,

Ff 3   and

Officers of China.

and either of these aboue named Officers, hath vnder him ten Auditors, chosen amongst those, whom they hold the most discreet and best practized in affaires ; who ease and helpe them in the expedition thereof. These Auditours are in the function of their places of great esteeme thorough the whole Countrey; they assemble vsually, at the lodging of the *Comon* or Vice-roy, in a stately Hall, appointed to hold the Councell: Fiue of them sit on the right hand of him that doth precide, and fiue others on the left, those which are on the right hand are the most ancient, and haue precedence before the others; Moreouer, their habit doth shew the difference; for they carry a girdle garnished with gold, and hats of a pale colour, where as they on the left hand, haue only siluer to garnish their girdles, and weare blue Hats. But both the one and the other, together with the President, carry before their brests, and on their shoulders the Kings Armes, which are two Serpents imbroydered with gold. This marke is so necessary for them, as they dare not goe forth in publique, nor exercise their places without it. The History crownes these Iudges, and Officers of *China*, with the commendation which the vertues it makes mention of deserue, and especially for their admirable patience: They heare (saith the History) the parties very patiently, euen in the heate of their passions; and the confused trouble of many, yea, of those the heat of affaires doth cause to speake disorderly, doth not trouble this goodly vertue in them to beare without choller, those which are transported. And their words are accompanied with such an incredible sweetnesse, as they are gracious euen to those whom they condemne. Such are the Officers and Iudges of *China*, whom vertue and experience doth aduance to the dignity of the Realme, and not money and ignorance.

Other inferiour Officers.

Besides these six principall Officers, there are many others inferiour and subordinate to those, as the *Cantoc*, which is the great Ensigne-bearer; the *Pothin*, which is the second Treasurer; the *Pochniss*, or keeper of the Seales; the *Autzatzi*, or high Prouost: three Iudges of their Court, which are called *Hugtag*, *Txia*, and *Tontay*, who giue audience in their houses.

ses once a wecke, and before they open their gates, they cause three peece of Ordnances to bee shot off to giue notice that they are going to their seats: Imitating in the grauity of their Seats of Iustice, the wrath of the thunder of Heauen, which doth not only serue to aduertise innocents, but to be a terrour, and amazement to the guilty. They haue vnder them a great number of Prouosts, for the execution of Iustice: But they are not so absolute in their Iudgements, but there is another Iudge aboue them, who may reforme them: Hee is called *Hondim*, that is to say, a repairer of euill: It is also his profession to repaire it by his Decree, if the other Iudges haue failed in their Iudgements. The *Toivpo* is also of the Court, and after his example, that Office is erected in Townes that are remote: His care is to prouide for victuals, and to set the price. The *Quinchey*, which signifies in their Language, Seale of Gold, is an Officer which neuer parts from Court, if some businesse of importance doth not force him: Hee causeth the Edicts of peace to bee published, and such like which the King establisheth.

This in generall is the relation of the Officers of *China*: Let vs examine it now in particular, to know by what means they do exercise their places worthily. As soon as they are aduanced, they part to goe to execute them: The charges of their Voyage is defraide by the King, and likewise their lodging where they are to remayne: The which is so vast, as all the Officers of Iustice dwell therein, for the commodity of the publique, and the speedy execution of Iustice. The wages which they receiue, may well supply all their expences, with which they must rest satisfied, for to take any present from the parties, the Law so rigorously obserued within the Realme, forbids them expresly vpon great penalties and likewise the parties, who are not allowed to go and see the Iudges in their houses. They must repaire to the accustomed audiences to haue Iustice from them: When the Iudge is in his seate, the Vshers goe to the entry of the Hall, and name with a loud voice the party that comes for Iustice, and likewise deliuers what he demands. The party enters presently, kneeles downe before the Iudge, and pro-

A particular description of these Officers.

propounds his demand; or if it be in writing, giues it to the Register, who reads it; the Iudge ordaines presently what is Iust, and writes his Iudgement himselfe with red Inke, to auoid the faults which Registers commit: whereof in other places, they feele the inconueniences which happen to the prejudice of the parties: These Iudges are bound to goe fasting to their Audiences; and if their infirmities require some comfort in their weaknesses, they may only vse Conserues by way of Physicke: If it happens that they drinke any Wine before the Audience, they shall bee no lesse punished, then if they had committeed the crime of some violent concussion. Their Iudgements are executed in euery point without any fraud: In all matters the Iudges proceed by writing, and if the businesse bee of importance, they write the Acts themselues and the Depositions of witnesses: So as few men complaine of their Iustice, and there are few appeales to superiour Iudges. In their Iurisdictions, they register the number of the houses which depend of them, they set them by tens in a Table, in the which they write the names of the Inhabitants, and the Kings Decree; which enjoynes all persons of what qualitie and condition soeuer, to reueale presently vnto the Iustice, what they shall see committed by any of their Neighbours against the publique good, to the end they may be speedily punished. If any one of the ten leaues the Countrie, the Towne or Street, to goe any journey, hee ought ten dayes before his departure, to ring a little Bell or a Copper Bason, throughout the whole Quarter, to the end that if he owe any money, his creditors, may haue notice of his departure; or if any man hath lent him any thing, hee may come and demand it: If he seekes to steale away in secret, the Neighbours must watch, for in his absence the Iudges will force them to pay his debts. But there are few found that breake: The lawes strictly obserued in *China*, punish them seuerely: They giue them dayes for payment: If they faile at the first, they whip them in prison; if they do not satisfie at the second, they double their stripes and if they be obstinate till the third time, they beat him vntill he bleeds, and keepe him continually in prison.

For

of the King of China.   223

For this reason when some are troubled to pay their debts, they implore the helpe of all the World to be freed, and not able to obtaine their libertie in this manner, they sell themselues vnto their Creditors, to auoid the sensible stripes of the Whip. When as any Iudge goes forth in publique (the which happens seldome, their custome being to be much retired, for that by this meanes, they say, they are lesse diuerted, and maintaine their authoritie better) hee goes accompanied with all the Officers of Iustice, whereof the two first which goe in ranke, carrie vpon their shoulders two long Maces of siluer, for a signe that they are Officers of Iustice; two others which follow them, haue in their hands a long strait Reed, and carry it in like manner, shewing thereby that they must doe vpright Iustice, which the Iudge whom they accompany will performe: In the third Ranke are two other Officers, who also carrie Reeds, but they dragge them on the ground with long red Girdles; These are the Scourges wherewith they whip Offenders, if they encounter any: A fourth ranke followes them; these are two men which carrie two white Tables, in the which is written the name of the Iudge his office & qualitie: The rest of the traine are persons which accompany the Magistrate for honour. This pompe and conuoy of Iustice, is no vaine ostentation of these Officers, they liue as they speak, and are such as they appeare, that is to say, indued with vertue, exact and entire in their Offices, and of a life without reproach: But men are men, and no gods, which cannot run into vices, and the integritie of a Magistrate, being in an inconstant and changeable life, may erre, although it happens lesse in *China* than elsewhere. The King and his Councell haue prouided necessary remedies for this inconuenience, which punish those that faile, and keeping the rest in awe, make them to containe themselues in their duties; The charges of such Officers continue but three yeares, after the which they must giue an accompt of the administration thereof before Iudges called *Chaenes*. Notwithstanding the King sends Visiters yearely called *Lenthu* thorowout all the Prouinces of his Realme, men which are faithfull to his seruice, of great experience

The Visitor of the Court.

perience in worldly affaires, and of singular integrity. This Delegation is made so secretly, as it is not knowne to any, but to the King and President of his Councell, who causeth the Secretary of Estate to dispatch Letters, leauing a blanke for his name they send, and for the Prouince whither he goes: They adde vnto the Letters this necessary clause to the Visiters absolute power; *That whithersoeuer the Iudge or Loytias shall goe, carrying those Letters of prouision, hee shall be obeyed like the King himselfe.* These Letters sealed, the President addes the name of the Visiter, and of the Prouince whither hee is sent: hauing receiued them, he departs so secretly from Court and trauels so vnknowne, as no man vnderstands what he is, or whither he goes. He arriues thus vnknowne into the Prouince or the Island which hee is to visit, goes thorough the Country, trauels from Towne to Towne, and informes himselfe with all care and diligence, of the carriage of the Officers, euen from the Vice-roy to the meanest Auditour, and yet in this exact reformation, he makes not himselfe knowne to any. When he hath ended his course, and thinkes that hee hath sufficient proofes of the sincerity of some, and of the misbehauiour of others, he goes to the chiefe Towne of the Prouince, and there attends the day when such Officers meete in Councell. The which is once a moneth at the Vice-royes lodging, or in his absence with the *Tutan*. When they are assembled, he comes to the gate, commands an Vsher to giue them notice, that there is a Iudge which will enter, to signifie the Kings pleasure vnto them. The Vice-roy who conceiues partly what it may be, causeth the gates to be opened, leaues his seate, and accompanied with the other Officers, goes to receiue him, as his Superiour: He enters, carrying the Letters of prouision in his hand. These Patents strike terrour into some of the assembly, and the Iudges which are guilty shew by their pale countenances the markes of their offences; They cause it to be openly read: After which the Vice-roy riseth from his seate, makes many low courtesies and submissions to the Visitor, and all the rest doe the like. Then he takes his seate in the most eminent place, and lets them vnderstand by a

graue

graue and serious Oration, the subject of his comming, the care which he hath taken, to make his Visitation thorough the Prouince, and to enforme himselfe exactly and truly of their behauiours: Crownes the vertue and integrity of such as haue done well, with a thousand commendations, promiseth to make his report vnto the King, and to his Councell, assuring them of the recompence which their good seruices deserue, and in the meane time aduanceth them to the most honourable places of the Councell in the Prouince. After that these good men haue receiued from his mouth and hand this honest testimony of their vertue; hee doth publiquely reproch such, as he hath found defectiue and culpable, the basenesse of their traffique in the sale of Iustice, makes them to see the shame of their concussions, and sets downe in particular the number of their faults. The effect doth presently follow this shamefull reproach, hee thunders out against them the sentence of condemnation, depriues them of their Offices, and strips them of the tokens thereof, taking from them in the face of the whole Councell, the Girdle and Hat with a little brim: If their faults deserue a greater punishment, he leaues it to the judgement of the Soueraigne Prince, and to his Councell: for the Law of *China* forbids all Iudges, to condemne any man to death before they haue aduertized the King, and hee hath resolued what they shall doe. But thus they execute Iustice in *China*, vpon those which deny it to others: In this manner recompence being apparant there, yea, certaine for vertue, and punishment for vice, most men imbrace the first to enjoy its crownes, and flie the other to auoide the miseries which accompany it: and the Realme of *China* enjoyeth all manner of felicitie.

This wise policie is practized in *China*, to containe the Inhabitants in their duty: But Realmes like vnto mans body, are not only assaulted by home-bred Enemies; Strangers may ruine them, as the Sword kils the body of man aswell as the diseases which haue their spring & fountain within it. For this reason the Soueraigne Monarch of *China* furnishes his places with good Garrisons, and when need requires couereth

The guards & forces of the Realme.

the fields with armed men; settles forces vpon the Ports of the Sea, and opposeth against forreigne violence, the best, and most resolute troupes of his Estates, which preserue it against their designes and assaults. Let vs first obserue the vigilancie and greatnesse of his forces by land, and then we will speake of those at Sea. Euery Prouince hath his Councell of Warre, supplyed with the most valiant and expert men of Warre in the whole Realme; They dispose of the Souldiers according to occasions and occurrents, and cause them to be paid so exactly, as they lose not any thing in their Musters: For the Treasurers which keepe the Kings Cofers, haue commandement not to refuse them any thing. Their Townes are not fortified with Bastions, nor defended by strong Towres, The Monarch of *China*, practiseth the aduice of that generous *Grecian*, who said that the best defences of a City consisted in the valour of the Citizens: Yet they haue good wals inuironed with deep ditches, which they fill with water by the current of Riuers, when they please: The best fortifications which may defend them well, are the good Garrisons they put into them, who keepe a very strict Guard, not suffering any man to enter nor goe forth, without leaue in writing from the Magistrate, or Gouernour which commands therein: They shut the gates carefully, seale vp the locks, and neuer open them till after the rising of the Sunne, and that they haue acknowledged their Seales. Their Artillery which is excellent good (the vse whereof was first knowne to them before it came to vs) is vsually placed vpon the said Gates. The Captaines are Natiues of the Prouinces which they guard, to the end that the naturall loue to their Country, together with the duty of their charges, should augment their care for the preseruation of places. They lodge vpon the wals of Townes, where their houses are built of purpose, to the end they may be continually in their vocation; they doe it without contradiction or any resistance of the Inhabitants of the Townes which they guard, for the Law of the State hath depriued them of all meanes to reuolt, hauing forbidden them the

ear-

of the King of China.

carrying of Armes, or to haue any in their houses, vpon paine of death, not allowing any, but such as are in the Kings pay, who succeed in that qualitie from Father to Sonne. They are distributed by thousands, whereof euery hundred hath a Captaine and an Ancient, and all these haue one Commander, as with vs the Colonell of a Regiment. They practise often, to keepe the Souldiers in breath, lest Idlenesse should rust their Armes, and soften their courages: Their Armes are Harquebusses, Pikes, Staues with Irons, and Hatchets. The Horsemen vse other Armes; when they goe to fight they carry foure Swords at their Saddle pommell, they hold two in their hands when they charge, and make vse of them with great dexteritie: They likewise vse Darts and Launces. They haue beene accustomed to be inuironed with a troupe of Groomes, which are about them when they enter battaile, the which are nimble and well armed: Their valour consists in policie, and stratagems of war, where they imploy their minds more than their courages, to charge the Enemy openly. They are very bad Horsemen, and mannage their Horses with a whip and the voice; and haue no other bitts but a peece of Iron, which goes crosse to the mouth. Their Armes are light, and their courages heauy.

Thus this Cauallery makes not the best part of the forces of *China*, the which are so great, as they are sufficient to guard many Realmes: It is true that the vast and great Prouinces where they are established, containe euery one in its dimension, the extent of a Realme. That of *Pagnie*, whereas the King makes his residence, hath for its guard two Millions, a hundred and fifty thousand foote, and fourescore thousand horse. That of *Canton*, hath six score thousand foot, and fortie thousand horse; that of *Foquien* fifty eight thousand, and nine hundred foot, with two and twenty thousand and foure hundred horse. *Olam*, seuenty six thousand foot, and fiue and twenty thousand fiue hundred horse. *Quinsay*, fourescore thousand six hundred foot, and no horse, by reason of the scituation of the Country full of Mountaines and Rocks: *Oquian* likewise hath not any: Its guard consists only in sixe score thou-

The number of his guards and forces.

thousand six hundred foot. The Prouince of *Susuam*, hath fourescore sixe thousand foot, and thirty foure thousand fiue hundred horse. That of *Tolanchie*, neighbour to the *Tartars*, with whom the Kings of *China* haue many times had great and bloudy warres, is fortified with two Millions eight hundred thousand foot, supported by two hundred fourescore and ten thousand horse; these are the best and most warlike Souldiers in the Realme. *Cansay* hath fifty thousand foot, with twenty thousand two hundred and fiftie horse. *Aucheo* is guarded by fourescore and six thousand foot, and forty eight thousand horse. *Honan*, forty foure thousand foot, and eighteene thousand nine hundred horse. *Xanton*, hath seuenty six thousand foot, and ten thousand a hundred and fifty horse. *Quichen*, forty eight thousand and seuen hundred foot, and fifteene thousand three thousand horse. *Chequean* hath thirtie foure thousand foot, with thirteen thousand horse: and *Sansy*, the least Prouince of all the rest, forty thousand foot, and sixe thousand horse. All the which forces amount to fiue Millions, eight hundred forty six thousand, fiue hundred foot, and fiue hundred forty eight thousand horse. This World of men armed (if they were valiant) might conquer all the rest of the habitable Earth. But the History makes their courages inferiour to the Men of *Europe*. The most redoubted Warriours of Antiquitie, who haue conquered many Realmes in *Asia*, triumphed ouer *Africke*, and strooke a terrour into *Europe*, had nothing in their forces that might approch the number of the Garrisons of *China*: And truly the History should be suspected vnto me, and in a manner fabulous, if it did not proue the truth of its relation by the great number of Townes, and the vast extent of a Realme; which may containe fifteene well peopled, for that euery Prouince of *China*, hath its greatnes like vnto a great Monarchie. But these fearefull forces banish the troubles of their Estate; for they take Armes to enjoy rest and tranquility, and warre is many times made to haue peace: The Garrisons of the Sea Ports, and the Guards which are in the Rhodes or open Harbours, for the safetie of Merchants, are comprehended in this number. The King entertaines ma-

ny

ny ships of warre, well armed, which guard the Ports, and the Hauens to restraine the courses & spoyles of Pyrats. These Vessels are of diuers sorts: Some are very great, they call them *Ionsos*: Others are lesse, and like vnto our Frigats, they call them *Bancoens*: Some are larger than these, and haue many bankes; euery banke hath eight Oares, and euery Oare hath six men, they call them *Lanteas*.

To defray the expences of so many Souldiers, to pay the wages of the Officers of Iustice and Treasure, and to furnish the Royall Pallace with all things necessary, the Soueraigne Prince of *China* ought to haue a great and powerfull reuenue: He leuies it vpon Men, Houses, Graine, Mines of gold and siluer, vpon precious stones, Pearles, Porcelaines, Wools, Cottons, and Silkes. The men of these fifteene Prouinces, are for a great part exempt from all Tribute: as the *Loytias*, the Iudges, Officers, and Souldiers: Yet the number of such as pay, is not small: For the Prouince of *Pagnie*, containes two Millions seuen hundred and foure thousand Tributaries: That of *Canton*, three Millions six hundred thousand: *Foquien*, two Millions foure hundred and seuen thousand: The Prouince of *Aucheo*, two Millions eight hundred and forty thousand: That of *Olam* two Millions, two hundred thirty foure thousand: That of *Cinsay*, three Millions, three hundred and eighty thousand: *Susnam*, two Millions fifty thousand: *Tolauchie* six Millions, ninety thousand: *Cansay* two Millions, three hundred and fiue thousand: *Oquian* three Millions eight hundred thousand: *Honan* a Million two hundred thousand: *Xanton*, a Million nine hundred forty foure thousand: *Chequint* two Millions, two hundred forty foure thousand: *Quichew*, two Millions three hundred thousand: and *Sancij*, a Million six hundred seuenty thousand, and fiue hundred Tributaries. All these Tributaries doe euery one pay yearly two Mases; the Mase may be in estimation a shilling of our money, which is in yearely reuenew to the King for this Tribute alone, fourteene Millions two hundred fifty three thousand, a hundred sixty and seuen French Crownes. Besides this, the other Tributes raise his Reuenue much: The Mines of gold,

The reuenews of the King of China.

pay him yearely in fine gold, from seuenteene to two and twenty Carrats, foure Millions two hundred fifty sixe thousand nine hundred *Taes*, the *Tae* is in estimation an Italian Crowne. The Mines of siluer yeeld him in pure siluer, three Millions, a hundred fifty three thousand, two hundred and nineteene *Taes*: That of precious stones, a Million foure hundred and seuenty thousand *Taes*. The fishing for Pearles brings into his Cofers two Millions, sixe hundred and thirtie thousand *Taes*. The custome vpon Sents and Perfumes, as Muske and Amber, is worth a Million, and thirty fiue thousand *Taes*: That which is laid vpon Porcelins brings fourescore and ten thousand *Taes*: making in all this second Tribute, eleuen Millions fiue hundred, fourescore and foure thousand French Crownes: So as hitherto the reuenew in siluer, amounts to about six and twenty thousand Millions of gold. But the third Tribute of Graines, Salt, Wooll, Cottons and Silke exceeds all that. This powerfull and rich Monarch giues vnto his Subjects a very great quantity of Lands, which depend of the Crowne, vpon condition that they shall yeeld vnto him yearely, a part of that which they gather, which serues for the necessary prouisions of his Royall Pallace, and for the Officers of his Realme. From this Tribute they which are appointed to gather it, retire yearely, three score Millions, a hundred seuenty one thousand, eight hundred and thirty measures of white Rice, which is the most ordinary food of the men of *China*, and of their Neighbours: Nine and twenty Millions, three hundred nineti one thousand, nine hundred fourescore and two measures of Barley: Thirty three Millions, six score thousand, two hundred Measures of Wheate: Twenty Millions, two hundred and fifty thousand Measures of Mesline: Twenty fiue Millions, three hundred and forty thousand, foure hundred Measures of Salt: Twenty foure thousand Measures of Millet: In other Graine and Pulses, fifty foure Millions of Measures. The Silke which is wrought into Cloth, doth furnish him with two hundred and sixe thousand peeces of the rarest workes, and euery peece is fourteene Ells long: That which is in Masse, makes him fiue hundred and

of the King of China.

and forty thousand pound weight. He hath in Cotton, three hundred thousand pound weight: The working of Couerings for Beds, yeeld him of the best sort, eight hundred thousand foure hundred peeces: Raw-silke payes him the weight of foure thousand pound. The workes of Cotton bring vnto him six hundred seuenty eight thousand peeces of that stuffe, euery peece being fourteene Ells long; the raw Cotton yeelds him the weight of three hundred foure thousand, six hundred forty eight pounds: So as the value of these commodities, augmenting the summes of the Tribute in Siluer, make the yearely Reuenew of this great Empire, to amount to six score Millions of Gold.

These great and immense Treasures of the King of *China*, leuied vpon his Subjects, and the excellent prudence wherewith hee gouernes his Estate, and ordaines of so rich a Reuenew; haue made him to take for his Armes, two Serpents interlaced one within another; and the immense extent of so vast and fertile a Realme, full of all sorts of felicities, haue caused him to insert in his Titles, the quality of *Lord of the World, and the Childe of Heauen*: And truly seeing this Countrey, is a World in greatnesse and bounty, hee hath reason to tearme himselfe the Lord. The Kings are in effect doubly the children of Heauen, aswell by the benefit of their Creation like other men, as by the excellent priuiledge of their Soueraignty, which is the liuely Image of the heauenly. But the Monarch of *China*, in the vanity of his deceitfull Religion, and the false worship of his Idols, liues like a childe of the earth. Yet the greatnesse of his treasures, the power of his forces, the fertilitie of his Country, and the extent of his Estate, hath transported the pride of his spirit to that insolencie, as to contemne all the rest of men, and not to esteeme any but those of *China*. They of *Europe* are lesse opprest with his contempt. Hee saith often, and this vaine bragge is in the mouthes of his Subjects, that the men of *China* haue two eyes, that they of *Europe* haue but one; and that all the rest of men vpon the earth are blind.

Notwithstanding this defect, which is common to many

Princes,

The Armes & Titles of the King of China.

Embassadours how they are received in China.

Princes, yet the amity and alliance of so rich and powerfull a Monarch, deserues to be sought after by other Soueraignes; His Neighbours esteeme it and desire it. The *Tartar*, his capitall enemy demands it, and the King of *Spaine* hath held it profitable for the good of his Estate, and the glory of his Majesty. Thus when these Princes, send Embassadours vnto him to that end, or to treat of some important affaires, he receiues them, honours them, and giues them all kind of good reception. When they enter into the Realme, the Gouernour of the place by which they passe, assisted by all the *Loytias* and Captaines of the Country, goe to meet them, to let them vnderstand by their goodly speeches that they are welcome. If they arriue by Sea, although there be but a little space from the Port to the Towne where they land: Yet they will not suffer them to goe on foot, but they carry them in Chaires richly embroydered with Pearle, and couered with Curtaines of Cloth of Gold, by eight men, whereof there are some in the principall Townes, appointed to that vse: For the Law of *China* saith: *Let a forreigne Embassadour be receiued and honoured in the like sort, as if the Prince which sends him came into the Realme*. Being arriued they lodge them in a Lodging made for them, built like a Pallace, and royally furnished with all things necessary, where they are serued and treated at the Kings charge, and in like sort during their whole Voyage, whereas a thousand Souldiers guard and accompany them at the Kings cost. The day after their arriuall the Gouernour who had receiued them, goes to visit them, and after many honest complements, demands the subject of their Embassie, and hearing it, hee presently dispatcheth a Post to the chiefe Towne of the Prouince, where the Vice-roy remaynes, by whom he giues him aduice. The Vice-roy dispatcheth the same Post to Court, and writes vnto the King and his Councell, who sends a safe conduct to the Embassadours for their Voyage. Hauing receiued it, they take their way towardes the Court, accompanied with that number of Souldiers which we haue mentioned. They are fed and defrayed by the Kings Treasures, and wheresoeuer they passe they doe them all ho-

honour: When they arrive at the Royall Citie of *Tabin*, the ordinary abode of the Court; the Kings Councell being followed by the principall Knights, goe to meet him: The President of this Royall Councell makes a band apart, with a Kingly traine and pompe. If the Embassadours come from great Monarches, this great President takes the left hand: If they come from meaner Princes, hee takes the right, and in this ranke doth accompany them to the Lodging which is prepared for them, whereof the moueables and the preparation for the entertainment of Embassadours are in truth worthy of the greatnesse and magnificence of the King of *China*: By the way he entertains them with the encounters of their voyage, and the estate of their health; An Interpreter which they haue with them, assists him which vnderstands not the Language: When they are arriued before the Pallace where they are to lodge; the President leaues them, and at his parting giues them power on the Kings behalfe, to create a number of *Loytias* or Knights, and to deliuer many Prisoners condemned to die, for a confirmation and assurance that they are welcome to that Court. The law of *China* frees them from all manner of inconueniences, that is to say, that for what crime soeuer the Embassadour commits in the Estate, his person may not in any sort be molested: He spends some dayes in his Pallace before he hath audience, to the end that rest may refresh him from the toile of his Voyage. In the meane time the greatest of the Court inuite him, they let him see the best companies thereof, and the magnificence of their Feasts; After which they giue him a day to come to Audience: The King assisted by his Councell, and the chiefest men of his Court, giues it him in one of those stately Hals, whereof we haue formerly made mention; there he treats of the subiect of his Embassie, and after hee hath receiued an answere, returnes laden with Presents towards the Prince which sent him. His returne is as sweet and pleasing as his comming, hee is accompanied with the same troupe, defraide in like manner at the Kings charge, and wheresoeuer hee passeth receiued with the like courtesie and honour.

Hh But

Embassadours of the Tributaries of China.

But all Embassadours which come into *China*, are not entertained in the same manner: For such as come from Princes or Common-weales which are their Tributaries, are receiued according to their condition, and as depending vpon the Realme. When they arriue, one Iudge receiues them, lodgeth them, and defrayes them at the Kings charge; at the Court their reception is equall vnto it; the Iudge which entertaines them, demands the subject of their Voyage, and they tell it him: He doth aduertise the President of the Councell, and the President tels the King, who giues them a day of audience: But when they goe, it is on foot, or if their indisposition will not suffer it, they goe on horsebacke without a Bridle, hauing only a Halter, for a marke of humilitie and vassallage: They haue no other Company but the Iudge which receiued them, with whom they take their way to the Royall Pallace; When they are arriued before it, they attend in a spacious place; a certaine Officer of the Kings, who is like a Master of the Ceremonies who makes a signe vnto them afarre off, that they should march, and sheweth them the place where they should begin to kneele, to ioyne their hands, and to lift them vp on high in signe of adoration, and to lift vp their eyes towards the place where they tell them the King remaynes: Thus they approach vnto the Pallace, and enter it after they haue made fiue reuerences, or rather fiue adorations: They come into the first hall which is the manor of the Pallace, where the President of the Councell, Majestically set, and not the King (whom they see not) giues them audience, after which hee sends them backe without any answere, vntill he hath spoken with the King: Then his Maiesties pleasure is signified vnto them by the Iudge, who hath had the care of their conduct. Thus they returne as they came; without any honour, as in some sort Subiects to the Estate of *China*: For such Principalities or Common-weales, which send them, haue sometimes beene Prouinces of the Realme, but for that they were remote, when as the *Chinois* shut themselues vp within the inclosure of the Mountaines, with that great wall of fiue hundred leagues long, they gaue these Prouinces to those which now possesse

possesse them, reseruing a Tribute and Homage.

If the Embassadour of any Soueraigne Prince brings Pre- | Presents
sents to the King of *China*, and that the Law and custome of | brought by
the Countrey binde him to send his Passeport from *Canton*, to | Embassadours.
some Port or Towne of the Realme: The Gouernours of the
place where he arriues, receiue not the Present in their owne
But he lookes vpon it in the presence of a Notary, and some
witnesses, states it vp, and so sends it to Court, without handling
they giue vnto himselfe: It is to happen somewhat to passe from that
Embassadours which *Philip* the Second King of *Spaine* sent
vnto *China*. For it is expresly forbidden vpon great penalties to all persons which are in charge with it, that they neuer
ceiue any Present from any whatsoeuer, Nay not from their
neerest Kinsmen. But that the Embassadours which goe in
neere with it, Perhaps not heede such deliuered. The whole
seruice that the *Chinois* are men, and haue as good qualities,
as any other Nation vpon Earth. They haue with them Lear- | The learning
ning and the Sciences, which are the true ornaments of the | and studie of
minde; and that light which shineth in their men, in the obscure | *China*.
Labyrinth of great affaires. Their children are to be
instructed from their youth, in Colledges ordained for that
end. The Character which they vse, doth somewhat resem-
ble the Hieroglyphicks of the ancient Egyptians; for euery
one signifies a whole word, and sometimes a period. As for
example, they call Heauen *Quen*, which is a word of fiue
letters and yet ⿻ they write it by one alone painted in
this manner. ⿻ They call a Towne *Leombi*; and this
word is also exprest by one ⿻ letter only, or rather figure, that is to say, that ⿻ which followeth, which
is the reason they haue so great a number of Letters or Characters all different, which make six thousand. Their Realme
containes diuers kinds of Languages, yet they vnderstand all
by writing: For although that one thing be called diuersly in
many Prouinces, yet they write it after one manner thoroughout the Country: as a Towne which we said, was called
Leombi at the Court, in other places they terme it *Fu*; and
generally they write it in the same manner that I haue described

bed it. The people speake the common Language of the Countrie, but the learned and Courtiers, as they are all, haue one particular and familiar to themselues; they call it the *Mandarin*, which is as the Latine amongst men of Learning. There are few or none in *China* how base soeuer their condition be, but can read and write: For in their Country the qualities of the mind are in singular recommendation, and are much honoured, and carefully rewarded. They haue printing in perfection. It was inuented with vs. Homer before that the industrious *German, Iohn of Gutemberg*, taught vs the vse, in the yeare 1458, which was its beginning in *Europe*. The first moulds were cast at *Ments*. The first Booke which past the Presse, was that learned Worke of great Saint *Augustine*, called, *Of the City of God. From this Germany* carried it into *Italy* and elsewhere. Before all this, it had beene brought from *China* by Merchants which trafficke into that Country, who comming into *Arabia* the happy, past the Red Sea: After which they were in *Russia*, and *Muscouie*, where they left Bookes printed after the manner of *China* in the Characters of the Countrie, which were brought into *Germany*, and comming to the knowledge of *Gutemberg*, did furnish him with an example to imitate them, and to mould Characters: for the *Chinois* maintaine, and there is some colour, that all the rest of the World owe the inuention of Printing vnto them. It is writ that there were Bookes printed with them, aboue fiue hundreth yeares before that Printing came to the knowledge of them of *Europe*. The Paper which they vse is very fine and thin, they make it of the cloth of Canes or Reeds: Their pens are of the same Reeds, cut & pointed at the end like vnto Painters Pensils: They write from the right hand to the left, and draw the lines from the top to the bottome. Thoroughout all the Townes of the Realme there are Royall Colledges, where the youth is instructed, and in Butroughs there are Schooles at the Kings charge, where they teach them to reade and write, which causeth the meanest men, to make their children in their youth, to learne this honest and profitable exercise. They teach *gratis* in those great Colledges, Morall

and

and Naturall Philosophy, Astrologie; the Lawes of the Kingdome, with many other goodly and curious Sciences. The Regents or Readers are very learned, and the Schollers very studious: They know their great labour shall not be without reward; that the studie of Learning, by the good qualities which they infuse into their spirits, are degrees to mount into great places both in Court and Realme: For in the Court of *China* you shall find no ignorant men, and to be so in that place were a great infamy. The Visiters whom the King appoints repaire often to these Colledges, examine the Schollers, and honour such as they find diligent in their studies, with many recompences. This is the cause why this great Realme abounds in men of merit, and that their spirits thrust on with a desire of glory which is infallible, labour continually in their studies, and giue vnto the publique the profit of their rare workes. The Book-sellers of *China* are full of goodly peeces, the curiositie of Christians hath brought them into *Europe*, Heauen suffering it, to the end that the glory of their Authours should not be confined within the enclosure of the Mountaines and Wall, which shuts vp *China*. The Library of the *Vatican* at *Rome*, and that of the Royall Monasterie of Saint *Lawrence* in *Spaine*, haue many goodly Volumes of *China*: whereof some treat of Astrologie, of Morall Phylosophy, of the number of the Heauens, the motion of the Planets and of their influences; and the proprietie of stones and mettals, and of the secrets of Physique; Others containe the Lawes of the Kingdome, and the Reuenewes thereof, the Art of Warre, with the meanes how to conduct Nauall Armies, and many other Sciences, whereof the glory and profit: fils *China* with many felicities; and hath furnished the men thereof with precepts and meanes to gouerne free from the tempests and stormes of Ciuill Warres, whereas many others make shipwracke of the Estates which they possesse: For wee find in their Histories that for aboue two thousand yeares, they haue preserued and maintained their Monarchie, against the troubles which might rise therein, and about that vast extent.

But

But the vertue of the *Chinois* is not without diuersion, and the long rest which they enjoy with abundance of wealth, produceth delights among them, and guides their liues into the charmes of voluptuousnesse. The most ordinary which steales from their serious occupations a part of the time which should be deere vnto them, are their proud and stately Feasts, where they treate themselues deliciously: They make them in this manner. They giue to euery one of the guests (how great soeuer the number be) his table apart, where hee eats alone: these tables are of rare Art, the wood is exquisite, & the worke singular; they are inlayed with streaks of gold or siluer, interlaced so artificially, as they represent the figures of Birds, Fields, and Chases of diuers sorts; For the workmen of *China* in the excellency of their Art, are wonderfull industrious, and carry the prize aboue all the World. They couer not the tables with any clothes, the neatnesse and handsomenesse of the *Chinois* in their feeding needs not any; they lay on Carpets of Damaske, or such like stuffe, hanging downe to the ground; they place vpon the foure corners of the table many little open Panniers, wouen with fillets of gold and siluer, some are full of diuers sorts of flowres made of Sugar, represented to the life: Others carrie a pleasing diuersitie of many Beasts made likewise of Sugar, as Elephants, Lions, Stags, and Hindes; some are full of Birds of the same stuffe. In the midst of the table is set exquisite meate, which makes a part of the guests good cheere: this is commonly of all sorts of Fowle and Venison in dishes of Siluer and goodly Porcelane: they eat neatly and take their meate with Forkes of Gold and Siluer, neuer touching it with their hands: the Wine they drinke is vsually made of Palme; delicious to the taste, and lesse fuming to the head; the tables are set round, to the end the guests may see one another: Whilest they make good cheere in this manner, many Musicians and Players of Instruments giue vnto their senses the sweetnesse of their pleasing consort; some others represent the inuention of some pleasant History: their Banquets are neuer without a Comedy; the which is excellently well performed, the personages are very actiue, and the

apparell

apparell is proper to the representation: the Banquet is of all sorts of fruit, and comfitures in great abundance, whereof the vse is very common in *China*. The Courtiers and other men of *China*, doe often spend their time in these delicious Feasts: But particularly on the day of the great Feasts of their Religion, which they celebrate the first day of the Moone in *March*, they giue vnto their senses all the pleasures they can desire; they attire themselues in state, and weare the richest Iewels they haue; they plant great trees at their gates, like vnto the May-poles in our Countries, they hang before their houses many peeces of Silke and cloth of Gold: they crowne the streets with many triumphant Arches; they giue light vnto the night, with a number of lights which they hang vpon these trees: and they feast it perpetually.

The excesses are greater, when as the Courtiers or great men of the Realme entertaine their equals, or feast the Embassadours of some Soueraigne Prince: then their magnificence shewes it selfe with a greater lustre. The inuited hath many tables for himselfe, to the number of twenty: He eates at the first, and all the rest are couered with all sorts of raw meats, as Fowle of all sorts, Venison, Gammons of Bacon, and many others. When the Feast is ended, his seruants who hath entertained him carries them before the inuited to his lodging, where they leaue them with great Ceremonies. The Friends or Kinsmen of the house doe the honour; for he which is Master of the Feast, absents himselfe, and for good manners sake, according to the custome of the Countrey appeares not: they which vndertake this care for him (which are men of quality) conduct the inuited to their places in goodly chaires, vnder a Canopie of Veluet; but before they begin to eat, euery man takes his cup, and fils it with Wine, and after they haue made many great courtesies, they goe vnto the windowes, or to some place where they may see the heauens: they offer them to the Sun, and make great discourses in forme of a prayer, and demand of this goodly starre (who cannot but giue them light to see their drinke) constant prosperities for the inuited, and that the friendship which they meane to contract, may be

pro-

profitable and fauourable to both parties. Dissolute Feasts are stormy Seas, where amidst the delights of the body, the vertues of the minde suffer shipwracke. Wherefore, hee that hath left to men the Rules of good Gouernment, aduiseth them to goe rather to the house of mourning, and to the Connoy of Funerals, than to the pleasures of sumptuous Banquets; for that in the one they see before their eyes, the portraite of the end of man, and many times in themselues their owne vanities; and the other bewitching their spirits, steale them from themselues, and make them to forget their condition. It is true that the *Chinois* haue with many others this commendable qualitie, not to order the Estate lesse, than to gouerne, as they doe; with excellency and pompe, the magnificence of a stately Feast: although their licentious Religion doth not forbid them the entertainment of delights and pleasures which are enemies to solid vertues.

The Religion of the Court of *China*.

These men, who say, they haue two eyes, and esteeme others blind, are notwithstanding so blinde, as to hold pieces of wood and stone for gods fashioned into Idols by their own hands: For at the Court as well as in other places of the Kingdome they adore the workes of Painters and Grauers; they keepe in their houses Idols which they reuerence with a particular worship, and haue recourse to their vaine assistance in all their affaires: Their Temples one full, there are some which containe aboue 200. vpon diuers Altars, among the which that of the Deuill, hath alwayes his place, and receiues the like venerations and Sacrifices; not but that the *Chinois* know he is a Reprobate, an Enemy to Mankind, and the authour of the crimes which are committed, but they honour him in this manner, to the end he should doe them no harme, and not to be assisted by him. Besides these dumbe diuinities, they reuerence and pray vnto a great number of men already dead, who in their Realme haue exceeded others in the valour of Armes, in the light of Learning, or in the sanctity of an austere life, & retired in the solitudes of their religious Monasteries they call them *Pausocs*, that is to say, most happy, in which number they put many women, of the which they reuerence three

with

with a singular deuotion. The first they call *Sichie*, who came (as they say) from the Realme of *Trantheyco*, which is towards the West, and brought into *China* the Rules of a Religious life, and was the first inuenter of Cloisters, and of Religious Orders, who liue in common without marrying. Hee had his beard and head shauen, and his followers are so in like manner, and all the Monkes of *China* sing the glory of his name, and extoll the merit of his vertues aboue all the other Saints. The second subject in this ranke of singular holinesse, is a woman called *Canina*: she is worthy of her name, for the deuotion they bear vnto her in *China*, doth gnaw with an important Superstition the spirits of simple women. They say she was daughter to King *Tzonton*, who meaning to marry her to a Prince, as well as her other two sisters, being all children to this Monarch, she would not yeeld vnto it, pretending for her reason, that she had vowed a perpetuall chastity to Heauen. The Father incensed at this deniall, takes reuenge on her. Hee depriues her of her liberty, and shuts her vp into a great house like vnto a Monastery, & in contempt makes her to spend her time in base and abject things, causing her to carry water and wood, and to cleanse a great Garden which depended on this place; shee doth it, and labours with singular patience: But Heauen to whom she had made her vow, and for whose loue she was thus contemned (say the *Chinois*) eas'd her paines; It caused those blessed Inhabitants of those rich Vaults, to descend and comfort her, and sent many creatures to succour her: the Saints of Heauen came to draw her water: the Apes serued her as Groomes: Birds made cleane the Alleys of this Garden with their bils, and swept them with their wings: and wild Beasts came from a neere Mountaine to bring her wood. The King her Father seeing her one day serued by these new Domesticks, held her to be a Sorceresse; and resolu'd to purge by flame, the crime of her enchantments: whereupon hee caused this house to be set on fire; she seeing this goodly place burning vpon her occasion, would haue slaine her selfe, with a long Needle of siluer which she had in her haire, thrusting it into her throat: But suddenly there fell a great inundation of water, which quencht the fire: Then she left her designe, and retired into the Mountains, hiding herselfe in their Caues, where shee continued her penance. Heauen which protected her in this manner, would not suffer the cruelty of her impious Father to goe vnpunished: It strooke him with a Leprosie, and abandoned his liuing body to wormes, which did gnaw him, and made him to suffer many torments: *Canina* vnderstood it by Reuelation, Charity made her to leaue her solitary abode, to goe and succour her leprous Father: When the King saw her, he fell at her feet, to craue pardon, and worshipped her: shee holding her selfe vnworthy of adoration, would haue resisted, but not able to doe it in regard of the weaknes of her bodie, a Saint of Heauen put himselfe before her to repaire the errour, and to let him know, that the adoration was made only to him. At the same instant she returned to her Caue, and there ended her life in the like sanctitie. The *Chinois* hold her for a great Saint, and pray ordinarily vnto her to craue pardon for their offences. The third is a woman called *Neome*, who, they say, was descended from a most illustrious Family, in the Towne of *Cuchi*, in the Prouince of *Oquiam*: And as her Father sought to make her violate the vow of Chastity which she had made, and to force her to marry, she fled, and retired her selfe into the Desart of a little Island, which is right against *Ingoa*, where shee liued most holily, and did many *Miracles*, whereof they relate this, as the most famous of all. They say that a great Captaine, called *Cimpo*, Generall of a Nauall Army to the King of *China*, went to make warre against a Neighbour Kingdome: He arriued at *Boym*, with his Fleet; being ready to part, the Mariners not able to weigh their Anchors, were amazed at this encounter: They look into the Sea, and saw *Neome* set vpon them, and stay them. The Generall cals vnto her, and (as one diuinely inspired) intreats her to aduise him what he had to doe: she answers him, that if he would triumph ouer his enemies, and conquer their Realme, hee should lead her with him, for that they with whom he was to fight were great Magicians: Hee drawes her into his ship, weighes anchor, and hoists vp sayle, and within few dayes after

of the King of China.   243

after arriues at the Enemies Country. As soone as they discouered the Fleet of *China*, these Magicians flie vnto their Charmes, they cast Oile into the Sea, and by their illusions, make the *Chinois* imagine that their ships were on fire and burnt. *Neome* (who, without doubt, was an excellent Magician) defeated by more powerfull counter-charmes all that which they had done. Thus seeing that their Witchcraft was weake, and their Armes vnequall to those of *China*, they yeelded vnto them, and suffered the quality of Vassals, and Tributaries to the King of *China*. *Campo* whom the History notes for a judicious man, and a wise Politician, enters into some doubt of the sanctity of *Neome*, & holds her for a Sorceresse: to satisfie himselfe, hee requires some signe of her holy vertue, to carry as a Present to the King his Master. And intreats her to make a dry staffe, which he held in his hand to grow greene againe: she takes the staffe, and speaking certain secret words, makes it to grow green & to flourish, and moreouer of a most odoriferous smell, and so deliuered it to this Captaine, who blinded with Superstition like to the other *Chinois*, attributed the prosperity of his Voyage, and the good successe of his Armes to the holines of *Neome*, whose name hath beene euer since much honoured in *China*; especially by such as goe to Sea, who carry her Image vpon the proope of their ships, and they pray vnto her as the Diuinity, which gouernes the waues, commands the Sea, and pacifies tempests and stormes.

The Sunne and Moone are also the subjects of their adoration, they reuerence them as the Fountaines of light and comfort, and the causes of generation here below; but they beleeue a greater Diuinity which controlls them; for when they see that either of these stars suffers an Eclypse, they say that the Prince of Heauen hath condemned them to death, and that the feare of punishment hath thus blemished their light. Then they pray vnto this Soueraigne Prince, to pardon them and not to quench these Celestiall Lampes, which are so necessary for their life: They say that the Sunne is a man, and the Moone a woman. They hold Heauen to be the Creatour of all that which appeares vnto our eyes, and of inuisible things;

They worship the Sunne and Moone.

things; they expresse it so in the first letter of their Alphabet, as I haue formerly obserued, and they assure, that aboue these Celestial Vaults dwels an Immortall Gouernour, whom they call *Laocon Tzantey*, that is to say, the Gouernour of the great God; they qualifie him vncreated, incorporeall, eternall, and all spirit; they adore him with an extraordinary worship, & attribute vnto him the care of Supreme things, with whom they place another of the same nature, called by them *Cansaye*, who hath receiued from the first the gouernment of this part of Heauen, which lookes towards the earth, and holds in his powerfull hand the life and death of men. This second hath three Deputies vnder him, all three spirits like the first: They call them *Tanquam*, *Teiquam*, and *Tziquam*: These are the helps and assistants of his great Ministery, for the things of this inferiour World: For the first *Tanquam* is a waterish Diuinitie, or rather the fountaine of the World, he hath the charge of Raines, and his greatest exercise is to furnish the earth with water. *Teiquam* descends lower, towards our inferiour Regions. He rules ouer the Birth of men, disposeth of Warre, ordaines the Seeds, and causeth the Earth to bring forth the fruits which nourish men, and the beasts which inhabit it. *Tziquam* is their great *Neptune*; he spends his time in the ouersight of the Sea, retaines or thrusts on, as it pleaseth him, the fury of the waues; commands tempests, & hath a particular care of those which sailes. Wherefore all Sea-men adore him, Fishermen offer Sacrifices vnto him, and Marriners make Vowes, and at the returne from their Nauigations, represent Comædies in honour of his Name.

<small>Some marks of Christianitie in the *Chinois* worship.</small>

Amidst the abominations of this false worship of the *Chinois*, they obserue some steps and old markes halfe defaced of a better Religion: For in the diuersitie of their Images, they haue one which they hold in singular reuerence: Its formes is humane and majesticall: Out of the shoulders comes three heads equall and alike, which looke continually one on another, to let them vnderstand that they haue but one will. This may be taken for some steps of the mystery of the holy Trinitie,

tie, which the happy Apostle Saint *Thomas* had sometimes preached vnto them; when as going to the East *Indies*, where the Martyrdome which hee suffered crown'd his life with an immortall Diadem, he past by *China*, as the ancient writings of the *Armenians* report. But finding the *Chinois* much troubled with warres, hee past on, hauing briefly expounded the truth of the Gospell. In the same Temple where this Image with three heads is worshipped, they reuerence Pictures, not much vnlike to those of the twelue Apostles. The Christians which obserued these representations, demanded of them of *China*, what men those twelue Apostles had beene, and they had no other answere, but that those twelue personages had beene great Phylosophers, who had so earnestly imbraced vertue in this World, as it had caused them after their death to be taken vp into Heauen, and made Angels there. For a third testimony that they haue had some beames of the Christian verity, they reuerence in the same number of their sacred Pictures the Image of a woman, perfectly faire, which holds a Child in her armes, whom, they say, she brought forth without violating her Virginitie: And whose conception and birth were without the spot of any sinne; and they know no farther. The double cloud of the ignorance of the holy Bookes, and the sinne of Idolatry, hath hidden the rest from them. Yet all these markes expounded vnto them, by the eloquent tongue of some religious and feruent Christian, would be a reproach vnto them, that they are no more what they haue beene; and it would be no vnprofitable meanes to make the care successefull, which should be employed for their soules health: Besides that the excellencie of their spirits capable of reason, would giue the more free accesse: and their owne Oracles would support such workmen, to assist their good designes; for they haue a prophesie which saith; *That from towards the West the true Law should come vnto them, the which should carry them vp to Heauen to be made Angels there.*

Doubtlesse, the Court of *China* would be a pleasing abode for vs, in the conuersation of Courtiers, which are learned and indued with excellent spirits, and amidst the honest recom-

Of the death and funerals of the King of China.

compences which they giue vnto vertue. But the false worship of Idols, and the abominable superstitions which they commit, force vs to leaue it. It is therefore time to part, to turne our thoughts elsewhere; and to employ our labours in a more Religious occupation. Wee will doe it with the Diuine assistance of him who hath guided our workes hauing once related the Ceremonies, which are obserued at the Death and Funeralls of the Soueraigne Princes of this great Monarchie. When their King is dead, they wash his body in Arromaticall waters, they perfume his royall Habits, and clothe him more sumptuously than euer he went liuing: they set him in his Throne, to the end his whole Court may come and yeeld him their last duties, and deplore his losse. The first that present themselues are the Princes his Sonnes, if hee had any; after them comes the Queene his Wife, with the neerest of his Kindred; they kneele before his body, where they stay some time, and then retire with teares in their eyes, and sighes in their mouthes: The Chancellour or President of his Councell accompanied with all the Councellours of Estate, yeeld the like Funerall honours: All the Courtiers and Seruants of the Royall Pallace, are on their knees before the deceased, weeping for the losse of their Lord. This sad Ceremony being ended, they strip the body of his Royall Robes, and from his Throne they put him into a Coffin (it is the ordinary passage of the pompe of this World, from their greatnesse to the graue) made of rich odoriferous wood, shut vp so close as the aire cannot enter: They set it vpon a Table in the midst of the Royall Chamber, the which is most sumptuously hanged, and they lay vpon it a white cloth hanging downe to the ground, vpon the which lies the Picture of the deceased King drawne to the life: The Chamber of Presence is likewise richly furnished, and in it are set many Tables with a great number of Funerall Tapers, with the which they serue a great quantity of meate, for the Priests and Religious men of *China*, which come to sing after their manner, to pray, and to offer Sacrifices, for the rest of him that is dead in eternall vn-rest. To these vaine deuotions they adde many Sorceries, they bring

vnto

of the King of China.

vnto the Coffin a great number of little Papers painted, some of which they burne there presently, the rest they tie vnto the Coffin with little strings, the which they shake and moue continually, with such fearefull cryes and howlings, as a man can hardly heare them without terrour: They say, that by this franticke manner of succouring the dead, they send the soule of their deceased Monarch into heauen, to the number of those which are happy. This howling and spirituall noise of the Priests of China continues fifteene dayes, after which they conduct the Kings body to the Graue: the Conuoy is made in this manner: Before the body, march as many Priests and Religious men as are found in Court: They carry burning Tapers in their hands: The Princes Kinsmen follow the Conuoy, attired austerely in Mourning: They haue long Cassocks of wooll pitcht against their flesh, and girt about their loynes with cords: Their head is simply couered with a great Bonnet of wooll with broad brims, like to the Hats which they did weare in France, in the yeare 1625, the which is straitly obserued: For in China the Mourning consists not only in the outward shew, it passeth beyond teares and sighes, which are not performed but for fashion sake: The greatest, to obserue strictly the Mourning for the death of a Father or Mother, depriue themselues of their Offices: and the Vice-royes in the like heauinesse resigne into the Kings hands the gouernments which they had: to doe otherwise were no lesse shamefull and impious, then in our Countries for a Sonne to dance, laugh, and rejoyce publiquely, for the death of his Father: The Councell with the honourable markes of their dignity, march immediatly after them: and all the Officers of the Royall House and Court, assist in order, according to their places. In this pompe the body of the deceased King is carried to his Tombe, but not buried without traine; they burne in laying him into his graue the Pictures of many slaues, of a great number of Horses, of a heape of gold and siluer, and of some pieces of silke, which they belieue doe follow the dead into another life. Verily if these burnings in painting, be the markes of the foolish superstitions of the *Chinois*, they are

also

also of the mildnesse of their spirits, more humane then some *Barbarians* their Neigbours, who did really burne, at the interment of their Princes, the women and men which had serued them, and did prodigally cast into the fire the gold and siluer, and the precious stones which they found in their Cofers. This flash of fire ended, and the Pictures reduced to ashes; they goe downe and shut him into a little earth, who commanded a world of men and Countries: who might haue crowned his head with fifteene Diadems: For the Prouinces of *China*, which are so many, are in greatnesse and bounty so many Realmes: and in doing this they reduce into dust the greatest and most glorious pompe in the World. And certainly, seeing that all things are but dust, and that of dust hath bin made and fram'd the goodliest and noblest parts of the world, the men which are the Kings of the World, in laying them in the Graue they put dust into dust. For a lesson to Soueraigne Monarches, that in their stately Thrones, the Crowne and Royall Mantell couer only a pile of Earth inanimated, and a heape of liuing dust: If they haue not a great courage, a generous spirit and a religious soule: Then by these Royall and excellent qualities, they shall free their names from the dust of forgetfulnesse: And if by the common Law of Nature, the body which is but dust descends into dust, the spirit which was neuer dustie, shall goe and receiue in Heauen the immortall Crownes which those Kings deserue which are generous and pious.

FINIS.

Historia est pars Instructionis
Secundæ
Historia est pars Instructionis
Generalis

Historia

www.ingramcontent.com/pod-product-compliance
Ingram Content Group UK Ltd.
Pitfield, Milton Keynes, MK11 3LW, UK
UKHW020656260825
7573UKWH00054B/1295